FAMILIES IN DISTRESS

FAMILIES IN DISTRESS

PUBLIC, PRIVATE, AND CIVIC RESPONSES

Malcolm Bush

UNIVERSITY OF CALIFORNIA PRESS

Berkeley   Los Angeles   London

University of California Press
Berkeley and Los Angeles, California

University of California Press, Ltd.
London, England

© 1988 by
The Regents of the University of California

Library of Congress Cataloging-in-Publication Data

Bush, Malcolm.
   Families in distress.
   Bibliography: p.
   Includes index.
   1. Family social work—Illinois. 2. Problem families—
Services for—Illinois. 3. Child welfare—Illinois.
4. Community organization—Illinois. I. Title.
HV699.B88   1988   362.8′28′09773   87-162
ISBN 0-520-06094-6 (alk. paper)

Printed in the United States of America

1 2 3 4 5 6 7 8 9

To SCB, HFB, and Their Grandparents

Nourish beginnings, let us nourish beginnings.
Not all things are blest, but the
seeds of all things are blest.
The blessing is in the seed.

Muriel Rukeyser "Tenth Elegy. Elegy in Joy"

Contents

List of Tables

Preface

This book is about the variety of people and organizations who help children raised in troubled families. My initial interest in the topic was prompted by the debate, sharpened in the 1980 presidential election, over the proper roles of the public and private sectors in social welfare activities. I soon became convinced that the debate was far too narrowly focused, that it rested on unsubstantial caricatures about the nature of public and private organizations, and that it ignored the real complexities of the relationship between people in trouble and official and unofficial acts of helping.

The book is an attempt to widen the debate by introducing the concepts of citizenship and civic responsibility to the discussion. Thinking about people in trouble as citizens who happen to need help, rather than as clients whose only characteristic is their need, changes the ground of the debate. The altered perspective moves attention away from a narrow attempt to match a given problem with an appropriate service toward the underlying issues of rights, opportunities, and responsibilities in a democratic society. Civic responsibility implies the involvement of people in the debate about helping and in helping itself simply because they are citizens: they are affected by what is happening to other citizens and, to some degree, are responsible. I have no intention of describing a utopia. Rather the point is to show where civic action has been vital in the past, how it has been eroded, and where it is still essential. Underlying this approach is the premise that, though citizens may be only sporadically involved with social welfare issues and though the individual's role has changed with the changing division of labor (particularly since the New Deal), public and private organizations continue to act on behalf of people and therefore their actions should continue to be a concern of citizens. Moreover, people in trouble depend not only on organizations but also on other citizens, and the assistance of private citizens constitutes the vast majority of helping that occurs in our society.

I was introduced to issues in child welfare at the Center for Urban Affairs at Northwestern University during my graduate training. There, Andrew Gordon, Margo Gordon, Tom Dewar, and John McKnight led me from a comparatively narrow investigation of the experiences of children living in child welfare institutions to the broader issue of what constitutes appropriate social welfare strategies in a democratic society that is fully conscious of the perspectives of people on the receiving end of social welfare. Our conversations have continued, and I am particularly grateful for two weeks of intense discussion at the Center in the summer of 1983 with John McKnight, Tom Dewar, and Stan Hallett. When I moved to the University of Chicago, Harold Richman welcomed me to the Children's Policy Research Project (now the Chapin Hall Center for Children), where he provided the group of colleagues and the resources that made this book possible, gave me every encouragement, and made no demands. I have drawn heavily on other people's research at the Project—in particular from Mark Testa, who has shepherded so much of the project's work. Harold Goldman, who knows the child welfare world from more angles than anyone I know, was a constant source of information, constructive criticism, and advice. As Dean of the School of Social Service Administration, Margaret Rosenheim obtained for me a year's leave of absence in 1982–83, during which I wrote much of the first draft. That leave, and additional resources, were made possible by a generous grant from the Prince Charitable Trust.

My debt to my students is enormous. In particular, Scott Geron, Susan Grossman, Liz Krueger, and Fred Wulczyn were able and energetic research assistants.

Ellen Netting, Harold Goldman, and Richard Caputo generously shared the information they collected to write their dissertations.

It is impossible to name all the people involved in the practical world of child welfare who answered my questions and sent me data, reports, and other critical information. I am delighted to acknowledge my debts to the Children's Home and Aid Society of Illinois (formerly the Illinois Children's Home and Aid Society) who generously opened all their files for my research, to the members of the Illinois Action for Children, and to Roxille Glasco, who gave me valuable insights into the worlds of public and private child welfare organizations.

Haydn Bush, Bill Cannon, Joan Costello, Joan Gittens, Laura Epstein, Tom Dewar, Harold Goldman, and Harold Richman have read parts or all of earlier drafts, saved me from many errors, and given me sage advice. Any remaining mistakes and peculiarities of interpretation are mine alone.

My wife, Mary O'Connell, has advised on innumerable problems and has taken her green pencil to the text with the sureness of a surgeon wielding a scalpel. Her skill has been second only to her love and encouragement.

INTRODUCTION

Need and Response

In the biblical parable of the Good Samaritan, a stranger makes a response as a private citizen to a traveler robbed and beaten by thieves. A contemporary version of the robbery would set off a series of organizational and professional responses as police officers, paramedics, and emergency room staff became involved. The subjects of this study—families whose children the juvenile courts declare to be dependent, neglected, or abused—are the targets of a chain of organized helping. These organized responses developed over the last hundred years as private responses to need proved inadequate to the demands of growing cities. Today we analyze and evaluate those responses with a zeal that both demonstrates our desire for a finely tuned relationship between need and response and betrays our suspicion that responses can misfire.

This book argues that the current debate about public and private organizations and professional helping is misdirected. In the field of family welfare, better organizations and more highly skilled professionals have only a limited capacity to improve the lives of troubled families. Most face-to-face helping is still done by individuals who are neither professionals nor staff of social service agencies. The division of labor has not made their involvement any less vital. But these individuals, whom we shall call citizens, have another role in addition to their actual helping. Public and private organizations act on behalf of the citizenry, and for that reason groups of citizens should oversee how organizations define need, respond to need, and measure the results of their work. Citizen review of organizations is an important aspect of civic responsibility and participation. Civic participation in helping is essential because organizations and professions, responding to their own needs, can act in ways that hinder rather than help the distressed. The expansion of organized and professional helping has crowded out civic participation. More effective helping will depend on redressing that imbalance.

This approach helps us to rephrase the public–private debate. The reality of what is public and private is not fixed and is often ill defined. Moreover, the auspices under which an organization operates are not vital to the well-being of clients. Organizations vary in effectiveness, but when evaluated they do not divide neatly along public and private lines. Public organizations fail to be public in some ways that would help their clients. Private organizations are sometimes private in ways that make their lives, rather than their clients' lives, better.

People in trouble are also citizens. They are often called clients, but, we argue, the more they are clients the less they are citizens and the less chance they have of achieving a decent independence.

An emphasis on helping organizations sometimes obscures the relationship between poverty and other forms of trouble. Some families' troubles are caused or exacerbated by poverty. Many of the most troubled families in our study—families who come to the attention of the state through dependency, neglect, and abuse petitions in the juvenile court—are poor. The relief of poverty can relieve the accompanying troubles. But the current debate reduces issues of poverty to a discussion about welfare, especially Aid to Families with Dependent Children (AFDC). Even that narrow debate is conducted inadequately because it is based on a homogeneous image of poor mothers and the conditions in which they live. The distance between the poor and some of those who describe them maintains the caricature.

A most important aspect of contemporary social welfare practice is the categorization of recipients as clients. The word *client* frames a person's circumstances in a particular way. The word says that from the public's perspective the most salient aspect of a person is his or her need, and that the role of the instruments of public policy is to recognize and respond to that need. In this formulation, however, lies the seed of a problem. Treating symptoms of distress and recognizing and encouraging a person's capacity are different strategies with different consequences. At some point the former strategy has disadvantages for the subject of attention. To put the problem in a different language, the state of being a citizen—defined by its rights, responsibilities, and freedoms—and the state of being a client constitute a zero-sum game. The more a person becomes a client the more that person's citizenship is diminished. The obvious example is the hospitalized patient. A person used to making many of the decisions about his or her own life suddenly surrenders autonomy about the most personal and minute details of that life to other people. The gain, for a temporary period, is often worth the price. But sometimes it is not.

There are a number of reasons for the trade-off between citizenship and clienthood. The citizen is subject to general rules about a narrow range of behavior. The client is subject to particular rules about a wide range of behavior. The range in which a client's behavior is judged to be normal is narrower than that which applies to the citizen. Making a person a client reduces that person's freedom to act in the ways he or she chooses. One consequence is that the process of becoming a client very often reduces people's confidence, and hence competence, to act on their own behalf. This diminishment can occur even when the formal purpose for making a person a client is to increase confidence and competence.

Clienthood also reduces people's responsibilities for their own actions. Citizens are expected to act competently on their own behalf and on behalf of their families. Diminished responsibility is attributed to clients. That attribution can be a self-fulfilling prophecy. Diminished responsibility at the same time makes less necessary the other two attributes of citizenship— namely, the authority to act on one's own behalf and the opportunity to do so. For example, parents whose children have been taken away from them have been denied the responsibility, the authority, and the opportunity to be parents. In such circumstances their taste and capacity for being parents decrease.

This argument is partly practical: competence will flourish by its exercise, not its curtailment. It is also political in the broadest sense. If we apply to social welfare decisions the standard that the response to trouble should be appropriate to a democratic society, we will avoid various undemocratic phenomena. We will reject incarceration disguised as refuge and control disguised as diagnosis and treatment. The extreme example of the Soviet psychiatric hospital illustrates the potential for robbing people of their citizenship in the name of help. Moreover, we will avoid the substitution of psychological explanations of distress when economic and structural explanations are more compelling. This is not a matter of choosing a liberal over a conservative frame of reference. Citizenship also requires the acceptance of reasonable responsibility—a position that is alleged to be more in favor with conservatives than liberals. Moreover, the emphasis on maintaining citizenship should alert us to the possibilities for avoiding distress in addition to the possibilities for relieving distress.

Particular characteristics of contemporary social welfare suggest this emphasis. Quite simply, the chances of falling into clienthood are higher than they have ever been. Some help, for example AFDC payments, is given only after many aspects of a family's life have been inspected, and those inspections often turn up other "deficits." The opportunities for federal and state government to intervene in the lives of families are very great. Child abuse legislation has expanded the grounds for intervention in the lives of families, and accompanying it has been the massive growth of state welfare and family service departments. As the worst manifestations of distress have diminished from a hundred-year perspective, the newly enlarged agents of government and their private contractors have acquired the freedom to notice and respond to less serious manifestations of distress. Nineteenth-century volunteers struggled with orphans and abandoned children. Their contemporary professional equivalents are much more likely to be concerned with "acting-out" behavior and hyperactivity.

Lastly, the expansion of the helping professions has resulted in increased numbers of people who assess and rate problems. This increase has led—at a semipopular, sometimes pseudoscientific level—to very high estimates of the incidence of certain kinds of distress. Estimates of poverty are subject to stringent, though still fallible, checks. Estimates of child abuse and emotional disorders vary widely; high estimates for these rarely stand up to rigorous examination. The expansion of the professions has also increased the number of people whose self-image and economic interests depend on the fact of clienthood. If citizenship, as opposed to clienthood, is the status we cherish for ourselves and others, we must be able to see that the expansion of organized helping always carries with it the possibility of increasing clienthood at the expense of that citizenship.

Like clienthood, the issue of citizenship arises anew with the expansion of the organs of social welfare in a democratic society. The issue this time, however, is the citizenship of people who are in no danger of becoming clients of the social welfare system. Our thesis is that the expansion of the formal organizations of social welfare has crowded out the space for direct civic action and that this development has adverse consequences for those in trouble.

We define civic participation as the process of hammering out compromises between differing interests and views by people directly affected. Via civic participation, judgments are made about public matters and responsibilities for the common good are assigned. Civic participation, then, is extrafamilial. Representative politics are an instrument of the citizenry but a compromise in the sense that they involve very little regular citizen participation. The formal organizations of helping are set up with the usually tacit consent of the collectivity of citizens as part of the division of labor.

Civic participation now takes place in the jury, the community council, ward or township meeting, and in some forms of voluntary action on behalf of people in trouble. It is more present in the city ward that organizes to ensure the safety of its streets and in the school parent council that has a voice in hiring and curriculum decisions; it is less present in the trustees of a voluntary agency who are separated by class, geography, and inclination from their agency's clients. Hence the blue-ribbon commission can be a perversion of civic responsibility. The exercise of the civic function may be episodic as the demands of the situation ebb and flow. But it involves the active personal responsibility of people who have no other qualifications except that the situation affects them, and that they as citizens are responsible.

Civic participation has some critical advantages. It brings together the actors and the acted upon. It therefore increases the possibility that a consensus will be reached on the definition of the problem, the appropriate response to the problem, and the preferred outcomes. Participation reduces the opportunity for the construction of caricatures of the problem or the people who experience the problem by reducing the distance between the helpers and the helped. Finally, it encourages the examination of the situation of the distressed so that the preconditions of deviance are as salient as the manifestations of deviance.

There are two other prime advantages to civic participation. The first advantage results because organizations operating under legal mandates administer only certain kinds of assistance; thus some kinds of direct, noncoercive help are outside their capacity. Some helping, in short, will occur only if people outside the formal systems become more involved. The second advantage has to do with the quality of formal helping. Many formal organizations have honest and elaborate systems to monitor their actions and the consequences of their actions. But the framework an organization employs to view a problem is merely one of several legitimate frameworks. Civic review of formal helping holds out the possibility that other legitimate perspectives (that organizations either cannot or will not recognize) will receive their due.

Setting the Scene

This book is about children and families who "get into trouble" and the organizations that try to help them. We concentrate on what happens to children who are officially called abused, neglected, or dependent and on minors requiring authoritative intervention. The last category (known in some states as minors or youth in need of supervision) consists mainly of adolescents who have so much difficulty getting on at home that they or their parents ask for help. Many of these children come from poor families, so we are also concerned with "welfare" or families who receive payments under the Aid to Families with Dependent Children provisions of the Social Security Act. A few of these children are mentally disabled and a few of them have committed delinquent acts. We deal with welfare, mental health, and delinquent behavior to the extent that they illuminate the condition of our central characters.

Most of the story is set in one state, Illinois. Most helping agencies are organized on a community, city, county, or state level, so a statewide analysis takes in much of the action. We look at federal legislation, budgets, and judicial decisions when they affect the state. The story gets so tangled in places that the action in one state is problem enough. But our single-state focus prompts the question of how the Illinois experience compares with other states. The answer to that depends on the particular subject of the comparison.

Illinois is a northern industrial and agricultural state and shares many of the demographic characteristics of such states. In child welfare it has sometimes been accused of lagging behind other states and has sometimes been in the forefront of reform efforts. In the late nineteenth century, for example, Michigan, Wisconsin, and Minnesota adopted the "Michigan plan," whereby the state assumed primary responsibility for dependent children and housed them in central child welfare institutions prior to placing them in foster homes or adoptive homes.[1] This measure was considered a reform because it kept the children out of the poorhouse and established some state control over private agencies. Illinois was considered backward for increasing its use of the "subsidy system," whereby the private agencies decided what to do with the children they chose to serve and the state merely paid a small subsidy for their care. But in 1899, Illinois established the country's first juvenile court and in 1911, along with Missouri, the first Mothers' Pension Act, the forerunner of AFDC. In states east of the Mississippi, private organizations were well established by the time public social service agencies were organized, with consequences for the contemporary relationship between the two sectors. Illinois, for example, has several long-established,

---

1. For a history of public policy for children in Illinois, see Joan Gittens, "The Children of the State: Dependent Children in Illinois, 1818–1980s," Chapin Hall Center for Children, University of Chicago, 1986.

large sectarian social service agencies that wield special power in the field of child welfare. This phenomenon is less common in western states. The particular division of labor between different types of organization is different in each state. But there are broader trends, problems, and solutions that have their counterparts in most states.

The Response to Need

This book seeks to understand the contemporary synthesis of need and response in that part of social welfare concerned with a particular group of troubled families. The concentration on one aspect of social welfare allows us to unravel some quite complicated problems. Some of the issues and conclusions, however, can be applied to other areas of social welfare. Our concern is to lessen the disjunction between need and response. We will be equally interested in situations where there is a reasonable mesh between the two: where, despite the complexity of the problem, a person, a group of people, or an organization has figured out a way to tailor the response to the need.

We discount bad intentions as the major cause of the disjunctions (although there are plenty of examples in all fields of social welfare where scandals have caused great hardship and suffering). It is more useful to consider the relationship between need and response as a dialectical process, where contradictions produce syntheses that both address the situation and carry within them the seeds of further contradiction.

One major source of tension derives from the changes caused by the passage of time. The nature of need, definitions of need, and the response to need change and the history of each of these affects the present. For example, some writers suggest that the welfare programs devised in the 1930s to prevent the breakup of single-parent families had, by the 1960s, begun to encourage the formation of single-parent families. It is a sign of our lack of historical imagination that we are surprised by such twists of fortune. We should not be startled that the relationship between a particular manifestation of distress and the response to it has changed in a thirty-year period, especially when many other aspects of social and economic life have changed as well. We need to place the contemporary debate in a historical context to capture the effect that history has on the present. For the moment we can illustrate the constancy of change with a few examples.

The changing demography of need.   Need that begs a response is a moving target for two reasons: different people have different definitions of contemporary problems and the demography of need changes. Thus the definition of contemporary need is partly a matter of choice. Any particular definition will be fallible and temporary.

Some children come to the attention of the state because they are dependent. This designation can mean that their parents are dead or have abandoned them, or that still caring parents cannot afford to look after them. Destitution was the domestic condition that troubled township and county officials at the formation of the United States. A destitute family that could not afford to put a roof over its head or food on the table had to be provided with those necessities.

The state still worries about destitute children and destitute families, but the causes of destitution have changed. The changes in this century are the most dramatic. In 1920, there were 750,000 full orphans (children who had lost both parents) in the United States. That figure amounted to 1.9 percent of the child population under eighteen.[2] At the same time there were 6,400,000 half-orphans who had lost one parent, and that figure was 16.3 percent of the child population. By 1980, that number had fallen to 60,000 full orphans (0.1 percent) and 2,955,000 half-orphans (4.5 percent). But as the number of children who are orphans has decreased, the number of illegitimate children has increased. In 1960, 5.3 percent of all births were to mothers who had not married. In 1979, 17.1 percent of all births were to unmarried mothers. The percentage of births to unmarried women in the black community was 54.6 per-

2. U.S. Bureau of the Census, *Statistical Abstracts of the United States* (Washington, D.C.: Bureau of the Census, 1978 and 1979), 79 and 357; and *Statistical Abstracts: Colonial Times to 1970,* pt. 1 (Washington, D.C.: Bureau of the Census, 1975), 52.

cent.[3] Out-of-wedlock births contribute to the form of family distress contemporaries worry about most, but separation and divorce also cause distress. In 1950, for every 1,000 married white women, 56 were either separated or divorced. By 1980, the combined separation and divorce rates had risen to 115 of every 1,000.[4] In the nonwhite community the separation and divorce rates were higher in both years. In 1950, 168 nonwhite women were separated or divorced for every 1,000 married. By 1980, 414 black women were separated or divorced for every 1,000 black women who were married.

These trends had their impact on the number of children who were living with their mothers only. In 1960, 4.7 percent of all white children in the state of Illinois were living with their mothers only. By 1980, that figure was 10.4 percent. In 1960, 25.8 percent of black children were being raised in female-headed households, but by 1980, 43.1 percent of black children were so situated.[5] The increases are demonstrated in another national statistic—the recipients of AFDC or welfare. In 1960, a total of 803,000 households received AFDC payments, and those households contained 3.0 percent of all children under the age of eighteen. In 1980, the number of households receiving aid had risen to 3,842,534, and those families included 12.2 percent of all children under eighteen.[6]

The change from orphanhood as the major cause of dependency to separation, divorce, and out-of-wedlock births has several consequences. Shelter and food are no longer the central issues, although the quality of the shelter and the sufficiency of the diet that can be provided on AFDC checks remain nagging questions. Instead, the precipitating conditions of the dependency become part of the problem that has to be solved. The social welfare task changes from that of seeking out and aiding

3. Andrew Hacker, ed., *U/S: A Statistical Portrait of the American People* (New York: Viking, 1983), 56–57.
4. William Julius Wilson and Kathryn Neckerman, "Poverty and Family Structure: The Widening Gap Between Evidence and Public Policy Issues," Department of Sociology, University of Chicago, February 1985, 56–57.
5. Mark Testa and Edward Lawlor, *The State of the Child: 1985* (Chicago: Chapin Hall Center for Children, University of Chicago, 1985), 20.
6. Hacker, *U/S: A Statistical Portrait,* 189.

all dependent children to that of reducing the number of dependent children. The public's sense of concern for the plight of helpless children is tempered by bursts of outrage at the behavior that leads to the dependency. The enthusiasm of the white majority for alleviating destitution wanes as the perception grows that such destitution is increasingly a black, rather than a white, problem.

The changes in the nature of dependency are the most important demographic changes in child welfare. Another change commanded sporadic attention in the nineteenth and first half of the twentieth century but has risen to prominence since then. The incidence of child abuse may or may not have increased since the phenomenon was redefined in the early 1950s, but the number of reports of suspected cases has increased dramatically.

Illinois passed a child abuse reporting law in 1965, and in 1970, some 683 cases of child abuse and neglect were reported under the act. By 1984, the number of reported cases had exceeded 67,000 and child abuse was a major part of the child welfare debate.[7] In the 1970s, the sexual abuse of children drew the attention that physical abuse had attracted a decade earlier.

One consequence of this fresh interest in abuse is a change in the perception of family trouble. In the 1930s, child neglect—the failure to carry out the essential functions of a parent—was seen in the light of mass poverty. By the 1970s, it was often seen as a watered-down version of abuse.

The case of abuse illustrates problems of fact and interpretation and points to a major change in the field of child welfare. This change is the clarity of the conditions that invite an organized response. The destitution of homeless and hungry children was an unambiguous problem that cried out for attention. But today neglect describes the largest category of children who require attention, and neglect is more ambiguous. It is ambiguous because neglect in one area of a child's upbringing does not necessarily indicate neglect in another; a dirty child might receive all the affection he or she needs. It is also ambiguous because the determination of what situations warrant interven-

7. Testa and Lawlor, *The State of the Child*, 72.

tion requires observation and judgment. Starvation and home-lessness are comparatively self-evident conditions. Neglect is self-evidently undesirable in the sense that we easily make the judgment that we would not wish our children to be neglected. It is, however, a phenomenon about which it is harder to make the judgment that imperfect and coercive state interventions are preferable to the unattended condition. It is a calculus in which the answer to the question whether the need should be acted upon depends on the effectiveness of the response.

Changing responses to need.   In the late eighteenth and early nineteenth centuries a few destitute families were given outdoor relief—financial assistance in their own homes. Some were assigned by the township meeting or the county court to a family that was prepared to take them in for a price. Destitute families could be put in the care of a person who contracted to take care of all such families in the locality, or they could be indentured or placed in almshouses.[8] The set of arrangements that the successors of those township officials use today are similar in some respects. Families are still given help in their own homes. Others have their children removed to families who are paid to look after them, and a few children are placed in institutions.

The apparent similarities between the historical strategies and their contemporary forms conceal differences in style and substance. What does persist is controversy about the appropriateness of the strategies.

Foster care, or boarding out children in other people's homes, remains one of the principal alternatives in child welfare. But by the 1960s, some people in the field had decided that foster care was itself abnormal and could be justified only as an interim solution. For them, the longitudinal research findings demonstrating that some children remained in foster care for more than two or three years were a sign that foster care itself was a problem. The profession as a whole was disturbed by a parallel finding that those children who stayed in care for a long time were likely to

8. For a history of child welfare in the United States, see Homer Folks, *The Care of Destitute, Neglected and Delinquent Children* (New York: Macmillan, 1902).

experience a number of different surrogate homes.[9] The research also showed that children resented being moved from place to place, that after a couple of moves they felt extremely insecure, and that they began to resist emotional attachments to their surrogate families for fear the attachment would be broken.[10]

These findings resulted in an emphasis on "permanent" placements. Such placements could be at the child's natural home in situations where the family problems were solved or at an adoptive home. If these two preferred options failed, a third alternative was a stable, long-term foster home. This goal was so widely approved that in 1980 it was enshrined in federal legislation.[11] This reform represents one side of an argument about whether foster children should expect just a decent upbringing or a normal upbringing. That issue, in turn, hinges on the question of whether they are normal children in difficult situations or in some ways abnormal. While in practice the difference is usually a matter of emphasis, both positions have their shortcomings. The normalization position can obscure long-term handicaps that afflict some families and children. The opposite position can lead to an overemphasis on deficits and can obscure the person of the client.

The history of institutional care for dependent children is just as controversial as the history of foster care, but at least in theory, the battle seems to be over. It has now become almost impossible to argue the merits of institutional care for ordinary children. For some observers, even the institutionalization of the most disturbed children is a last resort.[12] The story of institu-

---

9. See, for example, David Fanshel, "The Exit of Children from Foster Care: An Interim Research Report," *Child Welfare* 50, no. 1 (January 1971): 65–82, and "Status Changes in Foster Care: Final Results of the Columbia University Longitudinal Study," *Child Welfare* 55, no. 3 (March 1976): 143–73.

10. This finding was the basis of a new theory in child welfare that children had psychological parents who might or might not be the child's biological parents, and that such attachments should be maintained at all costs. The term *psychological parents* was coined by J. Goldstein, Anna Freud, and Albert Solnit in *Beyond the Best Interests of the Child* (New York: Free Press, 1973).

11. Adoption Assistance and Child Welfare Act, 1980, P.L. 96–272, U.S. Statutes at Large, Vol. 94, 500–35.

12. See, for example, Malcolm Bush, "Institutions for Dependent and Neglected Children: Therapeutic Option of Choice or Last Resort?" *American Journal of Orthopsychiatry* 50, no. 2 (April 1980): 230–55.

tional care is also one in which the reform of one generation becomes the problem of another. In the second half of the nineteenth century, child welfare institutions replaced the much criticized poorhouse. In this century those institutions were themselves replaced by residential treatment centers. But institutional care has another characteristic: persistence in the face of criticism. At first sight the resurgence of the anti-institutional movement in the 1970s was extraordinarily successful. Between 1970 and 1985, the number of children in child welfare institutions in Illinois dropped from 4,127 to 1,998. The 1970 figure represented 30 percent of all the child welfare population placed outside their home. The 1985 figure represents 14 percent of that population.[13]

On the surface there is a steady progression toward deinstitutionalization. But the relationship between consensus and action is not always smooth. The critics of institutions won the rhetorical contest and reduced the number of children in child welfare institutions. But there have always been counterpressures—pressures to protect the community and pressures to treat children. The most recent evidence suggests that the reduction of long-term stays in children's institutions have been more than balanced with an increasing number of other forms of institutionalization. By one count, while the national rate of institutionalization for dependent and neglected children dropped from 441 per 100,000 in the 1920s to 112 per 100,000 in the 1970s, the rate for children in all forms of institutional care increased from 685 to 1,518 per 100,000.[14] This almost unnoticed development is largely due to the massive increase in short-term stays in the mental health and correctional systems; in the latter these stays occur under the labels of detention, shelter, and diagnostic care.

This unsuspected rise in institutional care points to another feature of the dialectic between need and response for children. Children's needs are subject to underexposure and overexposure. Whether a particular problem will get fair attention depends on who describes it, for what purpose, or whether it gets

13. Testa and Lawlor, *The State of the Child*, 47.
14. Paul Lerman, *Deinstitutionalization and the Welfare State* (New Brunswick, N.J.: Rutgers University Press, 1982), 140.

described at all. Children in institutions have been ignored for long periods of time. On other occasions they have been subject to intense scrutiny. The same is true for the victims of sexual abuse. The detrimental effects of inattention are obvious. There are also dangers to overexposure and to attention that springs from interests other than the child's. We will be concerned with both problems.

The most contentious response to troubled families is the provision of financial assistance. Charity or welfare has a long and convoluted history, and the issues are well rehearsed: whether poverty is the root cause of trouble or its consequence; whether cash assistance attacks the root cause or itself is a major cause of the problem. In the nineteenth century the debate was about "pauperism." In the mid-twentieth century it was about "the culture of poverty," and most recently it is described as the "cycle of welfare dependency."

Although the wisdom of providing financial assistance to poor families has always been debated, the circumstances surrounding the debate have changed in fundamental ways. In 1911, when the Illinois legislature passed the country's first Mothers' Pension Act, the purpose was to permit counties to pay "worthy" mothers, especially widows, a sum that would enable their families to stay together. The legislation owed a great deal to juvenile court judges who had watched thousands of children placed in institutions simply because their mothers could not afford to maintain them at home. The Mothers' Pension laws were translated into federal legislation in the Aid to Dependent Children provisions of the Social Security Act of 1935. In that year eighteen million Americans were relying on emergency relief and ten million workers were unemployed. The attack on AFDC that produced the cuts in the Reagan Administration's Omnibus Budget Reconciliation Act of 1981 reflected concerns about the number of families on welfare and the number of children growing up in single-parent families.

One logic used to justify the 1981 cuts was the assertion that the contemporary problem was solely the result of government programs that punished virtue and rewarded vice. Reliance on the job market, familial and private charity, and local public charity in jurisdictions that voted such aid would clear up the mess.[15]

The Reagan Administration lacked neither statisticians nor theorists to support its programs. But the programs were hardly an answer to the complexity of the problem. By contrast, between 1935 and 1981, two attempts had been made to balance the requirements of helping and encouraging independence. But the failure of Richard Nixon's Family Assistance Plan and Jimmy Carter's welfare reform program showed how difficult it was to achieve that balance in practice.[16]

Synopsis

These examples of changes in the history of need, and of the strategies for responding to need, have a parallel in another changing phenomenon. The people who do the helping and the organizations for whom they work also have a history. The response to need both follows the patterns of need and reflects other dynamics. Chapter 1 sketches the development of public, private, and civic helping in child welfare. The rise of the private social service agency in the second half of the nineteenth century was a reaction to the misery caused by rapid industrialization and immigration. The changing role of the private sector after the 1930s was an organizational reaction to the expansion of county and state government. That expansion was funded with money appropriated in New Deal legislation and derives, therefore, from the fact of the Great Depression. Such developments had the consequence of diminishing and belittling the role of civic helping.

This history gives us a background for addressing the contemporary interest in the health of the private sector. Chapter 2 attempts to go beyond the rhetoric and to examine the struc-

15. See Charles Murray, *Losing Ground, American Social Policy 1950–1980* (New York: Basic Books, 1984).

16. An insider's view of the Family Assistance Plan is provided by Daniel Patrick Moynihan, *The Politics of a Guaranteed Income: The Nixon Administration and the Family Assistance Plan* (New York: Vintage, 1973). The Carter welfare proposals are described in Lawrence E. Lynn and David deF. Whitman, *The President as Policy Maker: Jimmy Carter and Welfare Reform* (Philadelphia: Temple University Press, 1981).

ture, the functions, and the purposes of not-for-profit child welfare agencies. At other points in the book we will submit public agencies to the same scrutiny. The recognition of the dualism, public and private agency, does not, however, mean that the dualism is vital. It is merely a recognition that other people, including some very powerful actors, think it is vital. For us their assumption is a question among other questions.

These descriptions bring us to the primary issue: the relationship between need and response. The answer to the question whether the response meets the need depends on the criteria chosen to judge the issue. There are plenty of disagreements about what criteria are appropriate, and whether the criteria have been achieved. Our strategy is to start with the criteria the organizations themselves use when their staffs talk about good and bad agencies. We will see what those criteria actually mean when they are applied to real situations. We will discover that organizational definitions do not always make sense from the perspective of the people receiving help. This disparity leads us to some redefinitions.

One criterion that social welfare organizations talk about is *responsiveness* (chapter 3). Important meanings of this word include acting on a scale appropriate to the scope of the problem, responding to problems that most agencies would prefer to ignore, and activating the response of laypeople when the best solution lies in their hands.

Social welfare staffs are also concerned with *equity* (chapter 4). This issue has two aspects: the first is about race, reflecting a history of discrimination in child welfare. But a concentration on the equal distribution of all services obscures the critical differences between coercive and sustaining help, and between help that is necessary for people in deep trouble and help that keeps people out of trouble.

The second example of equity has to do with difficult clients (chapter 5). Social welfare workers ascribe the title "difficult" to clients who cause problems for their families, for themselves, and for the people who are trying to help them. Since "difficult" clients take more time and energy than "easy" clients, the notion exists that, in the interests of fairness, social welfare organizations should include in their clientele their quota of difficult clients. But that definition of fairness has the organizations, not the clients, as its subjects. In the same way, the usual notion of difficultness has to do with an organization's reaction to a child, not to the child's situation. If the children's condition drives the definition, we would be more concerned with the difficulty troubled children have being accepted in the world.

The most important criterion for the staffs of social welfare organizations is that of *quality* (chapter 6). Quality has to do both with particular outcomes and with particular processes. Some agencies are more concerned with one than the other. Their preference is often related to the particular work they are engaged in, and to their particular training. But it is very hard to trace the long-term results of child welfare interventions, and for the children the most important issue may be whether they feel sustained or well-cared for. Since they have a sense of what will sustain them, quality service may be service that allows them and their families some voice in the decisions made on their behalf. Quality then becomes a matter of who makes the critical judgments.

This set of questions takes us part of the way to thinking about the organization of help in the fullest relevant context. But to complete the picture we will have to step outside the "need–response" mind-set. The reason is as follows: if we acknowledge the tension between personal fault and situational explanations of distress, we should be able to explain some distress in situational terms. While services might ease that distress, the subject of the distress would prefer not to have got into trouble in the first place. This point raises the question whether the situation, particularly the condition of poverty, is a major factor in the set of events that brings families to the attention of the state for neglecting their children (chapter 7). We must also, in the process, respond to the argument that cash assistance produces the condition it is designed to alleviate.

The argument that services can produce the dependency they are designed to cure is of comparatively recent vintage, but like the debate on pauperism, it is here to stay. This more recent argument suggests that services that have the formal purpose of encouraging independence may, in fact, train people for the reverse. Writing about services for the blind, Robert Scott argues:

Many of the attitudes, behavior patterns and qualities of character that have long been assumed to be given to blind people by their condition are, in fact, the result of ordinary processes of socialization. The . . . organized intervention programs for the blind play a major role in determining the nature of this socialization.[17]

In this instance the helping organizations produce the traits they were established to cure. Our approach to this question is to ask whether professional social work conceives its task in a way that is likely to maximize its clients' chances for a decent independence (chapter 8).

We conclude with a reassessment of the terms *public, private, civic, participation, client,* and *citizen* (chapter 9).

17. Robert A. Scott, *The Making of Blind Men: A Study of Adult Socialization* (New York: Russell Sage Foundation, 1969), 3.

I

THE HISTORICAL BACKGROUND TO NEED AND RESPONSE

1

A Brief History of Public, Private, and Civic Helping

Introduction

This chapter describes the development of public, private, and civic organizations since the 1930s to set the scene for the discussion of contemporary organizations. Public departments of child welfare expanded massively after the New Deal and forced private agencies to redefine their role. In the process some forms of civic helping got squeezed out. But in the 1960s, civic interest revived in various guises, and over the next twenty years demonstrated that it had a vital role. Before we describe the last fifty years, we should note some of the major changes that preceded the recent period.

There has been a dance of public and private action in social welfare during the entire history of the nation, but what constitutes public and private, the degree of distinction and articulation between them, and what organized forms lie behind those labels have differed at various times. The sense that they constitute two sectors, fighting each other to establish their legitimacy and territory, is a very recent one. Moreover, there are two sets of activities that the two-actor game ignores: citizens acting privately for the welfare of their families, friends, and neighbors, and citizens acting publicly as an expression of the moral or political sense of the community.

The nature of public and private action in social welfare was governed until quite recently by the demands that social conditions imposed on a community. The large-scale development of social welfare bureaucracies added two additional interests to that of social conditions: the survival of those bureaucracies at a given size and the political attention that is drawn to operations that command a large percentage of state expenditures. There were times, however, when there was not a social welfare profession or social welfare agencies to stand between citizens and the community's action on their problems. Then the scale of the discussion allowed for (but did not guarantee) a civic dimension: the participation of individuals on the grounds simply that they were present (the problem existed in their locality), and that they, by virtue of being citizens, were responsible.

We have a scattered picture of what was done for dependent children in colonial times. Strategems varied in different towns and in different counties. But the key public institutions were the same—the town meeting and the county court. The key private actors were churches and individual families.

By the mid-nineteenth century these institutions and actors could no longer cope with the burgeoning number of distressed families. The situation had changed dramatically as a result of urbanization and immigration. Between 1790 and 1820, some 250,000 immigrants entered the country. Between 1815 and 1860, five million immigrants joined a population that in 1820 was only ten million strong. Not only was local oversight impossible, there were simply no public organizations that could deal with the number of neglected and dependent children. The dependent also became faceless: they were no longer part of the day-to-day lives of the nondependent.

The inadequacy of the public response in growing cities left a vacuum that was filled by a new expression of the private—the voluntary child welfare agency. There had been an organized response to children's dependency in the eighteenth century: the orphanage. Many of these were established by religious groups.

The voluntary child welfare agency that appeared in the second half of the nineteenth century engaged in a broader range of activities than the provision of institutional care, and it represented a mix of civic and religious motives. The first wave of child welfare agencies—the Children's Aid Societies in New York (1853), Baltimore (1860), Boston (1865), Brooklyn (1866), Buffalo (1872), and Philadelphia (1882)—appeared nonsectarian to their founders because they were Protestant organizations in a Protestant society. They represented the core beliefs of society as those involved saw them. But to German and Irish Catholics or to German and Eastern European Jewish immigrants, they were sectarian, and these groups responded by setting up their own agencies to ensure a proper upbringing for their foundlings, orphans, and dependents. The motive was straightforward and unambiguous: the reclamation of their own children.

Private child welfare societies did not constitute a private "sector" in the minds of the people who established them. But with the multiplication of those activities, a sense of the collectivity of private effort gradually emerged. The first organizational manifestations of a collective private effort were the Charity Organization Societies. Responding to the growing chaos of voluntary activity, they sought to bring order out of overlapping uncoordinated charities. One of their goals was to prevent an enterprising pauper from exploiting a number of charities in a manner not consistent with the best principles of relief work. The Charity Organization Society first appeared in the United States in Buffalo in 1877. By 1894, there were over 150 charitable organization societies in the country.

The societies were private in two very important ways. They were opposed to public relief, and their vision of help involved a private moral transaction between the solid citizen and the person in trouble. The concept of the private that was now summoned to bear on distress was the moral authority of established citizens speaking to the private, inner self of the poor. It was expressed through the process of "friendly visiting."[1] In some ways friendly visiting was a civic act, but friendly visitors acted upon the needy and lacked the critical civic element of acting for them and with them.

One contemporary phenomenon, the settlement house movement, was determinedly civic in the sense of trying to act among

1. For a description of friendly visiting, see Mary Richmond, *Friendly Visiting Among the Poor: A Handbook for Charity Workers* (New York: Macmillan, 1899).

rather than upon the distressed. In 1889, Jane Addams founded the first American settlement house, Hull House, in Chicago. The settlement house, unlike the Charity Organization Society, was concerned most with the context in which troubled families lived. First, its leaders saw the causes and relief of distress as dependent on a wide range of factors. Second, they were convinced that unless they immersed themselves in that context they would misunderstand it. They were, in the words of a recent commentator, replacing moral certainty with moral inquiry.[2] The need for moral inquiry stemmed in their view from the breakdown in ordinary communication between the social classes. Only collaboration between the classes could solve the problems of urban life.

The degree to which the higher civic and social life that Addams aspired to was created at Hull House can, of course, be disputed, but as her *Twenty Years at Hull House* makes clear, Jane Addams was attempting to solve urban problems by a radical effort to reintegrate the life of different sections of the community.[3] The aim was to create a decent community for the helper and the helped. Living in the community, the settlement house workers were acutely aware of what made life miserable for the poor, and they worked both to improve conditions and to create a lively communal life.

While Hull House was much closer to its constituents than the Charitable Organization Societies, the settlement house still raises the issue of how much it imposed its ideas and organization on the community. Thirty years after Hull House was founded, a new organization in Chicago attempted a different approach to its host community. The Russell Square Community Committee was the first experiment of Clifford Shaw's Chicago Area Project.[4] The project sprang from a concern with the

2. J. David Greenstone, "Dorothea Dix and Jane Addams: From Transcendentalism to Pragmatism in American Social Reform," *Social Service Review* 53, no. 4 (December 1979): 527–60.

3. Jane Addams, *Twenty Years at Hull House* (New York: Signet, 1910, 1960).

4. For a recent description of the Russell Square Community Committee of the Chicago Area Project, see Steven Schlossman and Michael Sedlak, *The Chicago Area Project Revisited* (Santa Monica, Calif.: Rand Corporation, 1983).

rising tide of juvenile delinquency, and from the Chicago School of sociologists' conviction that a sociological approach to organizing a community against crime might be more successful than a reliance on a psychological approach aimed at individual delinquents. While the theory came from outside the community, Shaw insisted that the local organizations be run and eventually financed by the community itself.

The Russell Square Community Committee was more of a local citizens organization than Hull House. The board of directors were all original residents of the community, and they decided which programs to initiate. Hundreds of local residents volunteered to raise money and help run the programs. The community supported the effort and made decisions about it. While Hull House organized programs for its community, Clifford Shaw organized the Russell Square community to run its own programs.

Jane Addams died in 1935, five years after the Russell Square experiment started. She died on the eve of a massive expansion of public action. That expansion sharpened the distinction between public and private and lead to a reinterpretation of the private role. The seeds of that expansion, however, went back a long way.

The early nineteenth century saw the development of state responsibility for ordinary children in the fields of education and child labor laws. In the second half of the century the public's regulation of dependent children also changed because of an ironic shift in people's perception of which welfare activities were suspect. Private institutions and orphanages were established out of a sense that the poorhouses were detrimental to the children entrusted to their care. By the late nineteenth century, a number of informed observers made the same charge against private institutions. So private parties were now responsible for the criticized response to dependency. This new attitude put the burden on government to redress the balance. Some states had a vehicle for monitoring public institutions. In 1863, Massachusetts established the Board of State Charities, and in 1869, Illinois followed suit with the State Board of Commissioners of Public Charities. Gradually the boards' powers were extended, and in 1899, the

Illinois board was given the power to inspect private as well as public child welfare institutions.[5]

The public's concern over the fate of dependent children was also a factor in the establishment of the institution that was to be the key arbiter of public responsibility for children in the twentieth century, the juvenile court. The first juvenile court in the nation was established in Illinois in 1899, and although its genesis and purpose are subjects of controversy, the lack of formal public responsibility for dependent children was instrumental in its foundation.[6] Timothy Hurley, who was partly responsible for organizing the coalition that pressed for the 1899 legislation, wrote twenty-eight years later:

> It [the juvenile court] owes its origin, in a large measure, to neglect on the part of the State to care for its dependent, neglected and delinquent children. . . . the State prior to the adoption of the Juvenile Court Law except in a few instances, allowed the care of its dependent, neglected and delinquent children to be assumed by private parties.[7]

The neglect Hurley was referring to had, in 1898, left 575 children in the county jail for minor offenses and, in the twenty months ending 1 November 1898, resulted in the commitment of 1,983 boys to the city of Chicago's House of Correction. Twenty-five percent of these boys were charged with truancy.[8] The city and the county had few responses other than incarceration or leaving children to the goodwill of private organizations.

Despite the large number of children who were unattended by either public authority or private agency, the establishment of this new public authority had been blocked eight years earlier by sectarian agencies determined to maintain full control over their own children. Unheeded children or not, the private agen-

5. Joan Gittens, "The Children and the State: Dependent Children in Illinois, 1818–1980s," Chapin Hall Center for Children, University of Chicago, 1986, 40.

6. For a discussion of this controversy and a revisionist critique of the radical attack on the juvenile court, see Mark Testa, "Child Placement, Deinstitutionalization and Social Change" (Ph.D. diss., University of Chicago, 1984).

7. Timothy Hurley, "Origin of the Illinois Juvenile Court Law," in The Child, the Clinics, and the Court, ed. Julia Lathrop (New York: New Republic, 1925), 320.

8. Ibid.

cies and the few public institutions already had the capacity to tread on each others' toes. The public sector's slowly increasing interest in private agencies, and in children who were not receiving appropriate help, started to arouse the suspicion of the private organizations that had themselves been formed to fill an earlier vacuum caused by the inadequacy of the public response.

Developing Public Agencies and Changing Private Roles

Public awareness of the inadequacy of the private and public response reached a high point in the debates over the first Social Security Act in 1935. From this point on our account of public and private organizations becomes local, focused on Illinois. The rise of public sector services is common to all the states. But the timing of that development, the reaction of the private agencies, and the view each sector takes of itself differ somewhat in various states. A nationwide account would conceal the detail that explains the dynamics of the changes.

In Illinois, between 1930 and 1960, the awareness that the private agencies could not perform the public function of being responsible for all children who needed care, grew slowly. The result was a demand for the creation of a public department to take the primary responsibility for all needy children.

The immediate response to the Depression in Illinois was the creation of a Children's Division in the Cook County Department of Public Aid, the county that contains the city of Chicago. This office was established because the voluntary agencies had exhausted their capacity for caring for the increasing number of children of relief families who needed placement. The division provided financial relief to the voluntary agencies who had run out of funds, and directly placed children whom those agencies felt they could not handle. The step was partial since only families on relief were entitled to support from the division.

The next step was the creation of a county agency supported by county and state funds to care for any child who needed help regardless of financial status. Legislation to that effect was passed in 1949 and implemented in 1955 as the Division of Child Welfare in the Cook County Department of Public Welfare.

In between those two events one of the leading private agencies in the state made the decision, to be followed by most of the other traditional agencies, that it would no longer play a semipublic role. In 1948, the Illinois Children's Home and Aid Society (ICHAS) decided to refuse to bow to pressure to take an increasing number of unserved children. In so doing, it consciously rejected the role it had assumed at its founding in 1883 to care for children who were left without help. ICHAS was forced to consider the issue because of the pressure on the society from a civic group, the Welfare Council of Metropolitan Chicago, to take in more children. A year after the society first made its decision, the director of the Welfare Council was still pressing it to take a larger responsibility for unserved children. In a letter to the society's board of trustees he wrote:

> When I told you that we estimated there are between 1,400 and 1,600 Cook County children in need of but not receiving foster care, I was not giving you a "rough guess." These figures were developed as the result of a study of rejected cases in our local [private] children's agencies carried on over a year's period.[9]

The society's resounding negative reply to this request was based on fiscal considerations, issues of quality, and the possibility of developing a new and interesting role. The board of trustees drafted a statement in 1948 in which it announced its decision to abandon the role of "semipublic" agency, a term the board actually used.

> Our proposed budgets for 1949 have crept over the $1,000,000 mark and we have been asked to carry a daily average caseload of over 1,000 children during the coming year. We are proud and appreciative of the trust imposed in the Society, but we cannot and have not looked ahead to the continuance of such heavy responsibilities.
>
> We shall be misunderstood if we are charged with sounding the alarm when we refer to the experience of the ICH and A in the depression of the 30s as one reason for taking this action at this time. We have no collective guesses about the business cycle

9. Letter from Wilfred S. Reynolds, Director, Welfare Council of Metropolitan Chicago, to Chauncey McCormick, Chairman, Board of Trustees, Illinois Children's Home and Aid Society (ICHAS), 15 November 1949, ICHAS Board of Trustees files.

ahead but we know from experience that we must never again risk the care of large numbers of dependent children on the uncertain revenues from contributions and endowments in a period of depression.[10]

Quality was another issue. The development of public agencies, the growing application of therapeutic ideas to social work practice, and a sense that the private agencies had taken on too much to do a good job combined to suggest a future that was more compact, more specialized, and more professional.

A distinguished director of the society, Miss Lois Wildy, looking back from the perspective of the mid-1960s after the establishment of a statewide department of children and family services, saw the 1948 decision in just those terms. Musing on the fact that between 1925 and 1950 the society's total caseload had ranged from 1,000 to 1,800 and that in between 1955 and 1964 it had dropped to between 700 and 500, she commented:

> This reduction in volume over the past forty years and the high increase in costs is the pattern of most voluntary agencies in the United States. In Illinois voluntary agencies assumed the major responsibility of child welfare services until about 1950. . . . During the period 1925–1950 this society was a quasi-public agency providing services throughout much of the State. The caseloads were high, many of the staff untrained. . . . Throughout this period there was a growing concern regarding the fact that children were removed too casually from their homes and parents and the high rate of case failures which pertained [11]

That was the past. In the future was the possibility of the society using and developing child welfare's new "specialized body of knowledge, values, skills, and facilities."[12] The 1948 statement of intent confirms Miss Wildy's reading of the society's history:

> It is our belief that the most useful future of private child caring agencies lies in providing the best possible service for

10. ICHAS Draft of Board Statement, 13 October 1948, Board of Trustees files.
11. Miss Lois Wildy, Executive Director, ICHAS, Report to the Board of Trustees, 24 June 1965, Board of Trustees files.
12. Ibid.

smaller (selected) numbers of children; and through research and demonstration, helping to push forward the limits of our present knowledge of children and their problems.[13]

Financial difficulties and concerns about quality do not, however, completely explain the change. The private agencies' decision to redefine their role was partly a response to a situation in which, as quasi-public agencies, they would be under increasing pressure to take black children. Nonsectarian, nonprofit agencies like the society were Protestant in origin, and while they gradually lost their denominational affiliation, remained particularistic in the sense that they served white children. So were the more robustly sectarian agencies. This particularism was not important in New York and other growing northern cities in the nineteenth century simply because the black population of those cities was so small. In 1880, blacks constituted only 1.6 percent of the total population of New York City, 1.3 percent of the population of Chicago, and 1.6 percent of the population of Boston. The foreign-born white population of those three cities, however, which attracted the attention of sectarian agencies, accounted for 39.7 percent, 40.7 percent, and 31.6 percent of their populations, respectively.[14] But by the mid-twentieth century, the situation was very different.

Between 1940 and 1950, the Cook County nonwhite population changed markedly. In 1940, nonwhite children constituted 8 percent of the total population under fifteen. In 1950, that percent had increased to 13, and the actual number of nonwhite children in the city doubled, jumping from 66,000 to 134,000. In 1940, nonwhite births in the city accounted for 8 percent of the total births, but by 1953 they accounted for 20 percent of the total. The fact that many of the unserved children in the county were black had been noticed as early as 1928. In that year civic groups and child welfare agencies created the Division of Child Placing for Negro Children in the Protestant Joint Service Bureau, an organization founded in 1922 to coordinate placement

13. ICHAS, Draft Board Statement, 13 October 1948, ibid.

14. William Julius Wilson, *The Declining Significance of Race: Blacks and Changing American Institutions* (Chicago: University of Chicago Press, 1980), 63.

services for Protestant and nonsectarian children in Cook County.[15] That division was created because the juvenile court increasingly found itself with just two options for black children: leaving them with their parents no matter how inadequate the home, or directing them to correctional facilities. In 1931, the population of children and youth in the Cook County Juvenile Detention Center was 21 percent black and the population of the State Training School for Girls was 26 percent black. At that time black children constituted 4 percent of the total state population under twenty-one and 10 percent of the urban population.[16]

The private agencies would not, in general, take black children into foster care. They particularly resisted accepting them into their child welfare institutions. This stance was maintained until the late 1960s. The development of public agencies then was partly driven by the lack of options for dependent black children. In 1945, four agencies, including ICHAS, took black children into foster care, but 71 percent of those children were served by the one public agency in the group, the Children's Division of the Chicago Welfare Administration.[17] A year earlier, the Chicago Urban League issued a report that highlighted the extreme reluctance of private institutions to accept black children.[18] As late as 1962, when the traditional part of the social work profession still regarded child welfare institutions as desirable placements, the number of black children in such insti-

15. A description of the state of black children in Chicago in the 1940s and 1950s can be found in "Facts Establishing the Need for a Child Placement Service in the Cook County Department of Welfare," Welfare Council of Metropolitan Chicago, September 1954. The Joint Service Bureau is described in detail in Merton Julius Trast, "A Study of the Joint Service Bureau of the Protestant and Non-Sectarian Child Caring Agencies of Chicago" (M.A. thesis, School of Social Service Administration, University of Chicago, 1934).

16. Council of Social Agencies and the Graduate School of Social Service Administration of the University of Chicago, *The South Side Survey: A Survey of Social and Philanthropic Agencies Available for Negroes in Chicago, Summary Report* (Chicago: Council of Social Agencies and Graduate School of Social Administration, n.d.), 6.

17. Council of Social Agencies of Chicago, *Survey of Resources for Negro Children* (Chicago: Council of Social Agencies and Chicago Historical Society, 1945).

18. F. T. Lane, *A Study of the Need of Facilities for Negro Children under the Supervision of the Juvenile Court of Cook County* (Chicago: Chicago Urban League, 1944).

tutions was minuscule. In that year sixteen voluntary child welfare agencies that had membership in the Welfare Council of Metropolitan Chicago and ran child welfare institutions reported a total capacity of 1,002 beds and a current population of 802 children; 21 of these children, or 2.6 percent, were black.[19]

Another change in clientele made private agencies reconsider their semipublic role. After 1935, a number of commentators noticed that the clientele of the welfare agencies was becoming more "difficult." The director of the Welfare Council in his letter to the chairman of the board of ICHAS in 1949 quoted a Community Trust study to demonstrate how much more difficult it was getting to find placements for dependent children:

> It can be said that the kinds of children coming to the attention of private child caring agencies in Chicago and the reasons for their coming have changed markedly. In general the children's problems are more difficult because increasingly they reflect the parent's inability or refusal to act for other than economic reasons. Although by no means all the children under the care of agencies come due to the incompetence or neglect of parents, an increasing number are coming with scars in the form of serious behavior and emotional problems resulting from broken homes and parental irresponsibility. . . . Proper corrective services for these deprived and emotionally disturbed children cost more both in money and intelligence.[20]

The increased difficulty, which was partly the result of ADC payments removing from the agencies' purview clients whose only problem was poverty, was at once a threat and an opportunity: it remains so today. The threat was that an agency might be inundated with clients who would not or could not respond to whatever the agency had to offer, and who left the agency staff with a sense of despair about their efficacy. The opportunity was that the more difficult the child, the more appropriate the application of the new techniques social work claimed it was creating. The inherent conflict in agencies' reactions to this new clientele

19. Welfare Council of Metropolitan Chicago, *Selected Information on Children's Institutions with Membership in the Welfare Council of Metropolitan Chicago and Serving School Age Children* (Chicago: Welfare Council, 1967), January 29.

20. Letter from Wilfred S. Reynolds.

could, in practice, be disguised by the ambiguity inherent in the notion "difficult." The agencies could use their definitions of that term to take clients they could or they wished to serve, and to reject clients who did not fall into those two categories.

The notion that the voluntary agencies might choose the clients they wished to serve was an essential part of this new sense of privateness and was a measure of the change that had occurred over a hundred years. Sectarian agencies had always chosen by religious and ethnic background but reckoned they were responsible for the subpopulation of children defined by those two characteristics. Within that limitation the child's need was the reason that serving the child was appropriate.

The new privateness had larger consequences than the choice of clients and more dimensions. It also had a more complicated history. Not only the clients had changed in the hundred years following the birth of the new agencies. The agencies themselves had changed. Their organization was no longer minimal. Fears of financial crisis to the contrary, they no longer existed from hand to mouth in the way they had in the last half of the nineteenth century. By the 1950s, they had a tradition of service to maintain, an increasingly trained staff, and, through the influence of their boards, a solid place both in the community of people concerned with family welfare and also in county and state politics.

The choice they made in the mid-twentieth century was not just to hand over to a developing public sector the task of providing for unmet needs. It was also to redefine private as professional and to exchange the particularism of serving one's own kind for the particularism of serving those people who might benefit from the specialized skills of trained social workers. This change took longer in the sectarian agencies than in the nonsectarian agencies, and was encouraged by public sector pressure on the private sector for the private sector to reduce its discriminatory intake practices. The first defense against that pressure for a sectarian agency was religious particularity; the second defense was technical particularity, which made it reasonable for an agency to pick clients who could benefit from what it had to offer.

What the agencies had to offer were new therapeutic skills.

By deciding to profess that knowledge, the agencies slowly took the road to being concerned with the private arena of the psyche rather than the private arena of the families and communities from which their clients came. Consequently, they became more interested in emotional trauma than dependency. In their former guise the limits of their resources defined the magnitude of need to which they would respond. In this new incarnation the nature of their resources determined the kind of need they would address. The definition of the problem now lay with their techniques, not with a common understanding of what a community wanted.

The new particularism and the developing professionalism had consequences for the civic involvement in family welfare. When the township turned into the large city, the interested citizen could not possibly watch and take part in the disposition of dependent children. A few such people remained involved either actively as people employed by the new child welfare agencies, or more passively, as members of the boards of trustees who monitored the agencies' development. But their wisdom, the wisdom of experienced citizens, was gradually to be replaced by the wisdom of the professional. This change left the nonprofessional with the much reduced roles of fund raiser and fiscal advisor. Professional knowledge began to delegitimize civic knowledge and substitute for it.

A Statewide Department of Children and Family Services

As the voluntary agencies became more professional, they reduced the number of clients they served. In the name of equity, rational administration, and clients' rights, the public agencies took up the caseloads the private sector laid down. In Illinois that public response was made in two stages. In 1949, legislation was enacted to create a Cook County agency to serve the "left out child." The legislation was implemented in 1955 in the shape of the Division of Child Welfare of the Cook County Department of Public Welfare. And in 1963, in response to several statewide investigatory reports, the legislature enacted a measure establishing a state department of Children and Family Services.

One of the reports that recommended the establishment of such a department was undertaken by the Illinois Commission on Children. This most recent form of a statewide civic group had its origins in a Children's Commission established by the director of the Department of Public Welfare in 1920 and a Commission of Child Welfare established by the governor in 1927. The other report was written by a legislative commission established in 1961 to study the public and private provision of child welfare services in the state.[21]

The two reports exhibited an impatience with the contemporary collection of partial solutions, a belief in the efficacy of a statewide response to child welfare problems, a belief in social prevention as well as fiscal prevention, and an implicit belief in the finitude of the need and the capacity of public resources to address the need in all its aspects. The reports were insistent that the state's hitherto minimal role, the provision of care for handicapped children with special needs in state institutions and its licensing function, was too weak a statement of the *parens patriae* power (the residual parenting responsibility of the state), and that a more powerful statement of the state's general responsibility for the welfare of children was essential:

> The government, as the instrument of all citizens of our state, has a primary responsibility to see to it that all basic social services needed by families and children are provided in all parts of the state and are equally available to all needing service, assistance, and care. The imposition by statute of duties in the public services carries with it responsibility for the provision of funds to discharge these duties.[22]

The irrationality and inequality of the prevailing system had to do with the variety of eligibility standards that different pri-

21. Illinois Commission on Children, *Report of a Committee for a Comprehensive Family and Child Welfare Program in Illinois* (Springfield, Ill.: Illinois Commission on Children, 1962); and Illinois Legislative Commission on Services for Children and Their Families, *Report* (Springfield, Ill.: State of Illinois, February 1963).

22. Illinois Commission on Children, *Report of a Committee*, 4.

vate agencies and different levels of government had developed. The 1962 Commission on Children Report argued:

> The service for children outside of their own homes is the craziest patchwork quilt of all services in Illinois. The child's qualifications must meet the specifications for eligibility of departments, divisions, tax-supported or voluntary agencies and County Juvenile (family) Courts to receive the services he needs. Instead of bringing to bear all the specialized services to meet the needs of the child, the referring person must shop around, offering the child first to one and then to another, hoping that the child's particular condition of needs and characteristics enables him to qualify for a particular service.[23]

The standards for admission that caused inequity in public services were veteran's status, geographical location, and parents' financial status. The receipt of AFDC qualified a family for child placement help from the Illinois Public Aid Commission. The receipt of General Assistance qualified a Chicago family for help from the Children's Division of the Cook County Department of Public Aid. Private agencies had eligibility standards involving religion, race, sex, age, and residence. These aspects of particularity were perhaps not surprising especially in a sectarian agency, but there was another particularity that had nothing to do with the demographic characteristics of agency and client. Private agencies were apparently also particularistic on the basis of the nature of the child's problem. The state had traditionally served physically and mentally handicapped children, delinquent children, and children whose behavior, though not delinquent, was a cause of concern. Both reports assumed that the state would continue to take the major responsibility for these children.

The client's rights in which the reformers were interested reduced to one major issue—the right of a child not to be in the child placement system unless that was absolutely necessary. The same sentiment had, of course, motivated the supporters of the Mothers' Pension Laws and the Aid to Dependent Children provision of the Social Security Act of 1935. The issue now was not so much financial security, although both reports paid lip

23. Ibid., 17.

service to that, but rather preventive measures of a service nature. Both reports noted that preventive services such as day care, homemaker services, and child and family counseling could maintain families that would otherwise break up. They also noted that voluntary agencies provided few of these services, and tended to concentrate on placement. This belief in a service solution was in line with the 1962 amendments to the Social Security Act, which provided for a doubling of federal support for social services by 1969, and as such represented a mainstream social work position.

A new public impetus was needed in the early 1960s to change the direction of practice in the state, because the private sector lacked the flexibility or the imagination to provide preventive services. That lack of flexibility was probably a consequence of a number of factors: the private sector's financial and professional commitment to institutional care, its increasing concentration on the skilled amelioration of emotional distress, and the consequent growing distaste for the comparatively unskilled tasks of providing day care and homemaker services. There was also the private agencies' developing sense that they were responsible for only that part of the problem they wished to tackle. This realization made it possible to regard the lack of attention to prevention as a rational choice rather than a sin of omission.

The New State Department and the Private Sector

The act establishing the Illinois Department of Children and Family Services was a public-inspired reform of a patchwork public and private system. An increase of public responsibility of this magnitude was also bound to affect the existing pattern of voluntary services. The act was also a partially coherent statement of what the appropriate relationship should be between public and private agencies. It was not, however, just a public sector statement about that relationship because the legislation was enacted only with the consent of the private sector. The consent was crucial—as it had been crucial in the past when the state increased its commitment to dependent children. For example, the director of the Children's Division of the city of Chicago Department of Welfare wrote in 1949:

> All previous attempts at establishing a public program had failed because of the pressures against such a program which could threaten the private agencies. Even so, this agency [the public Children's Division] which had come in via the back door, agreed to have the private agencies place and supervise the children they selected to serve, in return for the public per-capita payments.[24]

The power of the private sector, or more accurately the veto power of a handful of the largest agencies, was similarly a factor in 1963. The executive director of a prestigious nonsectarian agency, who was herself in favor of a statewide department for reasons of equity, was convinced that the largest sectarian agency in the state, Catholic Charities of Chicago, had held up the establishment of such a department in the past: "Monsignor Kenneth Cooke stopped a state department of child services for years because he was frightened that the State would take Catholic kids. He changed his mind when the task became too big and too black."[25] At the time of the setting up of the statewide department, then, the private agencies contained supporters and detractors of a broader statement of public responsibility. The private agency sector was not homogeneous. There was still room for civic voices (represented in the Commission on Children and the Welfare Council of Metropolitan Chicago) to call for a major change in the organizational structure of children's services. As the market in which these services operated filled up both with a growing public sector and a private sector expanding on the proceeds of purchase of service agreements with the state, the room for that civic voice to be heard independently of formal public and private interests diminished greatly. The Commission on Children was disbanded in 1985 because a few powerful legisla-

24. Roman L. Haremski, "Logical Features of Public Agencies in Behalf of Children" (Paper presented at the National Conference of Social Work, Cleveland, June 1949).

25. Interview with Marion Obenhaus, former Director of the Chicago Child Care Society, 31 July 1980.

tors wished to recreate it in a way that put it completely under the control of the General Assembly. The Welfare Council of Metropolitan Chicago was folded into the United Way of Metropolitan Chicago during the 1970s. It thus became a part of a fund-raising body for a select group of private agencies, thereby losing the role of a voice for the needs of the entire community.

The necessity for private sector consent to establish the Department of Children and Family Services meant that the legislation was bound to be a compromise between the private sector and the public sector view of the world. The compromise was based on the belief that the environment in which the old private agencies and the new public agency would operate was large enough to allow both groups to work as they chose, without coming into conflict over resources or clients. In the language of the sociological analysis of organizations, the organizational environment was seen to be rich rather than lean. Ten years later that was no longer the case, and much of the subsequent history of the two sectors can be explained in terms of the decline in the richness of the child welfare environment.[26] It was no longer a service providers' market.

In simple terms the legislation provided for a broader, more active public role centralized at the state level, in return for a promise of a more consistent and higher level of public financing of private agencies. The public sector would take primary responsibility for the new fields of preventive service, and the private sector would maintain its traditional placement activities. There were bound to be ambiguities and tensions in such an agreement. They were particularly present in the issues of territory—which organizations were to do what—and of the appropriate level of the public financing of the private sector.

The division of territory was accomplished in the section that required the Department of Children and Family Services to provide "direct child welfare services when not available through the public or private child care facilities"[27] and in a subsequent

26. For a substantial discussion of "rich" and "lean" organizational environments, see Howard E. Aldrich, *Organizations and Their Environments* (Englewood Cliffs, N.J.: Prentice-Hall, 1979).
27. An Act Creating the Department of Children and Family Services, 1963, 52.

section that required the department to place a child "as far as possible, in the care and custody of some individual holding the same religious belief as the parent of the child, or with some child care facility which is operated by persons of like religious faith as the parents of such children."[28]

The language itself is not particularly ambiguous. But the division of labor it envisioned contained the seeds of ambiguity. The department was to command the new field of preventive services and share the provision of foster home care with the private sector. The private sector dominated the field of institutional care. Before long the service decision as to whether a particular child needed a particular service (and if a placement service, whether a foster home or an institution) became a jurisdictional issue. The ambiguity about what particular service a child needed and which criteria were to be used in making that decision became critical in the debate about the merits of institutional care. The state's service decision to reduce the number of children placed in institutions was by extension a decision to reduce a major part of the private sector's work. This debate came to a head in the early 1970s. In this situation the act was ambiguous because it gave no final professional authority to either sector for the cases in which each sector had a different view as to what constituted appropriate services.

The arguments about institutional care were particularly bitter because the traditional private sector increasingly regarded institutions as their critical area of specialization. As purchase of service expanded in the 1970s, the private agencies specialized in a number of different ways, but in the early 1960s specialization was a code word for the therapeutically oriented residential treatment centers, where the presence of psychiatrists and psychologically trained social workers increased the cost of care. Specialization allowed the private agencies to do the sensible thing in the face of a new competition—to begin to disaggregate the child welfare market and reinforce their claims to part of it. The private agencies were quite aware of the market implications of the development of the public sector and the need to protect themselves by specialization. In 1966,

28. Ibid.

the director of the Illinois Children's Home and Aid Society, in rejecting the possibility that the society should withdraw from institutional care, pointed out that such a move "would leave us with an unbalanced program, put us in direct competition with the state, and probably result in our receiving children referred from public agencies with the least promising possibilities for improvement under foster care or adoption."[29]

Specialization through the provision of institutional care was, however, a two-edged sword. The possession of an institution in normal times protected an agency from competition because few agencies without institutions possessed the capital resources necessary to build one. In times when institutional care was under attack, however, the possession of an institution had drawbacks. While it was comparatively easy to change the character of an institution in response to the market, it was much more difficult to change in a noninstitutional direction because the mere fact of possessing an institution tied up a large percentage of assets in a nonliquid enterprise.

The division of services between sectors was one aspect of the division of clients. The other was control over the disposition of each individual child. The Juvenile Court Act of 1899 gave the court the right to assign a child to a suitable state institution, private citizen, or private association. The only restriction on this right was the requirement to take the child's religion into account when making that assignment. The 1949 amendment to the Juvenile Court Act, which permitted the establishment of county child welfare departments, included a section that allowed a commitment to a state institution or a county welfare department only if private associations would not accept the child for care.[30] The court could not refer to a public agency unless it had first offered the child to a private association. This guarantee of the private agencies' source of clients at a time when public service was expanding slowly turned out to be impractical because the private agencies had neither the capacity nor the inclination to serve all the clients they were offered. The section was repealed in 1963 on the

29. Spencer Crookes, Executive Director, ICHAS, Minutes of the Kinney Report Review Committee, 29 November 1966, 2.
30. 1949 Amendments to the Illinois Juvenile Court Act, sec. 7, par. 2.

advice of both commissions, thus putting the legal disposition of children firmly in the hands of a public body, the juvenile court.

The autonomy the private sector gave up in 1963 was, however, largely symbolic. The sense of the time was that many counties in the state lacked adequate child welfare services, and that even well-served counties had a paucity of particular kinds of services. The massive expansion of federal and state money for child welfare had only just begun, and no one seems to have been concerned about the possibility that, in the future, a child placed with the public department might mean one less child placed with a private agency.

That possibility turned into a reality in a very short time. The setting up of a state department of children and family services gave the public sector the opportunity to do what the private sector had declined to do in the 1930s and 1940s—to attempt to provide child welfare services equitably across the state. The belief in publicly funded services had reached its zenith in Washington with the 1962 amendments to the Social Security Act; public agencies, though not most private agencies, had begun to respond to the issue of discrimination. A former director of the department described the first eight years as the "golden age" when the philosophy "which was focused on extending the programs of the department to every part of the state with the greatest efficiency held sway."[31] Private child welfare had left large numbers of children unserved, and the public department had the confidence that it could fill in the gaps quickly and effectively.

The next ten years proved that the Department of Children and Family Services could exand rapidly. In the year before the department started its operations, public agencies were giving services to some 7,800 children and families in Illinois. In 1967, the figure was 15,400; in 1970, 22,100; and in 1972, 27,000.[32] The increase was partly a result of natural expansion—that is,

31. Edward Weaver, former Director of the Illinois Department of Children and Family Services, remarks at a seminar at the School of Social Service Administration, University of Chicago, 9 June 1980.

32. Mark Testa and Fred Wulczyn, *The Child in Illinois: A Series of Research Reports*, vol. 1, *The State of the Child* (Chicago: Children's Policy Research Project, School of Social Service Administration, University of Chicago, 1980), 43.

by geographic extension and by more intensive coverage of counties already served—and partly a result of the department taking on responsibility from other public agencies. In 1969, the department gained close to 2,000 children in a single day when it absorbed the caseload of the Children's Division of the Cook County Department of Public Aid. In 1974, the Department of Children and Family Services took responsibility for two other groups of children as part of a decriminalization policy: minors who had violated an order of the juvenile court by repeating a status offense, and adjudicated delinquents under the age of thirteen. Prior to this date both groups of children had been the responsibility of the Department of Corrections. In the first ten years of the Department of Children and Family Services, its budget increased 600 percent, from $14,400,000 in 1964 to $84,500,000 in 1974.[33]

There was another reason for the tension. The financial boundaries between public and private were becoming confused as the private sector became increasingly dependent on the public sector for its income. This dependency eroded one of the private sector's most distinctive features. The advantage was that in times of inflation and reduced private income relative to the cost of services the private sector maintained its size. The disadvantage was that it faced the possibility of cooptation and absorption. At the same time that the private sector worried about its growing reliance on public dollars, it also argued with the public sector to increase that source of revenue.

State support of private charities had a long history. As early as 1839, the state was subsidizing the LaSalle Charity Hospital by the appropriation of five acres of land. Between then and 1879, the state subsidized a number of other individual institutions by this "separate bill" process. In 1879, with the enactment of the Industrial School for Girls Act, the state moved to a system of authorizing counties to make monthly per capita payments out of county funds to such institutions. The state became reinvolved financially in 1943 when legislation allowed the state

33. Illinois Department of Children and Family Services, *Biennial Report* (Springfield, Ill.: State of Illinois, 1964); and Illinois Department of Children and Family Services, *A Family: Every Child's Right* (Annual Report) (Springfield, Ill.: State of Illinois, 1975).

auditor to reimburse counties for 50 percent of the funds expended by them for the care of dependent children. By 1963, the authorized county payments were being made at the rate of $70 a month, a sum considered very inadequate. The inadequacy was compounded by the facts that a year previously there were a total of ten counties that had never participated in the program, and that sixteen additional counties were not participating that year. The 1963 act establishing the Department of Children and Family Services was intended both to increase public support to the private sector and to establish a clear principle for the amount of those subsidies. The act achieved the first, but not the second, goal.

The ambiguity about the level of financial support is in the language of the statute. The legislation mandated the department to "establish and maintain tax-supported child welfare services and extend and improve voluntary services throughout the state, to the end that services and care shall be available on an equal basis throughout the state to children requiring such services."[34] Both the commissions involved in the 1963 legislation had recommended that the new department should reimburse the private agencies for their services at rates "based on the actual cost of such care."[35] That stipulation did not mean the department was to pay the actual cost, but that in deciding a rate, it should take cognizance of the actual cost. The final language of the statute was just as vague. It provided that the department was empowered to "make agreements with any other department, authority or commission of this State, any State university or public or private agency, to make and receive payments for services provided to or by such bodies."[36]

The spigot to facilitate the flow of public money to the private agencies was in place, but the rate of flow remained undefined. The results of this tension were a series of arguments, lawsuits,

34. An Act Creating the Department of Children and Family Services, 1963, 52.

35. Report of the Legislative Commission on Services to Children and their Families, 1963, 52.

36. An Act Creating the Department of Children and Family Services, 1963, sec. 23.

and mutual recriminations. While these were colored by the specific child welfare politics of the state of Illinois, they reflected tensions inherent in the state's increasing financial commitment to child welfare services. This situation was common across the country. Gradually the private agencies swallowed their misgivings about public support and demanded increasing public subsidies. The public sector resisted in order to control the expansion of their own budgets but eventually gave them much of what they had requested. In 1976, the leading private agencies in Illinois succeeded in obtaining legislation that they had favored for some years, which provided that the Department of Children and Family Services would pay 100 percent of the reasonable cost of designated child welfare services.[37]

An important consequence of the disputes and competition about clients and resources was that the private sector, which was increasingly heterogeneous in terms of organization and outlook, became for political and rhetorical reasons a collective entity that stood in opposition to the public sector. Led by one or two of the largest agencies and by its professional representative, the Child Care Association of Illinois, it increasingly acted as an entity in political and budget matters, particularly over the issue of the rates the state paid for placement care. In 1964, when it was founded, the Child Care Association had public and private sector members and put a lot of its energies into staff training programs. In 1978, it expelled the public sector members and hired a new director; he, in turn, hired a lobbyist to represent the association in the state capital. The lobbyist was also the lobbyist for the two largest sectarian child welfare agencies in the state, and took the professional stance that the private sector's job and right was to get as much money out of the state as it could. (This lobbyist, ironically, preferred the appellation "voluntary sector" to "private sector.")[38] The two sectors' sharing of clients and resources brought their daily activities closer together. Their different roles, different histories, different views of the world, and the fact that the sharing occurred only after fierce competition took the willingness out of that

37. Public Act 79-1481 [Ill. Rev. Stat., Ch. 23, S5005(a)], 1976.
38. Interview with Tom Nolan, Lobbyist for Catholic Charities and the Child Care Association of Illinois, 31 July 1981.

cooperation. It led them to exaggerate the distinctions between them as each sector elaborated its own particular merits.

New Criticisms of the Expanded Public Sector

The early 1970s marked another turning point in the pattern of the organized response to need. For a variety of reasons, the bloom began to fade on the state initiative that had started ten years earlier. The reasons were partly fiscal. Illinois, as every other state, began to feel the effects of the fiscal crisis that had been concealed for a few years by the extra revenues inflation brought into state treasuries. The reasons were also bureaucratic. As the Department of Children and Family Services became established, it succumbed to a host of pressures that edged it away from its initial intention of moving resources to preventive services. We shall discuss these pressures in other parts of the book, but they were so great that in 1973 a reform director, Jerome Miller, argued that the department had lost touch with its client families and that only drastic change could turn the tide. Miller's solutions were decentralization, deinstitutionalization, a move to community-based services, and the creation of a cohort of nonprofessional advocates to prevent children getting lost in the system.

This reform effort came to an abrupt halt for a variety of reasons; some reasons had to do with issues that were common across the nation and other reasons were purely local in character. But the problems were only just beginning. In the next few years a series of investigations pointed to mishaps that raised questions about the department's basic competence.

In November 1976, the American Humane Association, which the department had hired to conduct an evaluation of its services to severely abused and neglected children in Cook County, issued a report that criticized most aspects of the department's work.[39] The team of investigators discovered a pervasive confusion within the department as to policies and lines of authority, a breakdown in communication and cooperation between the

39. American Humane Association, Children's Division, *Evaluation and Consultation, Cook County CPS Program, Illinois Department of Children and Family Services* (Chicago: American Humane Association, 1977).

department and its Cook County (i.e., its major metropolitan) operations and between the department and its contracting private agencies, a dramatically high rate of emergency removal of children from their homes (the tragedy of which was demonstrated by the subsequent findings of no neglect in half of the cases), the abandonment of natural parents whose children had been placed in foster care, a weak and disjointed supervisory system, and case records that failed to allow a minimal reconstruction of the facts of each case. An internal department report conducted in 1978 reported much the same set of problems,[40] as did an investigation by the Better Government Association in 1979,[41] a major unpublished report by an investigative reporter for a local newspaper,[42] and another internal report in 1981.[43]

The national sense that the bureaucracy was now one of the critical problems in child welfare led to the passage of the Adoption Assistance and Child Welfare Act of 1980, an act that laid out in minute detail how state agencies were to monitor their child welfare services.[44] But there was more to the new situation than the failure of organizations. It was now arguable that, for the first time in the history of action on behalf of troubled families, the limits of public action as expressed through the work of public and private organizations had been reached. These limits are best illustrated in the issue of child abuse, an issue that fueled much of the expansion we have described.

In 1965, in response to the new national awareness of the

40. Carole J. Alexander, "An Analysis of the Cook County Children in Foster Care Two Years or More, Under the Age of Thirteen," Report for the Illinois Department of Children and Family Services, Chicago, Illinois, October 1978.

41. Better Government Association, Child Advocacy Project, *The State and the Child in Need. A White Paper* (Chicago: Better Government Association, 1979).

42. Mike Anderson, Draft Story on Child Protective Services in the Illinois Department of Children and Family Services for the *Chicago Sun Times,* 23 July 1979 and 25 November 1979. For reasons that are not clear, an editorial decision was made not to print these stories. The reporter was an experienced reporter who had previously published many stories of this kind.

43. Extended memo from Rolland Kulla, Deputy Assistant to Gordon Johnson, Deputy for Program Operations, Illinois Department of Children and Family Services, "Results of Region 2B CWS Case Inventory," 16 January 1981.

44. Adoption Assistance and Child Welfare Act, 1980, P.L. 96-272, U.S. Statutes at Large, Vol. 94, 500–35.

incidence of child abuse, the legislature enacted its first Child Abuse and Neglect Reporting Act; this legislation enjoined certain professionals who might be in a position to detect child abuse to report suspected cases to the Department of Children and Family Services and granted them immunity from civil and criminal suits for so doing.[45] It further enjoined the department to investigate all such cases as were reported. In the 1960s, that was not a heavy burden. In 1969, only 632 suspected cases were reported statewide. But during the 1970s, the number of people required to report cases and the department's responsibilities for such reports increased considerably. In 1980, the department projected 86,000 reports of suspected cases for 1982.[46] Moreover, it was mandated to commence investigations on all cases within twenty-four hours of the report, complete a preliminary investigation that included an evaluation of the family situation within seven days of the report, and determine whether the report was "indicated"—that is, accurate or unfounded—within sixty days of the report.[47]

This mandate was exaggerated, impossible, and ill conceived. It was exaggerated because only half the calls received in any one year were determined to be valid. Moreover, only a small percentage of the valid calls were of the type the public normally conceives of as abuse: deliberate and physical maltreatment that resulted in serious injury. The mandate was impossible because—despite the extra workers hired to investigate reports and the sophisticated computerized tracking system that could reveal in an instant whether a reported case came from a family where there had been previous reports of abuse—the task was beyond the resources of a department of any conceivable size. It was also impossible because it was driven by the assumption that all cases of child abuse could be prevented. The task was misconceived because it brought the massive resources relevant to the most severe cases of abuse to

45. "An Act for the Reporting of Certain Cases of Physical Abuse, Neglect, or Injury to Children and to Make Appropriation in Connection Therewith," Illinois Revised Statutes, 1965, 665.

46. Testa and Wulczyn, State of the Child, 67.

47. The Abused and Neglected Child Reporting Act, Laws of Illinois, 1980, 1686–89.

bear on comparatively minor cases of neglect. This focus strained the department's resources and morale and reduced the resources and attention paid to other parts of the department's mandate. It caused the unnecessary and unjustified invasion of many families' privacy and an inevitable rise of false positives—conclusions that neglect existed where in fact it did not.

In some ways the Child Abuse Acts were a vestige of the hopes of the 1960s that, if it had sufficient resources, the Department of Children and Family Services could resolve all the problems of severely distressed families. The legislation also indicated that no section of the public was prepared to accept the state's inability to prevent or "cure" all the worst cases—that is, the infliction of severe injury on children. (Between 1981 and 1985, deaths from child abuse in Illinois averaged around seventy a year.) In consequence, the common reaction to widely publicized cases of abuse were stricter and more extensive laws, which merely widened the gap between what was mandated and what was possible.

From the mid-1960s, physical child abuse illustrated the limits of mandated action. A decade later, the problem of child sexual abuse reiterated the lesson. Once again there was a real and disturbing problem, whose boundaries were considerably wider than had been suspected. But once again the overdefinition of the problem—for example, the inclusion of attempted sexual touching into definitions of the most serious sexual abuse—resulted in a state response that was clumsy, damaging to innocent parties, and incapable of focusing on the worst end of the spectrum.

The emphasis placed upon child abuse was caused by more than the natural and entirely proper revulsion at the phenomenon. It was also a potent device for expanding the child welfare bureaucracy in hard times. The issue allowed skilled administrators in the Department of Children and Family Services to increase the resources at their disposal while the real incomes of other state departments were declining. At some level this was merely good advocacy; at another level it showed a lack of awareness of the negative consequences of this emphasis.

One more phenomenon, the department staff's qualifica-

tions, raised the issue of the competence of the public department. In 1969, the Bureau of Family Services in the federal
Department of Health, Education and Welfare, as a part of a
move to promote hard services (day-care centers and homemakers) in preference to soft services (counseling), dropped many
of the regulations governing the practice of social work. These
regulations included casework standards such as the ratio of
supervisors to workers, the frequency with which social workers
should make visits to their clients' homes and the level of training required of new workers.[48] In 1971, the Department of Public Aid in Illinois took advantage of this ruling and separated its
service responsibilities from its payment responsibilities so that
it could hire less qualified workers for the latter. The Illinois
Department of Personnel followed suit in 1974 and reduced its
educational and experience requirements across the board, making it possible, for example, for a clerk-typist of three to four
years standing to become a social worker. The public departments were trying to save money.

This change combined with an exodus of middle- and upper-
level staff during a particularly controversial directorship
changed the nature of the staff at the agency and helped to create
the impression that the public sector did not care about quality.
Such an impression fed the perception the private sector had
been encouraging for some time that the private sector was the
standard setter. The private sector assumed that quality meant
the possession of a professional staff who had been trained in
recognized schools of social work, and by that standard the Department of Children and Family Services was worse off in the
mid-1970s than it had been in the late 1960s. However, in its
unadorned state this criticism ignored the complexities of what
quality meant in reference to social welfare services. It also ignored the fiscal issue of whether the quality the private sector was
aiming for was within the financial reach of the entire system. If it
was not, the unequal distribution of resources between the clients
of the two systems raised the issue of equity. We shall examine
the issues of equity and quality in chapters 4 and 5.

48. The policies and politics surrounding this change are discussed in Martha Derthick, *Uncontrollable Spending for Social Service Grants* (Washington,
D.C.: Brookings Institute, 1975), 19.

Public and Private Organizations and Civic Participation

We end this chapter by summarizing the aspect of this history that has to do with civic participation. Before we do so, however, it is worth noting that starting in the late 1960s there was a burst of reform activity connected with the issue of citizenship. The reformers came from different parts of the child welfare system and used different languages to describe their concerns, but a common thread ran through their efforts. That thread had to do with the situation of individual clients in their families and communities and their situation in the child welfare system. Some observers believed that a client family's ability to define its own problems, address them in a familiar setting, and receive relevant help was being eroded by the expansion of public authority and the therapeutic model adopted by the professional private agencies. The reformers aimed to redress the balance between a person's clienthood and his or her citizenship. The analysis was both a matter of dynamics (the situation is worsening) and definition (what had previously been called "help" seemed suspect in the light of changing class, racial, and political opinions).

The criticism grew narrowest, and therefore clearest, in the legal system, where lawyers operating under the mandates of Title II of the Economic Opportunity Act of 1964 argued that children appearing before the juvenile court were regularly robbed of their Fifth Amendment liberty rights. The issue came to a head in *In Re Gault,* which was argued before the Supreme Court in 1967.[49] In that case the Court ruled that the special circumstance of juvenile courts exercising the *parens patriae* power for the best interests of children was not sufficient reason for the denial of due process mechanisms; nor was that power likely to be hampered by the exercise of these mechanisms. The courts were also concerned about the detention of juveniles in mental health facilities that did not provide treatment. In 1966, Judge David Bazelon ruled in *Rouse v. Cameron* that people involuntarily committed to mental hospitals had a constitutional

49. *In Re Gault,* 387 U.S. 1, 87 S Ct. 1428, 18 L.Ed. 2d 527 (1967).

right to treatment because the deprivation of liberty involved in the committal was executed for the purpose of helping, not punishing, the client.[50] In Illinois that principle was used to remove children from mental health facilities to which they had been admitted on the basis of a voluntary agreement without a hearing. Later it was used to regulate the service rendered to children who fell between the cracks of the correctional, mental health, and children's services departments.[51] Also in Illinois, legal aid attorneys argued due process and equal protection grounds to obtain Spanish-speaking caretakers and social workers for Hispanic clients.[52]

The attempt in the social service agencies to restore a client's citizenship became more complicated because much more lay at stake than the definition and application of liberty rights. In particular there were the issues of what constituted a client's community for the goal of keeping a person in his or her community, and what constituted knowledge in situations where expert knowledge and citizen's knowledge pointed in different directions. For some people, community had to do with family—children should be served in their own homes whenever possible, and placed with relatives or friends if the home proved inadequate. When that goal failed, community meant geography—children moved out of their homes should retain a geographical identity with their home community. Community could also mean identity of racial characteristics. That meant black agencies for black families, and opposition to placing black children with white adoptive parents. More loosely, in mental health and child welfare services, the expression meant placement in a setting other than an institution—the community was any part of the community of citizens not living in an institution.

The restoration of citizenship through the recognition of the validity of nonexpert knowledge expressed itself in advocacy programs, where a client's account of his or her difficulties with

50. *Rouse v. Cameron,* 373 F. 2d 451 (D.C. Cir. 1966).
51. *In Re Lee and Wesley,* 68 J(D) 1362, 6383, and 15850, Juvenile Division, Circuit Court of Cook County, 1975.
52. *Burgos et al. v. Ill. Dept. of Children and Family Services et al.,* 75 C 3974 (U.S. Dir. Northern Dist. Ill. East Div. 1976).

other bureaucracies, especially the police and the schools, could be seen as a crucial part of the evidence. The recognition of the validity of nonexpert knowledge also expressed itself in self-help groups for parents who abused their children, and the use of former clients, clients' friends, and parents to perform an agency's service functions either as volunteers or staff. In the last two examples advocates argued that the participants' personal and communal experience and their personal stake in the outcome of the helping made them both knowledgeable and appropriate helpers.

The other side of the coin of this recognition of the citizenship of people in trouble was a distrust of professional knowledge and a denial of its efficacy. That distrust came in varying degrees. For the officials at the Department of Health, Education and Welfare in 1969 who relaxed the rules surrounding the practice of casework in order to divert funds to hard services, it meant a clear preference for environmental over personality explanations of distress. The same was true of reformers in the service agencies. Legal aid lawyers tended to distrust personality explanations because of the slipperiness of definition and the weakness of the evidence used to demonstrate the existence of personality defects. More in the middle were the new youth service agencies that owed their existence to the concerns (and resources) of the 1960s. Some of these agencies had been started by people whose experience was in the streets in poor neighborhoods among runaways, drug addicts, and disillusioned or bored suburban adolescents. Many of the staff of these agencies expressed hostility to old-line traditional agencies and the formal practice of therapeutic techniques. Despite this attitude, some of these staff still saw their chief role as counseling—that is, facilitating their clients' individual adjustment to their environment. For that reason the youth agencies were progeny of both the professional agencies and the settlement houses.

The institutional provenance of these attempts to restore community and citizenship was not restricted to either the public or the private sector. By the end of the 1970s, Cook County had eleven black and two Hispanic agencies devoted to serving their own racial groups. A handful of suburban agencies—new agencies had become established in the suburbs because the traditional agencies had not kept up with shifts in the population—treated volunteers and family as interchangeable with staff in the face of professional opposition and licensing standards. More widespread was the creation of professional agencies who were responsible to a suburban township and who had been established in the 1960s and 1970s to tackle a community-defined need, most often the problems of runaways, drug addicts, school dropouts, and minor delinquents. The public department was not immune to the rekindled interest in a client's rights and his or her community, as the directorship of Jerome Miller had shown in Illinois. But as the imperatives of professionalism weakened the impulse in the private sector, the consequences of a large centralized bureaucracy weakened it in the public sector.

This history of the growth of public and private service organizations starts with the inadequacy of a special form of civic participation found in small townships to meet the needs of an increasingly urban country. There is no reason to believe that a restoration of local civic participation will make the existence of these organizations unnecessary, but one of the arguments of this book is that some restoration of civic functioning will improve the condition of people in trouble. The specialization of labor, however, and the fact that the greater part of the population works in a marketplace outside of their homes means that the eighteenth-century township is an inadequate though vivid model.

The historical account does help us to shape a contemporary notion of the nature and the place of civic participation. One lesson is that contemporary civic action has a variety of forms and is found at different levels of the social structure. The sectarian agency, in its time and place, bore some important characteristics of civic action. In a society where heterogeneity was the salient characteristic of large cities, and where city government did not recognize that heterogeneity, the sectarian agency provided a refuge for the newest immigrant groups. The sectarian agency spoke the immigrants' language and shared their religious and cultural traditions. It provided a common historical referent and understood the place the immigrants inhabited in American society. As the larger society began to recognize its heterogeneity, and as it became apparent that some groups were excluded from functioning subsocieties, the sectarian agency became less an example for the whole.

This history also spotlights groups who would have welcomed the name "civic." One such group was the Committee on the Left Out Child, a collection of citizens who recognized a problem ignored by existing organizations, and who accepted the civic responsibility to fashion and implement a solution. By today's standards that group of people was remote from the lives of the black families they tried to help. But their acceptance of some responsibility for the problem was a genuine civic response. It was disinterested, being motivated neither by professional or organizational concerns.

The civil rights lawyers, working through individual and class action suits, belonged to the same tradition. They were fighting for the restoration of some children to their families and to their home communities in the face of well-intentioned but insensitive state action. Their suits stemmed from a recognition that benevolent state action could take children to places that were strange, lonely, and hidden, and that this could happen even when their parents could, with some help, cope with their situation themselves.

The most enduring figures in this story are the families who took in dependent children. Their official names and legal standing have changed from time to time. On occasions their services were unnecessary, and on occasions children found them unwelcoming or even harsh environments. But for many children they were good substitutes for homes, and in those circumstances they were expressions of civic responsibility. Today foster parents and adoptive parents take on children in trouble, at a net cost to themselves, to provide those children with a better opportunity to make it unscathed to the adult world.

These examples help us to fill out a working definition of civic participation. It involves an expression of active responsibility by people who are close enough—or make themselves close enough—to those in trouble to see the problem in terms the clients recognize. It also entails help whose goal is the restoration or preservation of the citizenship of those in trouble.

This history contains an irony. Public and private agencies

expanded because the existing civic effort was found wanting. At first the new helping organizations contained some of the useful characteristics of civic helping. In time they lost a number of those characteristics and discouraged what civic help was available. The manuals of professional helping even made that helping illegitimate. Private agencies diminished civic participation when they exploited their private status to enable them to choose the problems they wished to tackle with the skills they wished to exercise. Public agencies did the same when they allowed their size to hide from them the lives of the families they served, and when they used their bureaucratic power to conceal their activities from the body of concerned citizens. But this conclusion takes us ahead of our story. We must now look at some of the contemporary forms of these organizations.

2

The Nature of Private Social Welfare Organizations

Introduction

We are accustomed to the dichotomy "public and private" as it applies to organizations. It is a central characteristic of the way in which we think about the means of production of goods and services, and it is a familiar distinction to people who are concerned with social welfare and social services. In the world of social welfare it is a hotly debated issue. Some participants argue that private agencies are the ideal vehicles for ministering to those in trouble and that public agencies are a necessary evil. The argument continues that the long-term trend has been one where the public agencies have encroached on the private agencies and that the balance must be redressed.

Our history shows that the scale of government action has expanded dramatically in this century, but that the image of a behemoth gobbling up a powerless private sector is fanciful. The critical issue in the debate as it is now structured is the determination of the right balance: the point on the continuum between purely private and purely public action that is most useful (for either the clients, society-at-large, or the taxpayer) and that best suits our political convictions. This debate is ubiquitous; we have to address it. But one of the major purposes of our inquiry is to demonstrate that the public debate is being fought on the wrong battlefield. It is important to ask who should respond to need, but the public–private continuum, as it is now defined, is a comparatively trivial issue. Public and private agencies are not trivial; they are the vehicles for helping people who need help and who do not get it from other sources. But our analysis of the contemporary world of helpers and helped will show that, given the current structure of formal helping, a greater emphasis on either public or private agencies is not germane to the condition of those who need help. That is the conclusion of the argument. In order to get there we must stake out a broader debate.

The chief problem with the current construction of the public–private debate is that the lack of careful definition of terms has had the practical effect of excluding very important parts of the puzzle. To a great extent, the term *private* has been undefined, and the public realm has been assumed to be coterminous with the boundaries of government agencies. Very different phenomena collect under the rubric "private." That term has sheltered the defense of the right to privacy against intrusive state action, and the view that a policy of laissez-faire is appropriate to many forms of social distress. The term embraces organizations that have no public role and organizations that use public funds for public purposes. We have seen how the structure and purposes of organizations have changed. We have also seen how the meanings that attach to unchanging phenomena change. As a result we cannot assess the contemporary reaction to distress without examining the critical terms.

In this book we are concerned with four sets of actors. The first set is the group of people who make up for themselves the familial and the familiar. This title is not a long-winded way of referring to the family. It includes immediate family, relatives, and those who surround the lives of particular families in a familiar way. It is a cautious phrase that recognizes that the term *family* needs reconstruction to embrace changing social and demographic trends. *Familial* recognizes actors inside and outside the residential unit. It embraces the nuclear family; the single-parent family, which contains two or three generations of adults (and where there may be important adult males who, wherever they live, are a comparatively constant presence in the life of the group); and the divorced family, where a child may have active parents who live close together or far apart. It also includes the world of older teenagers whose connection to the traditional family unit is tenuous but who have other connections—that is, friends, lovers, and unrelated older adults. We will refer to this group as being the "private arena of the family." Note that sometimes when the glories of "the private arena" are being extolled in political argument, either this group is not included (this happens when *private* really means the structures of the market economy), or only a subset of this group is included in the commendation. Remember, too, that whereas the private arena of the family is generally regarded as "a haven in a heartless world," for the ancient Greeks this private was a place of "de-privation," and for the neglected child or the restive adolescent it can be a place that does not sustain. We accept the principle, however, that public and private action should be designed to maximize the capacity of families to sustain their children.

The second set of actors, which will be the major subject of this chapter, is the private organization. These organizations are sometimes labeled voluntary (which they are generally not), not-for-profit (a useful though not exhaustive description), or just private. (The latter term certainly means private as in "not of government" but is ambiguous as to other strands of meaning.) We exclude from this category private, for-profit organizations simply because they are not important actors in the world of those who help distressed families. This is a major exclusion and shows the limits of our inquiry, not the limits of our topic. In some fields of social welfare profit-making organizations are crucial actors (medicine is the key example), and for all families the actions of the corporate world help to create the conditions in which the family is set. They create the economic conditions and increasingly the social conditions. The advertisement of the McDonald's hamburger chain as a convenient location for children's birthday parties is merely the latest in the list of functions that have moved out of the home into the marketplace.

"Private" agency suggests another characteristic to people familiar with social welfare: many such agencies are characterized by a commitment to professional standards. Such professionalism may be demonstrated by the training of the higher echelons of the staff or by training that also reaches into the lower half of the organization. This trait does not make the job of definition any easier. The nature and role of professional activity in social services also require scrutiny.

All the habitual terms for this group of agencies are somewhat unsatisfactory. We will arbitrarily adopt the term *private agency* to describe them with the caveat that the adjective *private* raises the sort of questions we have just discussed.

Government agencies, the third set of actors, pose fewer problems of definition. They are federal, state, county, city, and township organizations that are funded by tax revenues for a publicly declared purpose and that report to legislative bodies. County and juvenile courts, who are important actors in this story, do not share the last characteristic. These organizations pose one important definitional question. The group is usually referred to as the public sector. The question is simply, how public is the public sector? Is it the place where public affairs are discussed openly, or even the place where members of the public influence the way in which decisions are made? Or has the public sector become private in the sense that its structures and actions are opaque, and that it responds to itself, not its public?

The last group consists of civic actors. For this group our task is that of construction. Our premise is that the incidence of citizens collectively and directly exerting authority and responsibility for those in trouble has declined. The task is to sketch the consequences of that decline and to analyze situations where civic authority is exerted. From this empirical exercise we will construct an argument for the revitalization of that set of activities. That argument is, however, our conclusion, and to get there, we have to dissect a number of social welfare issues in fine detail. But since the topic of the book is the broad range of activities aimed at those in trouble, not all of the subanalyses will point to civic action.

By devoting a chapter to the structure of the private sector, we do partially buy the logic of designating one group of organizations in that way. The key question in the public debate about the private sector is about its independence and vitality in the face of the expansion of government activity. We will look at that issue. But we must also compare the assigned and the actual characteristics of the sector and ask whether the collective designation makes sense. Do the organizations that fit under this umbrella share common traits? Are those traits important?

The detailed interactions of the four sets of actors occupy much of the book. This chapter is about the structure of the private sector and the significance, or lack of significance, of that structure.

Private Agencies in Illinois

There have been a variety of attempts to characterize the private social welfare sector. In 1908, an American view of private welfare was set out by Benjamin K. Gray in a metaphor of parallel bars, where the private sector was viewed as a "pioneering yardstick and advocate, by which to measure similar government services."[1] Six years later on the other side of the Atlantic, the Fabian Sidney Webb used a metaphor whose impact came out of a different political tradition. The voluntary agency, he thought, should be used as an "extension ladder placed firmly on the foundation of an enforced minimum standard of life, and carrying onward the work of the public authorities to far finer shades of physical, moral and spiritual perfection."[2] While the moral advantage lay with the private sector in both schemes, in the first instance that sector was the model for public action, and in the second, public action was the sine qua non of the welfare endeavor. Some more recent attempts to categorize the phenomenon have concentrated on descriptive characteristics rather than overall purpose, stressing the degree

1. Benjamin K. Gray quoted in Ellen Netting, "The Sectarian Social Service Agency and the Meaning of Its Religious Connection: Three Case Studies" (Ph.D. diss., University of Chicago, 1982), 13.

2. Sidney Webb, "The Extension Ladder Theory of the Relationship between Voluntary Philanthropy and State or Municipal Action," *Survey* 31 (7 March 1914): 704, quoted in Netting, "Sectarian Social Service Agency," 13.

of client involvement as a distinguishing mark, legal accountability for clients, and the character of the clientele themselves.[3]

Some distinguishing characteristics also mark differences within the private sector. They include the traits of traditional and nontraditional, sectarian and nonsectarian, professional and less professional, and the presence or absence of a distinct and functionally important geographical base. Few of these characteristics on their own determine the sum of an agency's nature, nor are they all equally important. Moreover, they omit the variable of size, which probably determines, as much as any other single factor, the character of an organization.

The question of differences among private agencies is a good place to start a discussion of the private sector: if the private sector is comparatively homogeneous in respect to key traits (and is different on at least some of these measures from the public sector), the public–private debate takes on an importance it would not otherwise have.

The material for this analysis is a group of private child and family service agencies in Illinois. The group of 200 agencies had purchase-of-service contracts with the Illinois Department of Children and Family Services in 1980. The information about them comes from the department's 1980 contract manual. The contract book is a fairly good representative of Illinois child and family service agencies. It does, however, underrepresent agencies concentrating on youth services (which in 1980 were largely funded through federal delinquency prevention grants funnelled through state agencies), and it does not represent agencies like the Boy Scouts, church youth clubs, summer camps, and sports teams that serve "normal" children. Illinois, in turn, is a fairly good representative of the nation in terms of the range of private agencies active in the business of child welfare. (It is less representative in terms of the political status of private agencies because, like other states east of the Mississippi, the private

3. See, respectively, Ralph Kramer, "The Future of the Voluntary Service Organization," *Social Work* 18 (November 1973): 59–69; Alan Pifer, *The Nongovernmental Organization at Bay,* Carnegie Corporation Annual Report, 1966; and Philip Kotter and Michael Murray, "Third Sector Management—The Role of Marketing," *Public Administration Review* 35 (September–October 1975): 467–72.

Table 1 Number and Percent of Agencies Offering Particular
Services

Services	Agencies	
	Number	Percent
Institutions and group homes only	39	20
Foster care homes only	12	6
Institutions and foster homes	16	8
Counseling services only	58	29
Single-service agency other than above[a]	20	10
Several nonplacement services[a]	18	9
Multiservice agency[b]	15	8
Small child welfare grant to agency with major other funding and major other services[c]	20	10
TOTAL	198	100

SOURCE: Compiled from data in the Illinois Department of Children and Family Services Contract Book for FY 1980.
[a]These other services include adoption, day care, advocacy, homemakers, after-school activities, and baby sitting.
[b]These are mainly large traditional agencies that provide at a minimum institutional and/or group home placements, foster care homes, and separate counseling services.
[c]These other agencies include institutions for the developmentally disabled, YMCAs, community organizations, and community service centers.

agencies became firmly established before the growth of public service agencies. West of the Mississippi that is not the case, and that aspect of the chronology of the establishment of social service agencies affects the relationship between the public and the private sector.)

We shall start our description of this set of agencies with the characteristics of function and size. Tables 1–3 summarize these data.

The most striking aspect of these data is the skewed distribution of the size of the agencies. Of the 146 agencies for which there is client capacity data 95 (or 65 percent) served fewer than

Table 2   Distribution of Agencies Contracting with the Illinois Department of Children and Family Services with Particular Client Capacities

Client Capacity	Placement Agencies[a]		Counseling and Advocacy Agencies		Agencies: Total Capacity[b]	
	Number	Percent	Number	Percent	Number	Percent
1–14	23	24	18	28	31	21
15–24	8	9	21	32	29	10
25–49	27	28	16	25	35	24
50–74	17	18	8	12	24	17
75–99	9	9	2	3	12	8
100–149	2	2			5	3
150–199	6	6			3	2
200+	4	4			7	5
TOTAL	96	100	65	100	146[c]	100

SOURCE: Compiled from data in the Illinois Department of Children and Family Services Contract Book for FY 1980. Capacity is reported for all the agencies whose contracts report capacity.

[a]Includes institutional care, foster home care, and the supervision of independent living arrangements.

[b]This is the distribution of the total capacity of an agency whether it provides only placement services, only counseling services, or both.

[c]This figure is less than the other two totals since a single agency may be reported in both the other two totals.

fifty clients, and 60 agencies (or 24 percent) had fewer than twenty-five clients on their books. The income data naturally show the same trends. While most agencies receive money from sources in addition to the state's child welfare department, the size of the contracts from that department is a reasonable indication of the distribution of total income. Of the 200 agencies for which there is fiscal data, 150 (or 75 percent) received less than $200,000 from the state and 133 (or 56 percent) received less than $100,000. This core of small agencies contrasts with the handful of large agencies with many years of service that dominate the child welfare world. Ten agencies served 150 or more

Table 3   Distribution of Illinois Department of Children and
Family Services' Grants to Private Agencies for Fiscal Year
1980

Amount		Number of Agencies	Percent of Agencies
$1 –	$24,000	57	28.5
$25,000 –	$49,000	29	14.5
$50,000 –	$99,000	27	13.5
$100,000 –	$199,000	37	18.5
$200,000 –	$299,000	11	5.5
$300,000 –	$399,000	7	3.5
$400,000 –	$499,000	5	2.5
$500,000 –	$599,000	2	1.0
$600,000 –	$699,000	2	1.0
$700,000 –	$799,000	4	2.0
$800,000 –	$899,000	1	0.5
$900,000 –	$999,000	5	2.5
$1,000,000 –	$1,499,000	6	3.0
$1,500,000 –	$1,999,000	4	2.0
$2,000,000 +		3	1.5
TOTAL		200[a]	100.0

SOURCE: Compiled from data in the Illinois Department of Children and Family Services Contract Book for FY 1980.

[a]Tables 1, 2, and 3 have different totals because the contract book does not provide all classes of information for all the agencies contracting with the state.

clients, with the largest serving close to 1,000 children. Thirteen agencies received over $1 million from the state and had total budgets, either exclusively for child welfare or for child welfare and their other services, in excess of $3 million. This group of dominating agencies was itself overtopped by a single agency, Catholic Charities of the Archdiocese of Chicago, which received close to $2.25 million from the state, and had a total child welfare budget of about $13 million. The collection of Catholic agencies in the state signed contracts in 1980 totaling $8.5 million with the state child welfare department. If the Protestant agencies' contracts were totaled, that amount would exceed by far the amount for Catholic agencies. The Protestant agencies, however, do not act as a block on children and family welfare issues, whereas the Catholic agencies occasionally do act in concert.

The other major pattern described by these tables is the separation of labor in the voluntary part of the child welfare world. There are, in fact, two large classes of agencies with a small third class dominating the picture by virtue of the size of a few agencies. The key variable is whether the agencies provide placement opportunities for children outside their homes or services to intact families. Of the 198 agencies that reported the services they supplied, 67 (or 34 percent) provided placement services only—that is, they ran institutions, group homes, and/or foster homes. At the other end of the spectrum, 59 (29 percent) of the agencies provided counseling and advocacy services, with the vast majority providing just counseling services. The third class of agency is the multiservice agency of which there were fifteen. This class includes all the large multimillion dollar agencies reported in the fiscal distribution. The commonly accepted definition of a multiservice agency, and the one used here, is an agency that provides at a minimum institution or group home care, foster care, and separate counseling services—that is, counseling for children and families other than those in placement.

These patterns have several consequences. The tables show that very few agencies in the private sector are organized in such a way that they can behave as mini public sector agencies. Only the fifteen multiservice agencies provide a wide range of services. This situation does not preclude the possibility that groups of private agencies acting in concert could perform such a role. We discuss that possibility in chapter 3. The two major types of agency—agencies with placement services and agencies with counseling services—exhibit large differences of outlook and interest. Within the placement block are agencies that provide only institutional services, and their view of the world is influenced by the high cost of institutional care, the amount of money they have tied up in nonliquid assets, and hence the difficulty of diversification.

The counseling agencies' role in social welfare is complicated by the view that in an ideal world a public department's case-work staff would perform the counseling role for their clients. In practice, public agency social workers are too busy to do much counseling; consequently, the existence of counseling agencies is partly justified by the assessment that public agencies do not perform their task adequately. There is a theoretical division of labor that would reduce this conflict between the public agency and the contracting private counseling agencies. That division would allocate case management responsibilities to public agencies and all service responsibilities to private agencies. Such a notion raises the theoretical problem of whether expert knowledge and decision-making power rest with case manager or counselor. Another important characteristic of this division of labor is that nonplacement, noncounseling services are heavily underrepresented in the private sector. These services—especially day care and homemaker services—are regarded by some people as effective preventive services. The minor role these services play in the large private agencies reduces the political weight behind a shift of resources to prevention.

The concentration of capacity and income in a comparatively small number of agencies has other political consequences. The handful of large agencies does not constitute an oligopoly in the strictest sense—four or so firms producing a substantial proportion of the products of a sector—but they are not far from that position. The placement services described in Table 3 were made up of 5,742 separate institutional, group home, foster care, or independent living arrangement placements or client slots. Of that total, 3,016 (or 52.5 percent) were provided by ten agencies, each of which had a capacity of 100 or more placements. The remaining 2,726 placements were provided by eighty-six agencies. The dominant position of the large agencies is not an issue of the extinction of the smaller agencies. The 1960s and 1970s saw a marked increase in the establishment of new smaller agencies. It is rather an issue of the distribution of political power. Political power in the world of social welfare agencies is not automatically aggregated: the slight leverage of individual small agencies cannot be added up across all small agencies to create a significant degree of political influence in the absence of a strong effective coalition to collect, shape, and wield that power. In contrast the large agencies, by virtue of their longevity, political ties, and preeminent position have a considerable amount of political power in matters of state actions that affect their interests. This power derives partly from the largest agency, Catholic Charities of Chicago, having strong ties to key members of the state legislature. For some of these legislators, child welfare issues that affect the Charities are assumed to be the same as, and are therefore subsumed in, the interests of the church. The large agencies also have more power because in a public system that is centralized at the state level a few key political actors are enormously powerful. This centralization gives disproportionate power to distinguished and eminent board members of private agencies who can influence those actors.

One consequence of this distribution of power and of the heterogeneity we have described is that the private sector is not a democratic collectivity that can act in unison on behalf of the collectivity of its clients. The private sector is not structured in such a way that it can naturally act as a buffer or intermediary between all its clients and the public sector. Its largest agencies are so large that they are subject to the same pressures that affect large public bureaucracies. Like their public counterparts, they find it hard to make small- and large-scale adjustments to their programs. Many of the other private agencies are so committed to a particular service that it is hard for them to assess the general relationship between need and response, and to reposition themselves to improve that relationship. Given these differences, it should not be surprising that the unity of the private sector is apparent mostly in its relationship with the public sector. That relationship is our next topic.

Fiscal Independence of the Private Sector

For many observers the key characteristic of a private agency is negative—it is not "of government." The model of being "not of government" is an agency whose affairs are overseen by a board of trustees, who selects an executive director to run an agency that determines its own agenda, with funds that it raises from private sources. The key to the independence is fiscal independence—the freedom to run its own affairs and plan its own agenda stem from that fact. The chief concern in the private sector since the late 1960s has been that, as inflation has outstripped private sources of revenue, and as purchase of service contracts with public agencies have increased, fiscal independence has been eroded. The degree to which the private sector has been or is private in this sense is the next question.

In the last chapter we discovered that the fiscal independence of the private sector has rarely been complete and that some degree of state aid has often been sought, especially for meeting some of the costs of institutional care. Such aid was sought deliberately and valued for the stability it brought; it was not seen as a challenge to the work of the organizations. A description of the income of the Children's Aid Society of New York in 1887 showed that the founder, Charles Loring Brace, valued equally the large bequest, aid from the city, and private contributions. It is an indication of the different temper of those times that he combined the latter two sources because they were distinct from endowment revenue:

> And yet we were glad that a good portion of our necessary expenses should be met by current contributions, so that the Society might have the vitality arising from constant contact with the public, as well as the permanency from invested property.
>
> If we take a single year, 1870, as showing the sources of our income, we shall find that out of nearly $200,000 recorded that last year, including $32,000 for the purchase of two lodging-houses and $7,000 raised by the local committees of the Schools, $60,000 came by tax from the county, $20,000 from the "Excise Fund" (now abolished), nearly $20,000 from the Board of Education, being a pro rata allotment on the average number of pupils, and about $9,000 from the Comptroller of the State; making $109,000 or a little over half our income, received from the public activities of the ninety-odd thousand received from private sources, about $11,000 came from our investments, leaving some $80,000 as individual contributions during one year—a remarkable fact, both as showing the generosity of the public and their confidence in the work.[4]

4. Charles Loring Brace, *The Dangerous Classes of New York and Twenty Years Work Among Them* (New York: Wynkoop and Hallenbeck, 1872). Reprint. (Washington: National Association of Social Workers Classic Series, 1973), 284–85.

Brace meant by "the public" the entire community, not just the faithful contributors. He saw the spending of even private money as a public trust, and he wanted the widest support to ensure not just vitality but also stability.

As the organization grows, State-aid should be secured for a portion of its expenses, that a more permanent character may be given it, and it may not be suddenly too much crippled by a business depression or disaster.[5]

The world in which Brace cheerfully accepted 55 percent of his society's income from public sources was different from the contemporary world; then the combination of public and private efforts only lapped the edges of destitution in large cities. As public and private service systems expanded to the point of overlapping each other, the receipt of public monies by a private agency became a more critical issue. The issue also sharpened as state authority became established for a wide range of activities that formerly the private sector could, with good logic, claim were as much their responsibility as anyone else's.

The fiscal environment in which private agencies operate today can be characterized in a number of ways. While some agencies still receive less government support than Brace's agency did over a hundred years ago, the general trend over the last twenty years has been for agencies to receive an increasing percentage of their income from public sources. In a 1980 survey of over 200 of its member child welfare and child and family service agencies, the Child Welfare League of America discovered that, between 1970 and 1979, the total percentage of these agencies' income derived from local United Ways had dropped from 27 to 16 percent; from sectarian federations, 6 to 4 percent; and from agency sources (endowments and private fund raising), 28 to 20 percent. The total amount of income derived from government sources had increased from 28 percent to 55 percent.[6]

We can illustrate these trends by detailing the fiscal experience of three large agencies in Chicago (see Tables 4–6). The

5. Ibid., 447.
6. Susan Hadas and Mary Ann Jones, *Sources of Voluntary Agency Income 1979–1980* (New York: Child Welfare League of America, 1981), 15.

Table 4 Sources of Income for Illinois Children's Home and Aid Society

Source of Income	Percent of total income for year						
	1955	1960	1965	1970	1975	1979	1985
Private fund-raising	22	21	22	19	12	11	15
Federated charities and foundations[a]	58	53	54	46	43	31	31[b]
Government[c]	[15]	[16]	[11]	20	34	50	43
Program service fees[c]				7	5	1	6[d]
Investments	5	9	10	5	5	4	5
TOTAL INCOME	$1.02 mil.	$1.12 mil.	$1.59 mil.	$2.19 mil.	$2.88 mil.	$4.88 mil.	$5.05 mil.

SOURCE: Figures for 1955 to 1979 are from the Society's archives.
[a]Most of this total is accounted for by United Way allocations.
[b]In 1985, foundation income is included in the private fund-raising line not the federated charities line.
[c]These two categories are not separated out until 1967.
[d]Some of this total includes indirect government funding.

Table 5 Sources of Income for Lutheran Child and Family Services

Source	Percent of total income for year							
	1950	1960	1965	1970	1975	1980	1985
Private fund-raising[a]	35	44	45	34	39	21	6
Federated charities and foundations[b]	21	25	25	25	16	11	21
Government	38	18	17	37	36	59	66
Program service fees	4	2	7	7	7	6	5
Investments	0.4	4	4	3	2	3	2
TOTAL INCOME	$0.27 mil.	$0.37 mil.	$0.60 mil.	$1.04 mil.	$1.77 mil.	$2.69 mil.	$3.97 mil.

SOURCE: Audited accounts at the agency collected by Dr. Ellen Netting for her dissertation, "The Church Related Social Service Agency and the Meaning of its Religious Connection: Three Case Studies," University of Chicago, 1982. The 1985 figures were provided directly by the agency.

[a]In some years this category includes substantial bequests. For example, bequests totaled $83,000 in 1965; $61,000 in 1970; and $293,491 in 1975.

[b]Most of this total is accounted for by United Way allocations.

Table 6   Sources of Income for Salvation Army Unified Command for Metropolitan Chicago, Northern Illinois, and Lake County, Indiana[a]

Source	Percent of total income for year		
	1975	1980	1985[b]
Private fund-raising	57	49	54
Federated charities[c]	15	14	12
Government	4	17	21
Program service fees	16	12	8
Other income	8	8	5
TOTAL INCOME	$9.26 mil.	$17.36 mil.	$17.82 mil.

SOURCE: Business Office at the Unified Command.
[a]This constitutes the income for both the Salvation Army's religious and social service operations. The Salvation Army does not distinguish between the two philosophically or fiscally.
[b]The percentages for 1985 represent figures for Metropolitan Chicago only.
[c]Most of this total is accounted for by United Way allocations.

Illinois Children's Home and Aid Society (ICHAS), an agency with an unusually large endowment, is very conscious of the issue of public funding. Between 1970 and 1979, its reliance on public funding went from 20 to 50 percent of its income. In the same period all its other sources of income declined in importance. Lutheran Child and Family Services exhibits a similar pattern in terms of public support. Its income differs from the ICHAS in its stronger reliance on private fund raising than grants from federated charities. The Salvation Army, where the percent of income from government funds is considerably less than the other two agencies, shows an even more dramatic trend. For a long time the Salvation Army eschewed formal government support, but between 1975 and 1980, its income from that source quadrupled.

The tables, however, point to an equally important trend. In a period of rapid inflation these three agencies, each of which provides labor-intensive services, maintained a mix of programs in 1980 that was similar to that of five, ten, or twenty years previously, and in the process, increased their real income. The

1979 income of the ICHAS was, in 1960 dollars, 58 percent higher than the 1960 income. As the controller of the agency put it, "the state has made our agency possible."[7]

The other side of the reliance on public money is illustrated for two of the three agencies by their 1985 budget totals. Between 1979 and 1985, the budgets of the ICHAS and the Salvation Army decreased in real terms largely as a result of federal restraints on social service spending.

Within the general trend of increasing reliance on government support there is a wide degree of variation in income sources. The 1979 Annual Report of Charitable Organizations to the Office of the Illinois Attorney General contains returns from fifty-nine Chicago area child and family service agencies (educational and sectarian agencies are not obligated to file returns). Of these, thirty-one reported that less than 15 percent of their income came from government sources, eight reported government support of between 15 and 40 percent, three between 40 and 65 percent, eight between 65 and 85 percent, and nine over 85 percent. With over half the agencies reporting less than 15 percent government support, the demise of the fiscal independence of the private sector might seem exaggerated. That claim, however, is sustained by the facts that the large well-established agencies that account for much of the private effort in child welfare have seen their dependence on government funds increase dramatically, and that the new breed of youth service agencies, who owe their existence to federal initiatives of the late 1960s and 1970s, rely almost completely on public sources of income. The agencies that do not rely heavily on government funds are community organizations, advocacy groups, and smaller counseling agencies that operate with low overhead expenses.

The relationship between the receipt of government funds and the freedom to act independently of government directives is the topic of the next section. Before we begin, though, we should point out that, whatever the relationship between fiscal independence and other kinds of independence, it is not a consis-

---

7. Interview with Joseph Devereux, Illinois Children's Home and Aid Society, 3 August 1981.

tent relationship. Sometimes the ability to act independently is highly correlated with the degree of fiscal independence and sometimes it is not.

The traditional organizations sense that their capacity to shape the world of child welfare (especially when they disagree with the policies of public agencies) is circumscribed by lack of financial independence. A few private agencies treasure their independence so highly that they have purposely reduced their dependence on government funds, either by moving out of services that attract substantial public funding (e.g., placement services), or by a joint policy of not expanding and relying on unusual sources of private support. Examples of this approach include United Charities of Chicago, which in some years has received up to 70 percent of its income from the United Way (because it turned over a substantial corporate and employees solicitation list to the community fund when the fund was first organized), and the Better Boys Foundation, a black agency (with a Jewish board of directors and serving a formerly Jewish neighborhood), which raised 37 percent of its 1980 income from its National Football League Player's Association Annual Dinner.

In contrast, some new agencies that lack a tradition and are heavily dependent on government funds might be thought of as decentralized units of the public sector. This situation is especially true of small counseling agencies whose staff used to work in government departments, and who took advantage of the increase in purchase of service funds to incorporate and perform the same tasks once removed from their former civil service positions. Some of these agencies are concerned not so much to increase their sources of private funding as to diversify their sources of public funding. Such agencies accept, as a condition of their existence, the need to respond to public sector policy shifts.

There is, however, a third group of agencies that accept large amounts of public money while entertaining no doubts about their independent identity. These are sectarian agencies whose sectarian identity is so strong, and whose internal structure is so hierarchical, that government funding is no threat to their private sense of themselves. This category includes both the Salvation Army, which still collects a large proportion of its revenue from private donations, and Catholic Charities, whose child and family division collects a large majority of its income from public sources and which would be quite happy to collect it all from that source. The Salvation Army maintains its self-image despite the fact that it serves anyone who needs help. (This catholicity as a religious belief might indeed be a crucial part of the Army's self-identity.) Catholic Charities retains its sense of identity in a situation where 50 percent of its child welfare staff and 50 percent of its child welfare clients are non-Catholic. In contrast the Jewish Children's Bureau guards its special character by collecting 50 percent of its income from the Jewish Federation and by serving mainly Jewish families with a Jewish staff.

The increasing reliance on government funding is thus not an unambiguous guide to the degree to which the private sector is, or perceives itself to be, private. The acceleration of that process causes concern because of some related developments. Reliance on public funds has a snowball effect. As government funding becomes the major source for a particular service area, United Way and other private funding is reduced as a conscious policy. Consequently, the public funds become even more important. Moreover, boards of trustees worry about the problem of raising funds from an agency's special constituency as the specialness of the agency—determined both by its mix of clients and the degree to which it is dependent on that constituency—diminishes. The constituency's loyalty is sometimes maintained through ignorance—by their dated perception of the actual work of the agency and of the agency's sources of income. White nonsectarian agencies whose clientele is increasingly black or Hispanic still regale suburban auxiliaries with tales of their few white adoptions. Sectarian agencies find it hard to convince their coreligionists that their chief function is not the maintenance of an orphanage.

In this situation, to return to our other definitions of *private*, boards' vision of the private arena of family and community is increasingly at odds with the actual private arena of the family and community of their agency's clients. One consequence is that boards are fed myths. Another consequence is that in moments of agency crisis, when boards are forced to recognize the reality of those clients, they may well lack the interest and empathy to resolve the crisis in a manner that benefits those real clients.

One last factor muddles the relationship between independence to act and fiscal independence. The esprit de corps of a private agency may not be particularly threatened by either change in sources of funding or a change in the mix of the agency's clients. It very often depends on the perception that the agency is a professional entity in contradistinction to the apparently increasing unprofessionalism of state agencies. The sense of professionalism constitutes another subset of "private," the private arena of the guild. The important function of this "private" is to allow a group of people engaged in the same occupation to regulate that occupation according to their own sense of what is proper and appropriate. In the case of a social welfare occupation, the needs of the client will be part of the equation that determines what is proper and appropriate. But the private arena of the client family and the private arena of the guild are quite distinct, and there is no guarantee that the influence of the latter will always be exercised in favor of the interests of the former. If, as we have suggested, the self-assurance that comes from professional status can survive fiscal dependence, the profession can presumably ignore the sensibilities of its clients when it so chooses.

Organizational Independence of the Private Sector

The characteristic that is at the core of most debates about private social welfare agencies is the ability to make decisions without outside interference, control, or regulation. This issue is one of degree since the organized private response to troubled families has always attracted some measure of public scrutiny. The privateness that allows private agencies to make decisions on what they consider the merits of the case is usually discussed in terms of licensing, reporting, contract, and regulatory requirements imposed on them by federal, state, or county government.

The relationship between the private sector and the public

sector in child welfare exhibits two tendencies: the public sector lacks the detailed control over private agencies' work that is sometimes attributed to it, but the public sector has a slow, cumbersome, but finally powerful capacity to determine what private agencies do with public money. Since private agencies accept a great deal of public money, it follows that the public sector is an important influence in determining a great deal of the private sector's agenda. But we should reiterate the condition for that influence—the private sector's voluntary decision to receive public money.

In the field of child and family services, the contract for the public purchase of private services is a critical test of the relationship between the two sectors. The licensing power—the power to demand minimum standards for the provision of service—is long-standing and widely accepted. The reporting power has a similar status, though the amount of detail that the public sector requires is often a nuisance to the large agency and a burden to the small agency. The contract, however, is the place where public and private agency roles are negotiated each year.

The act of entering into a purchase-of-service agreement that contains specifications as to the appropriate role of both parties is a process of very recent origin in Illinois. For a long time the private sector regarded the Department of Children and Family Services as a conduit for funds to allow the agencies to conduct their traditional business with more facility. A former director of the department recalled that as recently as 1975, when she informed a group of sectarian agencies that they had to sign a contract with the department, they had replied, "A contract is like big brother and we are religious organizations. You [the Department] ought to give us the children and trust us."[8] This argument has been updated to read that the private agencies contain a greater proportion of well-trained professionals than the public sector, and that, consequently, apart from licensing standards, the private sector should be allowed to monitor itself.

The existence of these attitudes attests to the importance the

8. Interview with Mary Lee Leahy, former Director, Illinois Department of Children and Family Services, 20 August 1980.

public and private sectors place on the contract relationship. The fact of contracts is in sharp contrast to earlier situations where private agencies determined their own agendas. But the word should not conjure up pictures of the buyer (the public sector) determining what, where, and when it will purchase from the seller (the private sector). We will discuss the possibility of a market in social welfare services later in the chapter. For now, we should note that there are significant limits on the department's power to dictate the terms of a contract.

The contract negotiating system is far removed from a system of requests for proposals, sealed bids, and the determination of the distribution of contracts on the basis of merit. One senior contract officer explained, "We treat old customers as if they are going to get a contract next time round."[9]

Not only is the Department of Children and Family Services severely limited in the control that comes from the power of being able to cancel or refuse to renew contracts. It also has little room to maneuver on the rates it pays for service and the amount of service it negotiates from any particular vendor. Rates for services other than institutional care are, by federal regulations for Title XX reimbursed services, constant for all contractors. The current differences in institutional rates have to do with differentials established years ago and are protected by the political clout of the large agencies. The department also finds it difficult to reward effective providers by increasing their contract capacity—that is, the number of clients they are authorized to serve. Some agencies do not want to expand and attribute their effectiveness to their maintaining what they consider an optimal size.

But the Department of Children and Family Services is also unable to reward or punish agencies who are concerned about their size. Its internal power is so diffuse that it is hard to organize a reward system based on capacity. While contract capacity is negotiated at the regional level, individual county or area officials make the decision whether or not to use a particular provider. Even area office decisions can be thwarted by the

9. Interview with Sonia Reed, Illinois Department of Children and Family Services, Chicago region contracting office, 16 September 1980.

caseworkers responsible for arranging placements if they have a different view of a provider agency than the office administrators. These differences should be negotiable at the internal contract review sessions held by the regions with key office managers before they negotiate with the providers. Such differences, in fact, are not negotiated because people at the area office level who have day-to-day experience of the providers simply do not show up to those meetings. Another consequence of those absences is that the department has very little information about an agency's performance to use as a negotiating tool. Even if that information were available, its use would depend on the latitude the department thought it had to reject poor providers and contract only with good providers. In fact, the department's sense of the collectivity of its providers is that it does not have enough good providers on its list to restrict or sever its relations with mediocre providers.

The final restraint on the department's control of contract talks is the inherent slipperiness of the definitions of what the private agencies will provide. An important example of this ambiguity has to do with the definition of clients in terms of the severity of their condition. It is an issue for two reasons: there is some disagreement between the two sectors as to whether each of them takes a fair share of difficult clients. In the interests of fiscal constraint and rational allocation of resources, the Department of Children and Family Services would like to allocate more resources for the service of the more troubled clients. For some years the department has maintained a category called specialized foster care—foster care that attracts high per diem payments—for the care of children who, without an extraordinary foster home, would be placed in institutions. These are homes where at least one adult is prepared to give the children full-time care and attention, and display a unusual degree of tolerance for aberrant behavior. This imaginative strategy runs into the difficulty of distinguishing between ordinary foster children, whose care in the late 1970s brought an agency $8 a day, and this specialized care, which attracted a per diem of double that amount. The department's contract office discovered that agencies were requesting specialized care fees for the least disturbed children and, moreover, were reducing the number of regular foster care slots they were offering the department. According to a department spokesperson:

> We mark a kid from one to four. Four equals murder and one equals the kid should stay at home. Many of the specialized foster care homes had ones. Why are we paying $16.42 a day just because they are above the age of thirteen? They get assigned wrongly because the worker has no place for the kids in regular slots. . . . We have as many regular slots as the agency will give us. The incentive for the agency is to go for specialized care and up to now there's no description of that.[10]

To increase its control and reduce the private sector's discretion, the Department of Children and Family Services decided to operationalize the category "specialized foster care" by insisting that only a child who exhibited at least three of a list of "troubled" behaviors could qualify for that designation. The list included such actions as taking drugs, running away, and firesetting. But the problem of definitions persists. Any one of these behaviors can exist in manifestations so minor as to not warrant attention and so major as to be sources of the most serious concern. When the criterion demands the child's involvement in at least three of the behaviors, the category becomes more differentiating and does give the department more control. But the department is still at the mercy of the regular and specialized foster care slots an agency says it has, and it runs into the definitional problem again the moment it attempts to make finer distinctions.

This example uncovers the different imperatives purchasers and vendors in social services face, and these in turn are the grounds for the claims and pleas for freedom of action that both sides make. The private agency provider of service is faced with the day-to-day task of looking after children, some of whom are troubled and some of whom require considerable attention. It seeks freedom to look after these children in a fashion it considers appropriate and consistent with the maintenance of the organization. It is, therefore, in its interests to exaggerate the difficulty of its charges, thus giving it some leeway and flexibility in

10. Ibid.

marshaling and allocating its resources. The public department, though, is the agency of last resort for children no one else wants to take; it is also responsible for the proper expenditure of state funds. The department is aware that some agencies would be more than happy to take children with few or no problems and still claim special rates for their care. Thus, the public department has an interest in underestimating the difficulty of its charges. This genuine clash of interests is an important part of both sectors' claim for more freedom.

Monitoring and Accountability

The details of what goes into a contract are one aspect of the distribution of power between the two sectors. The other aspect is whether any attention is paid to those details once a contract is signed. This is the issue of monitoring and accountability. It is a complicated issue and the light it sheds on public and private autonomy is less important than the effect it has on the lives of individual clients. We shall discuss that issue in chapter 6. But in terms of the two sectors, the apparent authority a contract gives the Department of Children and Family Services over the day-to-day work of an private agency is never realized. A contract that spells out the details of an agency's obligations is likely to reduce in practice to the flimsiest oversight: checking on paper that goals have been established for each client and that the process of achieving those goals—for example, that the number of planned counseling sessions are in fact happening—is proceeding according to plan. Even this degree of monitoring is unlikely in the majority of cases. Public department caseworkers with caseloads of eighty clients are often too busy for that paper monitoring, let alone for a series of conferences about their clients with the agencies providing services. The details of what actually happens in a counseling session, a foster home, or an institution are generally unavailable. Two attempts made in the 1970s to increase outsiders' knowledge of what went on between clients and social workers—an attempt to maintain an institutional evaluation unit in the department and a United Way plan to make random checks of case records and to interview the clients those records described—were killed by the opposition of the private agencies.

These obstacles to control do not preclude the possibility that an acute public social worker will develop a sense of a contracting agency's work. Nor does it prevent the Department of Children and Family Service from invoking the clauses of a contract if the department has enough information to suspect that an agency's work is extraordinarily deficient. But given the shortage of good placements and the amount of work an average worker has to do, an agency's work is likely to be subject to close scrutiny only if the department suspects a very high level of incompetence. Since budgets are easier to monitor than the quality of services, fiscal mistakes are likely to set off department investigations much sooner than poor performance. As one private agency director complained:

> I think the department should have a tough monitoring system for service and that it should think about outcome measures and feedback from clients and follow-up studies of effectiveness. They don't do that. They only notice whether supplies are necessary. Is a coffee pot an allowable expense when you are doing therapy with alcoholics?[11]

No general statement about the autonomy of the private sector will capture the variety of relationships that exist between particular private agencies and the state. The larger agencies will help determine the public agenda and have more latitude to resist it. Smaller agencies that rely entirely on public funds are much more in the position of vendors of contracted goods where deviation from contract could threaten contract renewal. One social work supervisor with contract and monitoring experience summed it up this way:

> There are three different groups of providers. With one group of providers we have most control and we call the shots. That's with things like in-home services, counselors, and homemakers and we tell them what to do. Then there is a middle group who

11. Interview with Ann Brown, Executive Director, Associates in Crisis Therapy, 17 July 1980.

provide institutional and group home care and have a long history of program planning. The department cuts people out of these providers for fiscal reasons. We may stop intake for a while to make the program change itself, though in general those programs go under for administrative and fiscal reasons, not for program reasons. We have little control over whether we contract with them. . . . Then the third kind of program are the traditional foster care providers like Catholic Charities and Jewish Children's Bureau and these are most out of our control. We did not have statements of what we could expect from them until last year.[12]

This analysis is borne out by the differences that exist in the contracts themselves. For fiscal reasons, the Department of Children and Family Services spells out more details in contracts for children in institutional care and, for political reasons, gives greater contractual authority to long-established larger agencies than it gives to new and smaller agencies. A typical contract for a new counseling agency reads:

The department caseworker maintains primary case monitoring responsibility with regard to service plans, quantity and quality of service and termination planning. The department caseworker is expected to coordinate service planning on new referrals with the agency as needed and appropriate. The department contract liaison provides referral information and delineates what services are expected from the agency.[13]

At the other extreme is a contract with a powerful, well-established agency for intervention and counseling in child abuse cases. This contract puts the responsibility and authority unmistakably with the private agency:

The agency is responsible for immediate intervention, and formulation and initiating the treatment plan. The agency will interpret the plan to the Department or referring source . . . the agency will make the decision as to whether to remove the child from the home in consultation with the department worker.[14]

12. Interview with Susan Demaree, Illinois Department of Children and Family Services, 31 July 1980.
13. Illinois Department of Children and Family Services Contract Book, 1980.
14. Ibid.

The state's day-to-day control over the private agencies with whom it contracts is much less than the anguished cries of government interference would suggest. Nonetheless, private agencies that wish to maintain their level of purchase of service funding have to move toward the major policy preferences of the state. An agency's decision to reduce purchase of service income in order to maintain broad control over its work is also a decision to reduce its size.

The private sector's relationship with the public sector, however, depends on more than the decision to accept or reject state contracts. When the private agencies acquiesce to state policies they dislike, the public sector rarely dictates all the terms of that acquiescence. The limits and the possibilities of both sectors' power can be detected in the policy shift over the use of child welfare institutions in the 1970s. The decision to reduce the number of institutional placements was a public sector decision and was implemented against the protests of much of the private sector. Between 1970 and 1975, the number of children in private child welfare institutions in Illinois fell by over 30 percent. During the course of that deinstitutionalization, however, the cost of institutional care as a percentage of a rising departmental budget remained constant. As the Department of Children and Family Services reduced the number of children in institutions, the private sector maintained their institutional income by demanding higher per diem rates for the smaller number of children in care. In short, while the private sector's professional views were overridden, their organizational interests were protected.

This brief excursion into the question of whether private agencies have succumbed to state control is meant to illustrate the fact of change and the limits of change. We shall discuss the relationship between the two sectors in much greater detail when we examine the effects of public and private efforts on the lives of the clients themselves. There is, however, an issue about the relationship between the two sectors and their clients that challenges one of the premises of the private sector's claims. Disputes often arise between the two sectors about who is to make the final decisions about a child. The two sectors regard this as an important issue for both long-term and day-to-day reasons. In the long term the question is about which sector stands higher on the professional hierarchy. In the short term it is a practical matter of who should decide what should happen to a particular child on any given day. Entwined in the private sector's claim for preeminence is an implicit belief that the public sector is an interloper in a private relationship.

This claim has a fundamental flaw. Children taken out of their homes and placed in voluntary agencies—whether by the actions of the parents, the voluntary agencies with the tacit agreement of the parents, or the juvenile court—are a public responsibility and always have been a public responsibility. They are a public responsibility in the general sense that the children as citizens have habeas corpus rights and the right to be protected against assault, and in the more specialized sense that, absent the effective guardianship of parents, the *parens patriae* power (the parenting responsibility of the state) is set in motion. In the nineteenth century, when a voluntary agency took cognizance of a child's plight and provided a surrogate home, it was generally considered unnecessary to evoke the *parens patriae* power. This action of a voluntary agency did not, however, formally invalidate the notion of the *parens patriae* power. At no time did voluntary agencies have a power or responsibility akin to that of natural parents or of the state. Rather the action of the voluntary agency rested on an implicit assumption of the community's approval. This assumption made the formal evocation of the *parens patriae* power appear to be unnecessary.

Charles Loring Brace related incident after incident when he and his co-workers found children on the streets of New York, in prison, or in slums; asked them and their parents whether they would like the Children's Aid Society of New York to find a home for the child in the country; and if there was agreement (or if the parents could not be readily located), put the plan into action immediately. By the 1970s, the situation had changed because some child welfare lawyers and public child welfare departments thought that it was necessary to exercise the *parens patriae* power formally when a child's liberty rights were at stake.

In current child welfare practice, children who do not live

with their parents and who live in placements arranged by voluntary agencies are a public responsibility because: (1) their placement away from home both theoretically and in practice triggers the *parens patriae* power; (2) in the vast majority of cases, the transition from living at home to living in a child welfare placement will be arranged by the juvenile court acting under the mandates of public legislation; and (3) in both foster care and institutional care the bulk of the cost of the placement will be borne out of public monies appropriated by the state legislature. The first ground for this claim has operated since the exposition of the *parens patriae* power. While the degree to which (2) and (3) have been the case increased over the course of this century, they both rest on the long-standing assumptions of (1). So although the state now pays much more attention to the operations of voluntary agencies, and although that increased attention is a source of dispute, some of the grounds on which that attention is justified are of long standing, and have not been the object of serious challenge.

There is one reason why this argument about the private agencies' relationship to children works better today than it would have a hundred years ago. Then some agencies had different grounds for claiming responsibility for the lives of troubled families. The trustees and staff of the German Catholic orphanage who agreed to accept a German Catholic orphan from their particular parish were acting in accordance with the expressed wishes of the child's community. The private agency that claims a similar authority today on the dissimilar basis of professional wisdom has a much weaker case.

But just as we should be cautious about the claims of private agencies, we should also be cautious about the claims of public agencies. Few would deny that in the last resort the state acting on behalf of the public has the authority to intervene in the lives of children who are in deep trouble. But the public agency is, as the phrase implies, an agent of the public. Its actions are justifiable to the degree that they accord with the public's wishes. Public and private organizations expanded in the void left by families and communities who could not or would not act on behalf of their troubled children. But in a democracy that failure or incapacity of social groups does not change the fact that their proxies are still proxies. For this reason the debate about the rightful place of public and private agencies is merely a bureaucratic debate. The public debate should be about the possibilities of reducing the need for proxies and the appropriateness of the proxies' actions when they are necessary.

The Private Sector as a Market

Another element of the "privateness" of the private sector is that the existence of private social welfare agencies makes possible a market in the delivery of social services. The existence of such a market would be important if competition produced efficiency and quality. Our immediate concern is with the issue of whether private social services create a market either among private agencies or between the private sector and the public sector.

In child welfare, clients are not consumers in a market sense. In general they do not choose which services they will receive, and sometimes they do not even choose to receive services. They do not directly pay for services. The potential market in social services for troubled families is in the arena where a government department contracts with a private agency for the delivery of specified services to clients at a per client/time unit cost or for the operation of a specified program.

At a theoretical level this arrangement has the characteristics of a market. The consumer (the state) determines what and how much it will purchase at what price, and the supplier (the private agency) decides whether to provide services of that kind, at that quantity and price. In practice these transactions are unlike the ideal market where price, supply, and demand move freely to an equilibrium.

Agencies, the suppliers, help to determine demand by the influence they exert on the state legislature about the kinds of clients the state decides to serve and the total budget allocated to serve those clients. Some of the demand for services is price inelastic and outside the control of the consumer (the state agency) because the legislature, for political reasons, has to respond to its constituents' demands for dealing with troubled and troublesome families. When this happens, the market consists of the same supplier, the agencies, and a different consumer, the taxpayer; but the relationship between the two is attenuated because it is mediated both through the legislature and the state bureaucracy. Both this market and the one that exists between the state and the private agencies are further attenuated by the actions of the juvenile court. In theory the court determines demand (the number of people for whom the state has to provide services) solely in accordance with its interpretation of the law. In practice the number of cases it is asked to adjudicate and the pattern of these adjudications are influenced by the knowledge of the availability of services, and by a sense of the overall budget demands the purchase of these resources is putting on the state.

If the state is regarded as the consumer, the public sector's capacity to choose a particular private agency from which to purchase service could create competition between private agencies for that business. Consequently, the quality of the services offered and the appropriateness of the service (by the state's criteria) might increase. In practice this possibility is circumscribed by the paucity of decent quality service programs in the private sector. Some state agencies consider that they do not have sufficient minimum quality contracted services to address the needs of their clients, far less sufficient services of reasonable quality. In practice poor quality agencies, as long as they keep their accounts in order, do not go out of business, and high quality agencies do not attract extra business. There are several reasons for this. As a state contractor explained: "Legally, we can cut off all providers, but in practice, we can't. They are part of the family. . . . [One year], we thought we would drop a lot then we started to get phone calls saying, 'where is my contract?' "[15] As we pointed out earlier, some of the good agencies resist larger contracts because they think expansion will change the character and perhaps the quality of the agency. They also resist more business because most of the pressure for expansion comes in the area of difficult children and such service has high institutional and personal costs.

On rare occasions the state can use market mechanisms to

15. Interview with Reed, 16 September 1980.

change directions. In 1973, the reforming director of the Illinois Department of Children and Family Services, Jerome Miller, ended a series of institutional contracts with one set of agencies and established a series of community service contracts with another set of agencies. In one year a thousand young people were taken out of institutions, and $2.25 million was transferred from institutional care to community services.[16] The circumstances of this transaction, however, suggest that it was a very special case, not an example of the flexibility the service market is capable of in normal times. The deinstitutionalized children had all been placed in out-of-state institutions whose sponsors and trustees had little political influence in Illinois. The new services were obtained not from existing agencies but from new agencies the director called into existence—a strategy that can be employed only on rare occasions. When the director attempted a similar redistribution of resources within the state, the private agencies were able to force the governor to terminate his appointment. Interestingly enough, a few years earlier when Miller attempted a similar massive change in directions within the wholly public juvenile corrections field in Massachusetts, he was successful. He succeeded mainly because he was able to persuade a group of influential citizens to his point of view—in this case the co-agent of change was not the market but civic action.

The effectiveness of the intra-private sector market is also reduced by the conscious differentiation of product. Some of the older private agencies are known to specialize in a particular area and their peers—other older private agencies—sometimes avoid getting into the same areas because they regard that area as the prerogative of the other agencies. The self-discipline works because the courtesy also operates in the opposite direction. There are also some examples of price fixing. In some services—for example, foster care—there is a single price for all private agencies. The suppliers, acting through their trade association, the Child Care Association, use political pressure to

---

16. See Harold Goldman, "Reforming Youth Services in Illinois in the 1980s. Governor James R. Thompson's Special Task Force on Troubled Adolescents" (Ph.D. diss., School of Social Services Administration, University of Chicago, 1982), 99.

influence the price level. In institutional care every agency gets a different rate, but the rate has to do with differentials established many years ago. The differences are an indication of the longevity of the agency (older agencies have higher rates) and an agency's political clout, not price competition.

In addition to the possibility of a market operating among private sector agencies, there is also a possible market operating between the private sector and the public sector. In practice this relationship has some of the limitations of the intra-private sector market, notably differentiation of product between the two sectors. The state provides virtually no institutional care, leaving that service to the private sector. The state is more likely than private agencies to serve black foster children. The state is also regarded by parts of the private sector as the placement of last resort. This differentiation is buttressed by each section's view of itself. The private sector's mandate is professional—it should serve those children who need the services it can provide. The public sector's mandate is legal—it should serve those children who by the decision of the juvenile court have to be served.

The other limitation the public–private market has in common with the intra-private sector market is a lack of information. The quality of a social service is measured by its effect on a client, but in many social services there are conflicting notions about what is a desirable outcome. Moreover, there is rarely clear-cut evidence about the efficacy of service rendered. While public and private sectors may exchange heated accusations about the merits of each other's performance, good data are hard to obtain, and data that might shed some light are rarely collected and even more rarely analyzed.[17]

An economic analysis—what is the economic pattern or dynamic of the distribution of labor between the two sectors—is still possible even if the usual analogy of the private market in goods is inadequate. Writing about the entire nonprofit sector, Burton Weisbrod has proposed the theory that, where there is

17. Some of the reasons for the lack of good data on the outcomes of child welfare services are discussed more fully in chapter 6. The situation may improve if the individual states faithfully and conscientiously implement the reporting provisions of the Adoption Assistance and Child Welfare Act of 1980.

not enough demand to allow the public sector to provide a particular set of goods if that involves higher taxes, voluntary agencies will supply those goods until the demand is high enough to trigger a public sector response.[18] The existence of a public sector service is, therefore, evidence of a particular level of demand, and the relationship between the two sectors has some market qualities. In many cases, of course, the demand for a particular nonprofit sector good—for example, baroque organ concerts or frog jumping competitions—may never be high enough to trigger that response. This theory does, how-ever, describe a wide range of "goods" that started off in the voluntary not-for-profit sector and ended up being at least partly provided by the public sector. It certainly describes the expansion of child and family services from the mid-nineteenth century to the present day. But there are important aspects of the current organization of those services that lie outside its explanatory power.

The theory is temporally bound because it is less useful in circumstances when fiscal restraint inhibits the expansion of ser-vices and when the dynamic that has to be explained is the way in which cuts are distributed among services. It is also inade-quate to explore situations where the key questions are about the comparative role of public and private agencies in a largely publicly financed system.

There is another problem with the argument. According to the theory, the agent in the transaction from voluntary service to publicly provided service is the consumer voter who is willing to pay higher taxes if the tax monies are used to support a service the consumer voter wishes to receive. A good deal of the change in the fiscal relationship between the private sector and the state was mediated through a much more restricted political process. In 1963, when the bill to establish the state department was enacted, child welfare issues were not broadly discussed in public, and the legislative action was taken as the consequence of the pressures of a few child welfare reformers and with the

18. Burton A. Weisbrod, *The Voluntary Nonprofit Sector: An Economic Analysis* (Lexington, Mass: Lexington Books, 1977).

consent of the leading private agencies. The legislative and judicial move in the mid-1970s to full funding of the reasonable costs of some services was accomplished by an even smaller group of people. The lobbyist for Catholic Charities insisted that the bill to provide full funding was a Catholic Charities bill,[19] and the court suit to enforce the provisions of the bill named the Charities as plaintiffs.[20] In this instance the sectarian organization was acting, not as an agent of its members' direct interests (in which case the action would have represented a considerable minority of voters), but on behalf of its bureaucratic interests. By the same token, the support of the Catholic laity for the actions of Catholic Charities existed, not because of the particular social policy the organization pursued, but because of a generalized support for the church. This support was particularly effective in a state where the Chicago Archdiocesan newspaper was quick to label as anti-Catholic any action of the state government contrary to the interests of any part of the church.

The Weisbrod progression suggests the expansion of grass-roots or taxpayer support for a service until the interests of a few become the interests of the many. It might be argued that the private agencies represent the interests of those who have no political voice. In this case, when the private agencies and their trustees request public funding, they are acting on behalf of a public constituency. Some private agencies do see their role in this light, but many do not. In those agencies whose worldview is bounded by their own direct service activities, the trustees' client is the agency, not the person who receives the agency's services. While some active trustees might have a well-developed sense of the place their agency has in the service system, few of them have a broad enough grasp of that system to question the premises underlying its structure. This ignorance prevents them from being spokespersons for a wider set of interests than the institutional interests of their agency.

19. Interview with Tom Nolan, Lobbyist for Catholic Charities, 23 September 1980.

20. *Catholic Charities of the Archdiocese of Chicago et al. v. Margaret Kennedy,* Circuit Court of Cook County, 76 L 22360, 1976.

Many trustees serve their agencies by organizing fund-raising auxiliaries in their home suburbs. For these trustees, the philanthropy has an even more telescopic character.[21] The auxiliaries are in the suburbs, the clients in the cities, and the auxiliaries' child welfare interests center on white adoption, which is a tiny part of the agencies' work. The privateness represented by this connection is the twentieth-century equivalent of the leisured gentlewoman of the nineteenth century, but in fact there is even less connection between the two worlds than that characterizing the philanthropic lady: she often knew her way around the rougher parts of the city.

Private agencies argue a noneconomic version of the Weisbrod thesis: the existence of a private sector permits the construction of a laboratory where service programs work as professionals believe they should. Once a particular technique or program has been perfected, it then serves as a model for the public sector. This justification for the existence of the private sector is not convincing. The existence of the private sector does allow for the occasional demonstration of what the profession considers good practice. It does not follow, however, that this demonstration constitutes a model for the whole. In the best of the private agencies where caseloads are small enough to allow caseworker–client contact, where the agency can choose the clients it wishes to serve, and where there is sufficient leeway in the budget to avoid the impression of harsh economy, the business of serving clients can approximate whatever method the profession holds in esteem. Outcomes are as intangible in these oases of calm as in the rest of the system, but the day-to-day operation of the system appears orderly, purposeful, and highly competent.

These agencies justify both the preferred methods of the profession and the existence of a private sector, because they foster the illusion that good practice is possible everywhere and that the private sector is the model of good practice. In fact, the resources available to the child welfare system, even in the best of times, make the "ideal" practice of a few agencies a mirage,

21. The phrase "telescopic philanthropy" comes from Charles Dickens's *Bleak House* in which the character Mrs. Jellyby, ignoring the neglected children at her feet, spends all her time lobbying for the interests of the natives in Borrioboola-Gha on the left bank of the Niger.

not a model for the entire system.[22] Those agencies are able to demonstrate that good practice, not necessarily because of superior skill, but because their private status and political power shield them from the responsibility of taking on oppressive caseloads and oppressive clients. This is not a marketplace where one segment performs better than another; it is a situation where the existence of the public sector gives parts of the private sector reserves of time and energy to conduct their business in a way they believe is consonant with the best professional practice.

The Possibilities of a More Perfect Market

The very limited way in which market forces are currently operating within the private sector—and between the private sector and the public sector—does not preclude the possibility that the work of the two sectors could be rearranged to make it more like a market. It might be possible for the public sector to become a purchasing agent, choosing among competing private agencies. In practice, however, as long as the defining context of child welfare services is the delivery of mandated services to mandated clients (who themselves cannot afford or might not choose to use those services), there may be little opportunity to restructure the system in a way that allows the interaction of price, supply, and demand to produce a more effective whole.

There are other reasons. The private and public sectors have, to some degree, different goals and different purposes. If the public sector purchased more service from the private sector, or if the private sector dominated the service system, some private sector goals would be achieved at the expense of some public sector goals. In the Netherlands, where private agencies dominate social welfare but where the government pays much

22. Michael Lipsky makes a similar point about ideal cases in the public sector in his book *Street Level Bureaucracy: Dilemmas of the Individual in Public Services* (New York: Russell Sage Foundation, 1980). Lipsky argues that since the ideal service cannot be delivered in public agencies because of the pressure of work, workers in such agencies select a few clients who are treated according to the ideal and who thereby justify the ideal.

of the bill, some advantages of privateness are obtained at the expense of public goals.[23] The major advantage is what the Dutch call "verzuiling," or vertical pluralism, in which the three major religious groups—Catholics, neo-Calvinists, and liberal Protestants—organize their own social welfare organizations along with their own schools, universities, political parties, trade unions, and other cooperative ventures. According to a Dutch government report, the disadvantages are the uncontrolled growth of small voluntary agencies, which has resulted in "a highly fragmented system with extensive duplication, inefficient services, inequities among groups and regions, and considerable over and underuse [of services]."[24] The report, titled *Knelpuntennota* or "policy bottlenecks," added:

> Constantly rising costs of subsidies reduce policy options and the possibility of change, making it difficult to fund any new or revitalized programs. In addition, inspection and supervision are spotty and restricted, limited to financial accountability with few means of assuring program quality.

In this case the expansion of the private sector, rather than rationalizing the relationship between service and need, widened the discontinuities between need and help.

The dominance of the private sector in the Netherlands also meant a lack of any government policy direction, despite the fact that the Dutch government, through subsidies and social insurance payments, paid almost all the voluntary agencies' staff and program costs. The private sector as a whole had neither the organization nor, more importantly, any compelling internal reasons to examine the universe of social services in order to rationalize the system. Moreover, the largely private system had little internal capacity to change directions when changing social circumstances suggested a different allocation of effort. This inability existed because the private agencies came under little or no collective scrutiny, either from within the private sector or from government ministries.

---

23. This discussion of the situation in the Netherlands relies on the description of Dutch social services in Ralph Kramer, *Voluntary Agencies in the Welfare State* (Berkeley and Los Angeles: University of California Press, 1981).
24. Ibid., 34.

The Dutch system differs from the American system, not only because most services in the Netherlands are provided by private agencies, but also because the Dutch have no tradition of central government interest in the shape and character of the social service system. These two characteristics are related. The way in which services are provided is bound to affect which services are provided. If the American system moved to a greater reliance on the private sector for the delivery of services, the habit of public influence would be challenged. In particular it would be challenged in the case of clients who are considered to be difficult to serve. The fact that the public sector acts as a service provider of last resort guarantees that some "difficult" children will be served, and it gives the public sector a distinct advantage in pressing the private sector to take its share of such children.

The credibility of the public sector would be diminished in another way if it were reduced to the role of paymaster of the private sector. The difference between the qualifications of public and private agency staff gives the private sector a plausible justification for resisting policy directions from the public sector and for resisting public sector evaluation of its work. At present the public sector can claim that its staff are qualified by experience to examine the work done by private agencies under purchase of service contracts. If public departments did none of that work, their actual and perceived competence would be severely reduced, and the private sector would probably claim, licensing and fiscal accounting aside, that it should monitor the quality of its own services.

The absence of public sector services would also enable the private sector to drive very hard bargains in purchase of service contract discussion. In these circumstances the private sector would probably bargain for private goals. The existence of state services limits the power of the private sector to take clients on its own terms. The absence of public sector services would increase the probability that the private sector, represented by its trade associations and the most powerful private agencies, would force the state to agree to its terms. On two occasions in the past twenty years, the private sector has threatened to dump its public charges on the public department's doorstep if the public sector refused to agree to certain contract demands.[25] This is an extreme scenario, but there are many possibilities short of this in which the private sector could force the public sector to back away from publicly determined policies for publicly financed programs.

There is a more fundamental reason why the transference of more responsibility and work to private agencies might not improve the condition of troubled families. Some forms of distress can be avoided. As we shall argue later, prevention is largely accomplished by public policy in the areas of transfer payments and education and housing services, and an economic policy that recognizes high unemployment as a major source of distress. These issues are not within the realm of private agencies and certainly not traditional social welfare agencies. A shift of responsibility from the public sector to the private sector would only increase the tendency for organized intervention to concentrate on the alleviation, rather than the prevention, of distress.

This chapter has described private organizations in organizational terms. The subject of the book is the relationship between organized help and clients. In part II we unravel that relationship for both public and private agencies. But we should take to that discussion a perspective on where the public and private debate fits into the larger issue of the relationship between need and help. To the client family, the most important aspect of "private" help might be help that respects their privacy, and that understands enough of their situation to offer useful help. There is no necessary relationship between a private organization and that kind of helping. The most important characteristic of public helping may be that "public" actions are

25. A former director of the Illinois Department of Children and Family Services related an incident when "the person running the largest multiservice agency in town [Catholic Charities] with 300 kids in placement, purely custodial care, no services . . . said that he did not want to accept the rates DCFS offered him. I said that he did not set the price, that I had to decide whether the state wanted to purchase services from him. The director of the agency said, 'If you don't agree I'll march 150 kids to your office [and leave them there].' I said, 'If you give me two hours notice we'll take the kids and have the T.V. cameras rolling.' Unless a public agency can say this you're in trouble. They have you over a barrel." Interview with Edward Weaver, 9 June 1980.

open to inspection, and that public officials can be held account-
able for those actions. Again, there is no guarantee that a public
organization will be public in this sense. The characteristics of
publicness and privateness of which organizations are proud
may not be the characteristics of public and private helping most
important to the rest of us.

II

JUDGING THE ORGANIZED RESPONSE

3

Responsiveness

Introduction: Responsiveness as Knowing

The business of social welfare agencies is responding to need, and they rightly value the accolade of being responsive. Responsiveness is not, however, a discrete internal characteristic of an organization. It is a characteristic of how an organization or a person acts in a particular situation: what constitutes responsiveness will be different in different situations. Consequently, it is unlikely that one actor, one organization, or one type of organization will always be responsive in every time, place, and circumstance. This chapter examines some commonsense definitions of responsiveness suggested by particular child welfare situations: child abuse, adoption of black children, inner-city families, and difficult children. This range of situations will give us a spectrum of meanings for the term *responsiveness*. We will discover that responsiveness is not the prerogative of either sector, and that the well-being of troubled families depends on the responsiveness of many other actors in addition to public and private service organizations.

The history of social welfare has plenty of examples of people who were responsive in their own way to different kinds of problems. Both the public and the private sectors have responded with insight and forcefulness to the changing character of distress. The private sector, as we know it, came into existence to tackle the problems of destitution in large cities in the middle of the last century. The public sector's greatest triumph was the creation of Aid to Dependent Children in 1935. In both cases a few individuals seized the opportunities provided by a particularly vivid and concentrated demonstration of need to persuade public and private bodies to respond to that need. The failure of the municipal response to destitution in large cities made the creation of private agencies the avenue for addressing the first problem. The resources and authority of the federal government made it the only possible avenue for a comprehensive response to the nationwide problem of poverty.

We can elaborate distinct meanings of responsiveness in different situations. Response as answer or reply to a situation is preceded temporally by response as sensing or being aware of a situation. Thus, knowing a phenomenon in a way it has not been known before and knowing it in what is later judged to be a more useful way are the necessary precedents for new action. In the recent history of child welfare this new understanding of problems and solutions has come from a variety of sources in a variety of contexts. In some cases new understanding has come from the assembly of new data. In the case of the reassessment of violence toward children in the early 1960s, the new knowledge was the result of technological breakthroughs in the production and interpretation of X rays. These discoveries in the 1950s established the connection between X-ray changes in the long bones in children and subdural hematoma. This, in turn, provided new grounds for distinguishing between accidental injuries to children and injuries inflicted by others. The knowledge was so compelling that, once it was described and elucidated, it was generally accepted and became the basis for major legislative and administrative action.

In other instances responsiveness as sensing the heart of a situation has come from the reinterpretation of old data or the setting of the known in a new paradigm. Deinstitutionalization in child welfare is a goal that dates as far back as the turn of this century. Releasing children from asylums and prisons has a longer history. The deinstitutionalization in child welfare, which occurred in the 1970s, was in a sense a reaction to the claims made for institutional care in the 1950s and 1960s that such care could be the therapeutic option of choice for particular children. The reevaluation of the 1970s owes something to the involvement of a new breed of lawyers in child welfare who regarded institutions from the incarceration end of the continuum rather than the treatment end. It is also indebted to the sociological view, as exemplified by the work of Erving Goffman, that total institutions are inherently demoralizing and degrading.[1] This revival of an anti-institutional perspective did not, however, command the universal assent that, for example, the revised view of child abuse commanded. Whatever the merits of deinstitutionalization—and most observers pay it some homage—it is clear that it was a perspective contributed from outside the mainstream of child welfare: within the mainstream the view of child welfare as a placement activity was paramount.

The other reforms of this period have a similar shape: responsiveness as reinterpreting the given. The two most notable reforms are the attempts to push service back to the level of the family and the community, and a skepticism of claims of professional skills, which has, as its positive side, respect for the possibilities of nonprofessional helping. The first reform meant supporting the child in the family wherever possible and, where that was not possible, encouraging the search for a caretaker among relatives and friends. The second reform included such tactics as encouraging the use of college students and "visiting families" as advocates and counselors for wards, particularly those who were trying to adjust to life outside of institutions. It also meant recognizing the central role that foster parents play for children whose families cannot cope; reform gave foster parents some limited voice and responsibility in the administration of the system.[2]

The intuition that lay behind these moves had to do with redressing some critical balances—the balance between common sense and professional knowledge; the balance between a recognition of the negative and positive effects of organized interventions; the balance between the environmental and psychological determinants of distress; and the balance between

1. Erving Goffman, *Asylums: Essays on the Social Situation of Mental Patients and Other Essays* (Garden City, N.Y.: Anchor Books, 1961).

2. Jerome Miller, director of the Illinois Department of Children and Family Services in the early 1970s, attempted to set up citizens councils to advise local units of the department. The first plans for these councils allotted a large number of council seats to foster parents.

the view that distressed families retain some capabilities and the view that they are incapacitated. In each case the reformers emphasized the first of these poles. Like the criticisms of institutions, these views were unlikely to come from the mainstream of the profession. They came most frequently from outsiders or recusants.

Another form of responsiveness is the declaration of the facts of situations of which most of the actors are aware but about which they are silent because the situations are difficult or even intractable. In these cases responsiveness is not merely being aware of a set of issues but insisting on their existence loudly enough to draw attention to them. Newspapers sometimes play this role, and sometimes it is a job the courts take on. In 1981, a judge of the Circuit Court of Cook County in Illinois played this role for a group of young dependent people who were mentally incapacitated and who had demonstrated some degree of difficult, if not delinquent, behavior. The Department of Children and Family Services had deemed these children too disturbed to serve, but the Department of Mental Health had found them not disturbed enough to serve. The court determined these children were, therefore, occasionally wrongly adjudicated delinquent and turned over to the custody of the Department of Corrections.[3] The initial case was brought to the Circuit Court by the Legal Aid Bureau as a due process issue. By court order, responsibility for monitoring the children's condition was handed over to the Legal Assistance Foundation, and the sitting judge enlarged the issue to that of the right to appropriate treatment. At various times the state departments named in the case moved for dismissal, but each time their motions were rejected.

3. The first order in this class action suit, *In Re Mary Lee and Pamela Wesley* [68 J(D) 1362, 68 J(D) 6383, 68J 15850, Juvenile Division, Circuit Court of Cook County], was made on 29 February 1972 and addressed the rights of juveniles temporarily admitted to mental hospitals by their parents. In this same order the Court appointed the Legal Assistance Foundation of Chicago attorneys and advocates for the children. The second major order, made in March 1975, set out detailed instructions on how the children were to be treated by the responsible social service departments. The final order, made in April 1981, vacated the terms of the previous orders but provided for the appointment of legal advocates for each child.

What is important about this example is the number of public and private child welfare agencies who found themselves unable to "notice" the conditions of these children. These departments' problems stemmed partly from the consistent refusal of a large group of private institutions to accept these children for care. The state's prelitigation response was to allow the children to drift into the Department of Mental Health and the Department of Corrections, not because the children's condition warranted those dispositions, but because the Department of Children and Family Services could not or would not find more appropriate placements. The only body with the authority to force attention to the situation—and indeed the only body with a theory of the problem—was the legal system. It was represented in this case by lawyers who came out of the civil rights and due process movements of the 1960s and by a judge who was unusually well versed in social welfare issues.

There are many other groups who respond by sensing and describing the characteristics of distress. In the 1940s and 1950s, an independent civic group, the Welfare Council of Metropolitan Chicago, analyzed and publicized the lack of provision for black children in the child welfare system. In the late 1960s, a black action group in Chicago called the Black Consortium, through its social welfare division, Catalyst, continued that effort. The youth service agency, Aunt Martha's, examined the organizational environment of the young people in its community to see what degree of adolescent trouble could be traced to unnecessary practices in the community schools. On a national level the Child Welfare League of America at the traditional pole and the Children's Defense Fund at the reform pole analyzed a number of child and family problems.

The list of organizations who respond by knowing, sensing, and reinterpreting is much more heterogeneous than the set of service-providing agencies. This fact should not be surprising. The kind of knowing and understanding we have described springs from a willingness to see the service system, not just in terms of activities that can be refined or improved, but from the perspective that contemporary definitions and premises are fallible. This curiosity can sometimes be institutionalized in organizations that have a formal commitment to such analyses, or it is sometimes an attribute of individuals who bring their conclusions to public attention.

Our account of responsiveness as "knowing" serves two purposes. It describes an important definition of responsiveness and demonstrates the variety of actions and actors the definition encompasses. This chapter analyzes a variety of social welfare situations to discover who, under what circumstances, makes an appropriate response to need. Such an exercise will lead us to a particular definition of civic actions—the actions of people so situated in respect to a problem that they can see complexities and opportunities not visible to more distant participants. In some of the examples, being situated requires being physically present. We will consider a number of important issues in the lives of children and youth, child abuse, the adoption of minority children, responses to conditions in decaying city neighborhoods, and organized help for very difficult children. This exploration will give us a chance to continue our attempt to define responsiveness.

Responding Appropriately: The Case of Child Abuse

The central meaning of responsiveness is answering. But the question of whether social welfare agencies really do answer the call for help is too dependent on definitions of the words *answer* and *help* to be useful. A concrete way to pose part of this question is to ask if particular agencies respond to distress on an appropriate scale—that is, on a scale appropriate to the nature and extent of the problem. An inappropriate response may be one that is insufficient or one that is an over-response. In the latter case there is the possibility of unintended harmful consequences. An appropriate response depends on an appropriate judgment of the situation; this question, therefore, can be phrased as the issue of who is in a position to make appropriate judgments.

The problem of child abuse illustrates the necessity for public action and at the same time reveals the disadvantages of such action. Child abuse, the actions of parents or other adults that severely threaten the physical health of children, is a nationwide problem that calls for coercive intervention to protect the lives of those children. In a free society, it can be argued, only the state should have the right to make such coercive interventions and only under the strictest rules of law. The argument can be made positively. The state has the responsibility and authority to protect life, and child abuse (in its most extreme manifestations) is life threatening.

There are also practical reasons why child abuse should be the state's responsibility. A state social service department is the only entity able to take cognizance of, and respond to or organize, the response to child abuse in every part of the state. The initial diagnosis of child abuse often depends on reports of previous incidents in the same family, and only the state has the capacity to assemble easily accessible and comprehensive information of this kind. The public agency, then, is the appropriate organization to make regulations concerning the response to child abuse, to collect information about child abuse, and to organize the response to child abuse. The response, the reaction to individual families, can be made by a variety of agencies as long as it is orchestrated by an agency with clear final responsibility. (In 1980, the Illinois Department of Children and Family Services contracted with thirty-five agencies including hospitals, traditional child welfare agencies, community groups, counseling agencies, and self-help groups to help individual families.)

Serious problems, however, do exist with the state response to child abuse. Although these problems do not outweigh the advantages, they are the result of some structural aspects of public action. The central problem is that, even taking into account the seriousness of the phenomenon, the state response to child abuse is an overresponse with deleterious consequences. The crux of that overresponse is that public servants and legislators in their official utterances treat all cases of child abuse as preventable and see all child abuse deaths as not only personal tragedies but unnecessary tragedies.

This seemingly commendable attitude misses the nature of the problem. The act of abusing a child is usually a private act. The results of that abuse are sometimes visible to the child's public—friends, neighbors, and teachers. But as the discoveries made by X-ray technology demonstrated, the results are sometimes invisible to the naked eye. Consequently, in a society where the privacy of family life is a protected right, some incidents and results of child abuse will go undetected. Sometimes, where the results are visible in bruises or scars or weight loss, state intervention will prevent further abuse and on some occasions will save lives. Sometimes children will die because warning signs were not noted or were misinterpreted, or because there were no warning signs. Despite the fact that some portion of child abuse is unreachable, the state has gradually expanded the scope of child abuse legislation as if all child abuse were open to prevention or treatment. We shall suggest some reasons for this situation and its consequences in a moment. First, we should describe some salient facts about child abuse.

The first specific child abuse act in Illinois was passed in 1965. It provided that certain specified medical practitioners, having reasonable cause to believe that a child coming before them for examination had "suffered injury or disability from physical abuse or neglect inflicted upon him, other than by accidental means," were to report their suspicions to the Department of Children and Family Services.[4] Since that date, the state's jurisdiction in child abuse has expanded in three ways: (1) an increasing number of people, designated by their professional titles, have been required to report suspected cases of child abuse; (2) the types of situation warranting attention have been extended and described in greater statutory detail; and (3) the action required of the state has been expanded and refined. In 1965, seven classes of people were mandated to report suspected cases of child abuse; by 1980, that number had reached twenty.

The circumstances that can set off a child abuse response include neglect. Neglect is currently defined by statute as being a situation in which parents do not provide for a child "the proper or necessary support, education as required by law, or medical or other remedial care recognized under state law as necessary for a child's well-being, or other care necessary for his well-being including adequate food, clothing, and shelter."[5] The

4. Illinois Laws, 1965, sec. 2, 235.
5. Illinois Revised Statutes, 1980, Supplement, chap. 23, par. 2053.

state is now required to respond to child abuse and neglect by initiating an immediate investigation when a child's immediate safety or well-being is endangered, and in all other cases, by commencing an investigation within twenty-four hours. The investigation is required to include:

> An evaluation of the environment of the child named in the report and any other children in the same environment; or determination of the risk to such children if they continue to remain in the existing environments, as well as a determination of the nature, extent and cause of any condition enumerated in the report.[6]

The inclusion of neglect, broadly defined, into the abuse statute is not inappropriate because neglect is less serious and abuse more serious. That relationship may or may not be true in any particular case. Rather the problem is that the abuse clauses, which strongly reflect the police power of the state and the medical interest in saving life, are aimed at a clear and present danger of the most threatening kind. They do not speak to the misery of children brought up in a combination of acute poverty, squalor, and parental inadequacy. These characteristics can, at their worst, produce terrible conditions. But they are not conditions that will respond to the flash of ambulance lights and the whine of police sirens.

This expansion of the state's responsibility has to be judged in the light of the subsequent expansion of the state's abuse and neglect work load. In fiscal year 1969, the total number of reports made to the state under the child abuse laws was 632. In fiscal year 1981, the number of actual reports was 21,054. The state's estimate for 1982, published in the state's 1982 social service plan, was 85,000 cases.[7] This dramatic increase suggests that the state's response was correct, that the number of cases of child abuse reported in the 1960s was merely the tip of the iceberg, and that the expansion of responsibility was justified by the real incidence of abuse. A closer reading suggests a modi-

6. Illinois Revised Statutes, 1979, chap. 23, par. 2057.4
7. State of Illinois, *Department of Children and Family Services 1982 Human Services Plan, Phase I: Human Services Data Report* (Springfield, Ill.: State of Illinois, 1981), 26.

fied version of that conclusion; some degree of expansion was justified, but the state went too far.

In 1960, thirty-six children under fourteen were murdered, and most of those deaths were child abuse—physical assault by a parent, relative, or other adult.[8] In 1983, the figure was fifty-three. The rate of child murders, a high percentage of which are child abuse cases, rose from 0.0125 per thousand children to 0.0207. Death from child abuse is, therefore, a rare event. Moreover, the number of reported cases is a poor indicator of the number of proven cases. A number of sources suggest that, of the reported cases of abuse and neglect, 50 percent are unfounded and about 10 percent of the total rank as severe abuse—abuse that warrants immediate state protective intervention.[9] Severe cases, involving deaths or serious injury, are a fraction of all cases. Yet the exceptional intervention prescribed for severe cases is prescribed for all cases.

The "better safe than sorry" justification glosses over the possibility that on this particular issue "more" is not safer. This policy has consequences damaging both to severe cases and to the general run of neglect and dependency cases. There is damage to severe cases because those children do not receive the attention they deserve. The amount of work mandated by the current statutes is beyond the scope of the current Department of Children and Family Services and, indeed, beyond the scope of any department of a practical size. Consequently, the department cannot be in full compliance with the reporting laws. For example, although severe cases receive the most attention, they do not receive the attention mandated by law.[10] Resources are diverted from serious cases in order to detect all cases. Fifty

8. Mark Testa and Fred Wulczyn, *The Child In Illinois: A Series of Research Reports,* vol. 1, *The State of the Child* (Chicago: Children's Policy Research Project, School of Social Service Administration, University of Chicago, 1980), 70.

9. See, for example, Testa and Wulczyn, *State of the Child,* 67; H. Frederick Brown, "Policies and Practices of the Child Protective Services System in Cook County," Jane Addams College of Social Work, University of Illinois at Chicago Circle, 1979; and Jeanne Giovannoni, *Defining Child Abuse* (New York: Free Press, 1979).

10. Irene Rizzini, "Report on the Child Abuse Case Load at Children's Memorial Hospital, Chicago, Illinois," School of Social Service Administration, University of Chicago, 1982.

percent of all calls nationwide to abuse and neglect hotlines are found to be unwarranted, and the annual cost of determining the status of those cases has been estimated to be $50 million.[11]

Less severe cases are affected because families whose problems are chronic, middle-level, or low-level neglect are subject to coercive intervention that can be justified only in life and death situations. They are also affected because the public discussion of the problems of neglected children, the largest category of child welfare cases, is preempted by the discussion and debate about child abuse. Families who should not be involved in the system at all become involved because of false complaints. Some reports of neglect are completely spurious—the work of ill-tempered neighbors or ex-spouses.

This overreaction is partly due to the way in which responsibility is handled by a public institution. Public, as opposed to private, organizations find it difficult to admit that they have reached the limits of their capacity to respond to critical social problems. That difficulty is intensified in the case of battered children. An individual private agency—or indeed a collectivity of private agencies—can beg the limitations of their resources. But public agencies are agencies of last resort, and the state is responsible for protecting life.

The state has perceived the problem of child abuse as a problem of knowledge—that is, of knowing where the abuse occurs, proving its occurrence, and distinguishing between accidental and traumatic injury. But this confidence in the ability of the state to know ignores three ambiguities in cases of child abuse: (1) deciding whether an injury occurred as a result of abuse; (2) knowing which state response will be best for the child; and (3) determining whether the state response, whatever it is, will be better for the child than leaving the family alone. The state is not at fault in trying to lessen the ambiguities by assembling as much data as it can, but it is wrong to act as if it will always resolve them.

And this point leads us to a more fundamental problem of understanding that can occur when the state is the locus of

11. Personal communication, Charles Gershenson, Director of Research, Children's Bureau, U.S. Department of Health and Human Services, 1983.

action. The problem of where to draw the line of state action—to determine where action has salutary effects and where it becomes ineffective or even harmful—is a political and moral decision that can be resolved only by the exercise of judgment based on incomplete knowledge. The judgment should be preceded by a debate in which people with responsibility and authority in the matter weigh the various sides of the question. But therein lies the problem. There is a public debate about child abuse, but it is not sufficient because it is not a civic debate. In problems like child abuse where one side of the issue (the deaths of children) is more compelling than the other side of the issue (the damage caused by the assumption that all such deaths are avoidable), the issue must be debated by those with knowledge, authority, and responsibility. But that does not happen. The legislature, responding to outcries about the death of a child, legislates greater state intervention. The Department of Children and Family Services goes along both because that means larger budgets, and because it is not immune from the prevailing political winds. Its actions on such sensitive issues affect the governor's political standing and such actions will, in turn, effect the governor's regard for the department.

In well-publicized abuse cases the department separates itself from its junior line workers. These workers often have the best understanding of the case, but it is in the department's political interests to blame them. The department finds it convenient to insist that the worker did not follow proper procedures and then to discipline or fire the worker. Sometimes these actions will be justified by the events, but often the insistence on following procedures is a denial of the ambiguity that exists in the case.

In other cases, at the crucial point when police, hospital staff, and workers meet a battered child and his or her parents, lack of knowledge of the family and the context in which the family lives can affect the diagnosis. In ambiguous cases the balance is likely to be tipped in favor of a behavioral rather than an environmental explanation. (A proper balance is particularly difficult to achieve in cases where abuse stems from sins of omission rather than commission—malnutrition, failure to thrive, and extreme neglect that is a threat to health.) The reason for this bias has to do with the remedies for different cases. Where the parents are at fault, there is the comparatively simple solution of removing the child from the home. Where the problem is rooted in the environment, the worker has no such simple solutions. But the popular demand for action creates a pressure to choose the most dramatic response—removing the child from home. By selecting that response, the system ignores the physical context of the family's life and chooses a false clarity over the real complexity.

The claims of omniscience that lie behind the growing legislative response can survive only in a context where the civic debate does not take place. The publicization of one side of the issue, the inflexibility of centralized public services, the difficulties legislators have in recognizing the limits of their efficacy, the institutional advantages of claiming competence, and the belief that increasing budgets and expanding mandates are relevant actions reduce the chances that the intricacies of the problem will be recognized. Without that recognition the civic debate is impoverished to the clients' disadvantage.

Innovations: Black Adoptions

Innovations have often shifted the course of social welfare activity. Successful innovations are often the vehicle for making the response more relevant to the need. The conditions for innovation have become an important part of the public–private debate, with the private sector claiming that it is more innovative than the public sector.

There are more searching questions, however, than whether the private sector is a source of innovation. That question is unsatisfactory because of the empirical difficulty of relating a particular characteristic of one type of organization to complex events, and because many important innovations occur in a context that is much broader than the context of one agency.

The question about innovation is best phrased by standing it on its head to read: what were the circumstances in which innovations in child welfare occurred? Since innovation is merely one characteristic of an action—that the action is in some ways new—a second question needs to be asked: how important was the action compared to other possible actions and compared to the character and scope of the problem that spurred the innovation? These questions require a detailed analysis of a particular problem.

Since 1950, major innovations have occurred in the field of adoption, where the focus of organized nonprofit activity has shifted dramatically from the placement of white infants to the placement of black infants and of older and handicapped children who were previously considered unadoptable. The work of finding adoptive placements for white babies has been taken over by consortiums of lawyers and doctors working for profit, and the ethics of that development are disputed. But the new efforts of public and private agencies to place minority and handicapped children in adoption have increased the options for those children.[12] For a variety of reasons, both public and private agencies made the change of trying to find homes for previously unadoptable children.

The questioning of traditional adoption practices in private agencies started in the late 1940s primarily for market reasons. Child Welfare League of America studies in 1948 and 1955 documented the declining availability of white babies for adoption and the fact that this trend was threatening some agencies with extinction. By 1959, the league had devised a solution—the provision of subsidies for adoptive parents who took difficult-to-place children, particularly children with expensive medical problems. In the mid-1960s, public and private agencies started experimental adoption programs. In 1966, the Chicago Child Care Society started a trial program of subsidized adoption, and two years later the state legislature enacted a statewide publicly funded program.

While market considerations had set the scene for this change, the change also had other antecedents. It was no accident that the Child Care Society was the first agency to respond to what was partly a racial problem. That society's charter committed it to the service of inner-city children, and its director

12. Adoption is a good option for dependent and neglected children in the sense that most adoptions appear to survive. Studies put the failure rate of adoptions at about 14 percent of completed adoptions. See the testimony of Theodore Levine of the Child Welfare League of America, U.S. Senate Hearings on H.R. 3434, 1979, 156.

used that mandate in the 1960s to increase the society's work with black clients. In 1967, the trustees of the Illinois Children's Home and Aid Society, (ICHAS) recognized their poor track record on black adoption and resolved to change the focus of their adoption division: "The background of our policy in recent years in the Chicago area has been to accept no more than one Negro child per month (for adoption) and a very limited number of children of other races."[13] The board resolved, "that in order to assist in solving the community problem the Society seek to step up its minority and mixed race adoption and experiment in various ways of attracting applications from families to consider these children." The ICHAS was as good as its word. In 1969, it placed 101 minority children in adoptive homes out of a total of 347 placements and maintained that change throughout the 1970s. In 1982, out of a smaller total of 238 adoptions, 79 were of minority children. Credit for this change belonged to the professional staff of the agency and to a few board members who had been shaken by the disturbances in the black community and had concluded that the ICHAS had not fulfilled its responsibility to minorities. (This was not a universal view. As late as 1981, some members of the board were less than enthusiastic about the change, prompting the director of adoptions to comment that "the Board wants nice little white babies for their friends."[14]

The change to subsidized adoption also represented a professional change of heart. For most of the century, adoptive parents and foster parents were distinguished not only by the different authority with which they held their children but also by class. Adoptive parents came from distinctly higher economic groups than foster parents, and most adoption agencies had strict prohibitions against foster parents becoming adoptive parents. This policy was partly a class bias—white infants deserved "adequate" homes—and partly a device whereby an agency could maintain its pool of foster parents.

The adoption of difficult-to-place children required a wider pool of potential adoptive parents; foster parents who were

13. ICHAS, Board of Trustees, Minutes of Meeting of 25 May 1967, 9.
14. Interview with Marjorie Topps, Director of Adoption Services, ICHAS, 22 July 1980.

already looking after children they wished to adopt were an untapped resource. So in the face of a newly perceived demand for adoptive parents, the quasi-theory that prevented foster parents being candidates was brushed aside. The profession recognized that parenthood did not necessarily improve by social class. A changing professional calculus also encouraged the move. As the director of a sectarian agency put it, "nowadays we prepare families rather than study them."[15] In this case innovation was a thoughtful reassessment of existing practice and a recognition that the practice was the problem.

Not all the private agency efforts were as successful, and one of the less successful efforts is instructive. In 1974, the Group for Action Planning (GAP), a consortium of twenty private agencies in the Chicago area, responded to the growing sense of crisis in adoption. The group had discovered that one of the Chicago area offices of the Department of Children and Family Services had on their books 900 children who were candidates for adoption. The likelihood that the office could make any noticeable inroads into that backlog was remote and so the consortium agreed to contract with the department to place some of those children. The consortium placed all the children it contracted to place, but that was only 50 children. Only three members of the consortium placed children, the three that already had private adoption programs. The effort was labeled a demonstration project but what was being demonstrated was not clear. In this case the apparent willingness to be responsive hid the fact that nothing much had changed on the private agencies' side. A slight increase in a few agencies' existing adoption programs was packaged as a major response by the private sector. But the effort was not commensurate with the problem. That incommensurability was hidden by the appellation "demonstration project."

The extra effort on the part of the successful private agencies and the parallel effort in the Department of Children and Family Services failed to meet the supply of difficult-to-place chil-

15. Gene Svebakken, Executive Director, Lutheran Child and Family Services, quoted in Rizzini, "Report on the Child Abuse Case Load," 7.

dren, particularly black children. The professional response, in short, did not solve the problem. In 1972, the protest of black social workers stopped the practice of transracial adoption, and the success of the black adoption program was slowed down by the apparent shortage of black adoptive parents. By the late 1970s, on any one day, there were 200 black children waiting to be adopted in Cook County; of that total, 70 were healthy black infants.[16] The cause of the shortage was the subject of much speculation. White agencies advertising in the black community had tended to portray adoptive parents as people of comfortable means, and this image may have discouraged working-class blacks from applying. Private agencies charged fees for adoptive services. The agencies saw themselves in a buyer's market for adoptive parents (an accurate assessment of the demand for white infants but not of the demand for other children) and had acted accordingly. Some white agency staff put the shortage of black parents down to apathy in the black community, and some share of the problem might have been due to simple demographics. The fertility rate in the black community is higher than the fertility rate in the white community, and this may have been a factor in the number of black adults seeking adoptive children.[17]

Whatever the cause, the best efforts of public and private agencies, which was a substantial improvement over previous efforts, could not solve the problem. When a solution did come, it came from a black Catholic priest who almost single-handedly increased the black community's awareness of the problems of dependent black children. In late 1980, the Reverend George Clements, the pastor of Holy Angels Church, one of Chicago's poorest black parishes, urged each black church to find a set of adoptive parents in its congregation and he himself applied to become an adoptive father. In July 1981, he adopted a thirteen-year-old black boy. The combination of the novelty of a Catholic priest adopting a child, Clements's efforts to publicize his solution in the black community, and the department's alacrity to take advantage of this unexpected access to that community

16. Interview with Joseph Devereux, Illinois Children's Home and Aid Society, 3 August 1981.
17. I am indebted to Harold Goldman for this observation.

produced the desired results, and the surplus of black infants quickly disappeared.

The story suggests a critical aspect of responsiveness. In the example of adoption the responsiveness that is the key to the problem of dependent children is the responsiveness required of the lay community to become adoptive parents. Only this personal and familial response could alleviate the problem. The task of the social welfare community was to find a means of producing that response and the answer came from a uniquely situated individual whose effort was initially personal but who could use an institution—in this case the Catholic Church—to magnify the effect of that effort. This example also shows that, even in the comparatively uncomplicated case of adoption, only a combination of individual and organizational actors is sufficient to tackle the problem. Nothing in this story suggests the unique capacity of either sector.

Understanding Context: Inner City Families

In the late 1960s, the unrest in the inner cities led to the realization that the child welfare system had broader responsibilities than the provision of surrogate homes for children whose families could no longer cope. At the same time poor, minority groups were demanding help in their own communities. The recognition of a fresh set of responsibilities and the change in programs to match those responsibilities were conscious and deliberate. Spencer Crookes, the director of the Illinois Children's Home and Aid Society (ICHAS), wrote in 1968 in a document entitled "Statement Concerning Relations with the Black Community":

> Recognizing the implications of the Kerner Report, that there must either be one society or an alternative of growing chaos in America, I believe that it is imperative on all institutions to do their utmost to combat racism. The Illinois Children's Home and Aid Society has a long-standing policy with respect to discrimination on the basis of race in its service program, on its Board, and in the employment of staff. It must be said that the problem of race has not been given priority concern partly because of the Society's broad concern for the welfare of all children and partly

indifference on the part of the white community to the problem as a whole.[18]

The director then described the framework within which the ICHAS would respond:

> Because of the specialized nature of its service, involvement of the Society does not readily lend itself to large scale programs within the inner city without a drastic refocusing of organization and service. There are, however, a number of steps that can be taken in keeping with our purpose and responsibility as a leading child welfare agency.

The second statement sounds like a major note of caution, but the director added examples that encompassed a broad range of activities. In addition to service activities such as promoting the adoption of black children, he suggested putting the ICHAS's money in black banks, offering expertise to responsible groups in the black community, and getting involved in legislation on issues of discrimination, rent supplements, fair housing practices, and even a guaranteed annual income. For a moderate-sized private agency with a long commitment to placement programs, this suggestion was a dramatic and large-scale change of direction.

In practice, while the ICHAS honored its commitment to pay more attention to the problems of the inner city, the scope of that enterprise came nowhere near the blueprint sketched by the director. In 1968, the ICHAS set up an adoption office in the black community and followed that in 1971 with a Mother's Enrichment Center. This latter facility was a drop-in center for mothers—open six hours a day, two days a week—where the mothers could discuss, and be taught about, issues of child raising while qualified staff looked after their children. The Society was contributing its knowledge of the burgeoning field of child development to the problems of the inner city. In 1972, the ICHAS started a program for pregnant girls and teenage mothers in an inner-city high school, providing counseling for the

---

18. Spencer Crookes, "Statement Concerning Relations with the Black Community," ICHAS, Board of Trustees file, attached to Minutes of Meeting, 18 September 1968.

mothers and care for the babies; their goal was to keep the mothers in school. And, in 1977, the ICHAS opened a Mother's Enrichment Center in one of the city's Hispanic communities.

While the changes fell short of the ambitious program the director set out in the late 1960s, they were not trivial, and they testify to the vigor and enterprise of the ICHAS. They demonstrated the ICHAS's capacity to respond to a new awareness of specific problems with specific proposals. But that accomplishment still leaves the second question about responsiveness: how close is the relationship between the response and the problem? In the case of black adoption and support programs for teenage mothers there is a very close relationship. The one program provided stable homes where none existed before, and the second increased the likelihood that the young mothers would one day be economically self-sufficient. In the case of the child development and mother's enrichment programs, the relationship is less strong. The case is important because a number of organizations in the 1970s justified new programs on the grounds that they were providing specialized, not ordinary, services to the urban poor. The programs were to be specialized, not just because poor children needed expert attention, but also because the agencies justified their particular character and their highly trained staff by the existence of these special programs. Some organizations were developed with the sole purpose of providing this kind of help.

At first glance these kinds of programs appear to be responsive in the sense that they address a community-felt need in the community itself. They are not placement programs, nor do they consist of giving poor clients therapeutic help from middle-class social workers in the workers' downtown offices. They contain an element of self-help—mothers joining together to encourage themselves to solve their own problems. And the programs were successful in the sense that some mothers used them, albeit in small numbers relative to the program costs. Responsiveness, however, is relative in two senses. It is concerned with the relationship between the character of a problem and the character of the response, and with the relationship between the scope of the problem and the response. In a field where resources are always insufficient, it is important to ask whether organized social welfare directs its energies toward the most pressing needs.

The historic touchstone in social welfare for a broad and appropriate response to human needs is the settlement house. Open to their communities twenty-four hours a day every day, the settlement houses defined their activities by the needs their staff perceived in the community rather than by specialized services the workers were trained to deliver. At Jane Addam's Hull House in Chicago, staff and volunteers investigated the city's garbage collection; studied sweatshops and lobbied for protective legislation; and provided day care, coffee houses, a gymnasium, rooms for family and ethnic celebrations, an education program for adults, equipment that enabled rural immigrants to start small farms, a boarding club for single women, advocacy for neighbors negotiating with insurance companies and employers, hospitals and stores, a cooperative coal-buying association, and a labor museum to preserve the artifacts and skills of European village society.[19]

The settlement house, though, is not necessarily the touchstone for contemporary social welfare. Many of the problems it tackled are now the domain of specialized organizations, each of whom have a few or even a single function. Moreover, the city and the state have regulated many of the activities that (while giving economic vitality to the growing city) injured people and communities. The specialization of labor in social welfare, and the expansion of the public sector might suggest that the broad approach is achieved by the collective efforts of a group of social agencies and is no longer proper for a single agency. As a corollary, the private agency that takes its specialized program to the inner city may be responding appropriately.

But the condition of the inner city demonstrates that the crisscrossing patterns of organized help fail to support some people, and the boundaries of that failure coincide, to a large degree, with the boundaries of economic class. It may be appropriate in middle-class communities to use the resources of welfare institutions to create meeting places for isolated mothers.

19. For Jane Addams's own description of Hull House, see *Twenty Years at Hull House* (New York: Pantheon Books, 1960).

Child development knowledge is doubtless lacking in the poorest communities, but in those communities to ignore the context of an individual's problems is to ignore much of the problem. The most destitute urban neighborhoods today can be more destitute than the crowded immigrant communities that Hull House was founded to help. These neighborhoods are characterized by high percentages of unemployed males, single-parent families, rapidly decaying private housing stock, lack of economic activity, and collapsing urban infrastructures. In them teenage boys are threatened by gangs and teenage girls by prostitution. The settlement house is not an anachronism in such communities. The lack of physical resources and the absence of other organizations with the range to make an impact on the deprivation give it a role.

The range is one clue to the usefulness of the settlement house in such neighborhoods. The other clue has to do with the way agencies choose their agenda. Settlement houses are nonprofessional in the particular sense that they derive their purpose from a close sense of what a destitute community needs rather than from the professional skills their staff possess. This approach results in a close fit between the totality of the need and the totality of what the organization offers. Such a goal does not mean the service meets all the needs but that all the service is directed at high priorities within the community. This trait is not a matter of the size of the organization as much as a recognition of the scale of the problem. Small organizations can recognize and respond to large-scale problems. But an agency blinded by a particular expertise and a one-dimensional definition of the issue will often miss the heart of the problem.

A brief description of a contemporary settlement house will show how little they have changed since the establishment of Hull House in 1889. The East Garfield Park and North Lawndale neighborhoods in Chicago's West Side have all the characteristics of the poorest urban neighborhoods. The area has an unemployment rate in excess of 40 percent, and the only new buildings (and indeed the only buildings in reasonable shape) are Chicago Housing Authority public housing and a few privately developed subsidized housing units. East Garfield Park, which is 99 percent black, lost almost 40 percent of its black

population between 1970 and 1980 due to neighborhood abandonment. In 1980, 40 percent of the remaining population lived
below the poverty line. The neighborhood is home to many of
the 150,000 persons in Chicago who in the early 1980s lived on
General Assistance checks of $144 a month.

In this neighborhood, Marillac House, a settlement house
established in 1947 and run by the Daughters of Charity of St.
Vincent De Paul, looks after 460 children each day in day care,
240 children in after-school programs, and 200 teenagers in the
evening; counsels 35 families in a child abuse program; distrib-
utes 1,000 food packages a month, provides summer nutrition
programs for school-aged children; runs a clothes and furniture
thrift shop; provides emergency formula and diaper service for
young mothers; links pregnant and postpartum teenagers to
clinics; and provides an elderly outreach program and check-
cashing privileges.[20] In addition, the sisters engage the media
and lobby the legislature on the conditions of such neighborhoods and the solutions to those conditions.

The day care and after-school programs allow mothers to
work while their children are protected from a threatening environment. The teenage program provides an alternative to membership in the "Vice-Lords" and the "Disciples," the two gangs
that dominate the neighborhood. The recreational and education programs in the orderly and well-kept former orphanage
provide one of the few reliefs from life among decaying and
abandoned buildings. The enterprise creates one hundred full-
time and part-time jobs that are filled mainly by people living in
the community. The jobs provide one of the few sources of
nonwelfare revenue. The settlement house thus allows some
semblance of ordinary existence for a population who, whatever
their own strengths and weaknesses, would find such an existence all but impossible under the conditions that exist in their
community.

All manner of agencies have responded in their own way to
the condition of the inner-city poor. What distinguishes these
agencies is the degree to which this intervention touches the

20. Interview with Sister Julia Huiskamp, Director, Marillac House, 2
March 1983.

heart of the problem or, more importantly, the heart of the community. This capacity, in turn, depends on whether their analysis of their role starts with a description of their special competence or with the general needs of the community their clients inhabit.

Accepting Responsibility: Difficult Children

Sometimes responsiveness is not so much a matter of the skilled perception of a problem as the acting on a problem that most agencies recognize but would prefer to ignore. In this section we will examine the organization of the response to "difficult" children. (We will discuss the appropriateness of the response in chapter 5.)

A few children come to the attention of the state who are so "difficult" that their care absorbs a great many resources, and no single agency wants to handle them alone. Responsiveness in this context is a matter of accepting responsibility and cooperating to fashion a joint solution.

In the early 1970s, a group of lawyers became aware of the situation of children who had connections with both the mental health and the child welfare systems. In August 1971, the Legal Aid Bureau of Chicago brought suit in the Circuit Court of Cook County on behalf of Mary Lee and Pamela Wesley and a class of similarly situated persons.[21] These children had been voluntarily admitted to mental health facilities by their parents. The issues in the suit were denial to the children of the rights governing admission and discharge for voluntary patients and the denial of adequate care and treatment. The essential problem was that the children were so difficult that neither the public nor the private sectors of the child welfare system wished to serve them. Consequently, the children had been sent to the Department of Mental Health. The children had previously been in both institutions and foster homes in the child welfare system, had not adjusted to those placements, and on a prior occasion had been signed into a Department of Mental Health facility by the Department of Children and Family Services.

21. *In Re Mary Lee and Pamela Wesley.*

During this "career," Pamela Wesley had been treated with thorazine and tranquilizers, and for an alleged battery she was tied to her bed for periods up to thirty-one days. She was then adjudicated a delinquent and was incarcerated by the Department of Corrections for two years. The challenge was how to deal with children who were neither mentally ill nor delinquent but who, because they were emotionally disturbed, slipped deeper into coercive systems to the further detriment of their own behavior.

Six years after the first suit was joined, the Department of Children and Family Services and the private sector organized a secure facility for these children within the child welfare system, a series of less coercive group homes, and a plan for a group of private agencies to cooperate in providing services that would help move the children to more normal, less restrictive placements. Only the secure facility lasted. Our analysis is about why the solution took so long to fashion and why it was so fragile. The attempt to set up a less coercive option for these children, which resulted in the establishment of the Joint Service Project for Adolescents (JSPA), illustrates the degree of cooperation necessary to produce such a response to disturbed adolescents.

The occasion of the problem was not the history of the girls in question—children had slipped out of the child welfare system into the back wards before—but a new sense that for some disturbed children such a disposition was unnecessary and unjust. The impulse to reevaluate the situation of disturbed youth was part of the general climate of deinstitutionalization. This case was fought out in court on due process grounds. The court outlined the conditions for a solution and insisted on their implementation. It was perhaps inevitable that the redefinition of care and treatment as coercion should come from outside the service system from people who did not have day-to-day responsibility for the children's care. The outsiders had a mind-set— legal theory—that could challenge the mind-set (or the inaction) of those in the service system. What was not so inevitable was that once the new view had been enunciated and legitimated in court, the change could be effected only by the constant and forceful pressure of that court. The organizational disadvantages of following the court's initial injunctions were so heavy that a constant reiteration of the court's position was necessary to persuade the service system that it was obliged to accept the change.

The County Division of the Circuit Court, to which the case had been transferred from the Juvenile Division, took an extremely active, quasi-administrative role in the young people's case. The judge who presided over the case, Judge Joseph Schneider, had a reputation for a subtle understanding of social service issues, and his interest was aided by the interest of the Legal Aid Bureau. The bureau was permanently attached to the case by order of the court as official advocates of this class of children.[22] The original order in the case, made in February 1972, found that the denial to the minors of their rights to contest continued hospitalization was in violation of the state's Mental Health Code. In March 1975, in the face of the Department of Mental Health and the Department of Children and Family Services' continued inability to make adequate provision for the children, the court, in a detailed thirty-three page order, directed the departments to adopt specific procedures to clarify the mutual responsibilities of the departments for the care of the wards. The order also set out rules for making the decision to hospitalize minors; rules for admission, inpatient, and discharge procedures; rules on the services that should be available for mentally retarded children; and rules about the administration of psychotropic medication.

The orders made in Judge Schneider's court were directed at the public departments and were largely responsible for the actions the departments finally took in regard to this group of clients. The private agencies became involved both because the Department of Children and Family Services asked them to consider providing services for these wards, and because in 1973, the Legal Assistance Foundation filed a separate case that alleged that the private agencies had denied treatment to state

22. This unusual action was based on the apparent failure of the juvenile court's guardian ad litem to fulfill his responsibility to the Wesley class of children. It had a precedent in a policy statement issued by the Illinois Department of Mental Health in August 1971, which called for the establishment of a public and private interagency body to address, inter alia, the question of child advocacy and the monitoring and evaluation of the delivery of mental health services to children and adolescents.

wards on the grounds of irrelevant characteristics.[23] The suit requested an order enjoining the department from using state funds to place children with agencies that had discriminated against other wards on the grounds of race, age, sex, degree of intellectual functioning, or emotional disturbance.

Thus the Legal Aid attorneys and Judge Schneider's court defined the problem publicly (the departments were well aware of it privately); through court orders, they provided the motivation for the agencies to respond. The next critical factor was the willingness of the Illinois Children's Home and Aid Society (ICHAS) to agree to provide the central service—a secure facility in the child welfare system designed to prepare the children for less restrictive placements. The ICHAS did this despite the fact that it had refused to serve such children in the past. In late 1972, the director reported to his staff, "We do not know too much about these kids from the data given. They sound like the children we currently turn down."[24] The director also pointed out to the board of trustees that the ICHAS did not in fact have staff who were trained to work with severely disturbed youngsters. "Our staff is not at the moment fully trained for this type of setting but will develop a crash program and then learn as we go along."[25]

The ICHAS's decision was a mixture of professional excitement at the opportunity for a new challenge, a sense of responsibility based on its claim that it had a special concern for the residential care of very disturbed children, and a practical sense of a good opportunity. The program was a good opportunity because the court's involvement meant it was a long-term venture and because the Department of Children and Family Services was promising to pay all the costs. The opportunity was also in line with the ICHAS's conviction that private service funded by the state should be the norm. The board of trustees summarized its attitude by declaring, "The Society feels it is important to cooperate with the state in this venture as it is the first time that

23. *In Re Debra Ford et al.*, no. 65, FCD 7665.
24. Spencer Crookes, Minutes of Program Heads Meeting, ICHAS, 25 September 1972, 2.
25. Ibid., Minutes, Board of Trustees Program and Planning Committee Meeting, 16 January 1973, 3.

the state has come to the private agency with an urgent request for help accompanied by 100 percent purchase."[26]

With enthusiasm, speed, and efficiency the ICHAS prepared to establish a home for twenty-five disturbed children. The state financial guarantees and other private guarantees were, however, the basis of the decision. Grants from private foundations paid for planning costs and the acquisition and renovation of a building. The state guaranteed 100 percent of actual running costs paid in advance. A condition, then, for the ICHAS's enthusiasm was the absence of any financial risk, and to a large degree the public sector shouldered the financial burden.

Despite the court's mandate and the ICHAS's enthusiasm, the project took six years to arrange. Much of that delay was the result of practical disagreements between the Department of Children and Family Services and the ICHAS. Some of the differences between the department and the ICHAS were due to the department's fiscal troubles and its inability to maintain policy decisions intact over the span of even a few years. The ICHAS had to negotiate with four different department directors between 1972 and 1977. Some of the differences had to do with different professional opinions and different bureaucratic pressures. At various times the department wanted to write into the contract a no-decline clause, which would have obliged the ICHAS to accept all the children referred by the department. The department also wanted a clause limiting a child's stay in the secure facility to six months. The ICHAS successfully objected to both those stipulations and to pressure from the department to involve the children themselves in some of the decisions about their care.

It is not easy to judge the merits of these issues. The Department of Children and Family Services was contracting not just with the ICHAS but with a consortium of private agencies. The department thought it was reasonable to expect such a coalition to guarantee the care of a given number of children. The ICHAS, though, feared that the referral of a large number of the most disturbed children to the secure unit would prevent any treat-

26. ICHAS, Minutes, Board of Trustees Meeting, 25 January 1973, 4.

ment. The department's insistence on a maximum stay of six months was based on its knowledge that the ICHAS had a record of keeping children institutionalized for much longer periods of time than the department thought appropriate. The ICHAS's resistance stemmed from its fear that the department had an anti-institutional bias, and that it did not understand the realities of the treatment of disturbed youth. The department's inclination to consult children about their care came out of a conviction that children had preferences and concerns that should be taken into account. The ICHAS's distaste for this position sprang from the professional conviction that only people trained in the appropriate psychologies could unravel the significance of even the most innocent client statements.

We shall discuss some of these issues in other chapters. What happened was that, just as the ICHAS won most of its fiscal conditions, it also won most of its professional conditions. It was, in important respects, responsive on its own terms.

The ICHAS's initiative was, nonetheless, the key to moving the children from coercive correctional and mental health facilities to a somewhat less coercive child welfare facility. This action was supposed to be the first step of a plan to move the children as close to a normal upbringing as possible. The next steps depended on another group of private agencies. Twelve agencies signed contracts to provide residential care for the project children—care that ranged from the ICHAS's secure facility to an independent living contract, a device whereby an agency supervises older adolescents living in their own apartments. The plan was not just to provide a range of placements but also to provide collaboration between agencies so that each child also received extra help at school or with any other critical aspect of his or her life. In each agency's budget there was an allowance for auxiliary services that would give the agencies the resources to provide the extra services. This part of the plan did not work. The agencies used only a small part of their auxiliary service budgets, and the interagency cooperation did not happen. In a few years all the agencies, except the ICHAS, left the coalition. As a United Way architect of the Joint Service Project put it, "When the chips are down, it's very hard for the private sector to act in concert. If they're going to act in concert, they must

have a trade-off. You can't rule out the weak sisters. You can't
have a common methodology."[27]

This history could be read as an exemplary tale of public and
private collaboration. In administrative terms it is, to some degree, such a story. The public sector financed a private sector
effort to provide decent care to a group of very troubled young
people. The private sector was the vehicle because, in this instance, it could move faster and with greater freedom than the
public sector. The public sector provided much of the money
because it had final responsibility for these children and because
the costs were too great for any private agency.

But the story can also be read another way. In this version
the court was the last ditch protector of the constitutional rights
of children no one wanted. The children had been refused entry
to private agencies and had fallen between the cracks of the
public agencies. The result was coercive treatment that was not
justified by their culpability or their condition. Under the most
detailed instructions of the court, the state and a consortium of
private agencies hammered out a plan that would give the young
people the opportunity to move to some semblance of a normal
independence. The plan collapsed because the private sector
could not produce the collaborative effort necessary to make it
work.

Both stories have some merit. The last one leads to the next
question: is collaboration an important aspect of responsiveness
and are the collection of private agencies able to collaborate?

Cooperation: The Private Sector Record

The Joint Service Project for Adolescents (JSPA) called
for collaboration between all parts of the social service system to
attempt the difficult task of moving disturbed clients from mere
maintenance to programs that gave them a chance to achieve a
greater degree of independence. Problems of this difficulty demand not only responsiveness from a single agency but cooperation from the entire system. The second stage of the JSPA initia-

27. Interview with Katherine Mortell, United Way of Metropolitan Chicago, 22 September 1980.

tive raised the question of the capacity of the private sector to organize private sector initiatives. In a state where 60 percent of the public child welfare budget goes to private agencies, the private sector has, de facto, a public role. That role is to some degree organized by the state by the pattern of contracts it signs. There remains the question of whether parts of the private sector (or indeed the sector as a whole) are internally capable of such organization. For example, can the sector cooperate internally to solve or alleviate some particular problem? If not, the private sector may merely be the collection of private agencies—no more than the sum of its parts. To put it another way, of what does the "sectorness" of the private sector consist?

The private sector in Illinois has a long history of formal and informal cooperation. Sometimes that cooperation had to do with saving the remaining resources and programs of fiscally weak organizations. There are many examples of mergers— one agency assuming the assets of another agency and one agency taking over the programs and the clients of a sister agency. On occasion, informal divisions of labor have been established between fiscally sound agencies. The former head of one agency recalls, "There was an agreement many years ago that Chicago Child Care would take the child up to six, Illinois Children's Home and Aid Society after six. There was also a plan that United Charities would counsel unmarried mothers and, if they wanted to release their babies, they would be referred to ICH&A."[28] She went on to warn that such agreements had their problems:

> These kinds of agreements tended to work and be in operation way beyond their usefulness. Once a thing gets institutionalized, it's almost impossible to get rid of it. These patterns no longer exist but nevertheless others will come along to take their place. . . . We need to be cautious about these kinds of arrangements, particularly in a fast moving society.

On one occasion, decades before the establishment of the Department of Children and Family Services, the cooperation took the form of an agreement to take formal public responsibil-

28. Harold Goldman interview with Marion Obenhaus, former Director of the Chicago Child Care Society, 1980.

ity for the care of a particular set of children. By the early 1920s, the Jewish agencies and the Catholic agencies in Chicago had arrangements by which the juvenile court would refer children to a central coordinating group for each faith. This group would then take the responsibility for placing the child with an appropriate affiliated agency. There was, however, no such organization for the Protestant and nonsectarian agencies. The juvenile court complained, therefore, that, although Protestant children were only 18 percent of the court's caseload, they were the hardest group to place.[29] In response to this problem the court persuaded the Protestant Church Federation to organize a coordinating office, and in 1922, the federation established the Joint Service Bureau of the Protestant and Non-Sectarian Child-Caring Agencies of Chicago. By 1928, the bureau had thirty-two member agencies and was handling over 1,000 referrals a year.

The gradual establishment of public responsibility for juvenile court wards made collaboration of this sort less urgent, and the recent history of cooperative endeavors has a very different pattern. One characteristic of the last twenty years is that attempts to merge agencies for service as opposed to fiscal reasons have failed. In 1969, three nonsectarian agencies, the Illinois Children's Home and Aid Society or ICHAS, the Chicago Child Care Society, and Child and Family Services began to discuss the possibilities of formal cooperation. The agencies believed that because they were similar, and because they served geographically different parts of the city, cooperation might be feasible. Such cooperation was expected to improve, through rationalization of effort, the combined effectiveness of the three agencies. By 1973, the group declared that it had failed. The deciding issue was how to maintain the loyalty and support of the three agencies' constituencies after a merger. The rationalization and improvement of service were finally not enough to combat the trustees' and auxiliaries' pride in their own particular organizations. As an observer from one of the agencies put

29. An account of the establishment of the Joint Service Bureau can be found in Merton Julius Trast, "A Study of the Joint Service Bureau of the Protestant and Non-Sectarian Child Caring Agencies of Chicago," M.A. thesis, School of Social Service Administration, University of Chicago, December 1934.

it, "The problem is that you have two elitest organizations. The existing social structures would have to leave."[30] The same observer concluded, "Out of all this came VIA—the Voluntary Interagency Association—where we share automobiles and insurance but not social work."

VIA in fact illustrates the only powerful motive for collaboration in this period: private sector cooperation to increase state-level political power under the rhetoric of the best interests of the child. The executive director of the ICHAS at the time of the establishment of VIA commented, "The creation of a consortium would give the agencies a collective clout in a state and a town where clout is an important factor."[31] With a perhaps unconscious honesty, the proposed name of the consortium changed with the changing purpose of the effort. The project started with the name Illinois Friends of Children. It was then changed to Illinois Friends of the Family, and was finally called the Voluntary Interagency Association.

The two other major collaborative efforts in the state produced organizations with the same purpose. In 1964, the Department of Children and Family Services and the private agencies founded the Child Care Association to discuss major policy issues and to organize training throughout the state. Fiscal pressures and the strains of the Miller directorate persuaded the private agencies to expel the department from the organization. By 1978, the association was effectively organized as the major representative of the private agencies in the state, and it had hired its own lobbyist to work in the state legislature. The association's main concerns were the interests of its member agencies, and their main concern was the rate of payment the department offered them for the provision of child welfare services. Only after the association had negotiated "decent" rate increases for institutional and foster care could it turn its attention elsewhere.

30. Interview with Joseph Devereux, 3 August 1981. A second attempt at a merger between ICHAS and the Child Care Society was made between 1977 and 1978. That failed again for lack of a compelling organizational incentive and because neither of the boards of trustees approved of the then director of ICHAS, who would have been in line to head the new organization.

31. Spencer Crookes, ICHAS, Minutes, Board of Trustees Meeting, 30 January 1975, 3.

The other major formal organization of private agencies, the Group for Action Planning (GAP), demonstrated a similar raison d'être. Founded in 1973 as a forum for Chicago area private agencies, the organization had an agenda that was consistently dominated by organizational rather than service concerns. In 1976, an agenda for future GAP activity listed purchase of service rate setting, a fair service evaluation system, and a proinstitutional public relations drive as key issues. The last two items on the agenda were: "11. Seek a system for interpretation of information to legislators that speaks strongly for the private sector. 12. Demand that the governor and legislature guarantee the involvement of the private sector in the planning and decision making for family and children's services in Illinois." None of the items mentioned substantive child welfare problems.[32] In the fall of 1979, GAP organized a retreat to discuss the organization; the blueprint that emerged from the retreat concentrated on the need to organize, lobby, and promote GAP interests. The one substantive section mentioned rates, peer review, and legal issues as subjects on which members could unite.[33]

There were occasions when GAP spent time on substantive service issues. We mentioned earlier the demonstration project on adoption. On another occasion GAP lobbied hard for continued service to eighteen to twenty-one-year-olds whom the Department of Children and Family Services wished to stop serving for fiscal reasons. But even some of its substantive efforts became exercises in self-protection. Between 1978 and 1979, GAP and the department conducted a task force on critical issues in foster care. The task force discovered that while 31 percent of the children for whom the department urgently needed homes were black infants under two years of age, only 3 percent of the placements offered by the voluntary agencies were for children of that description. Yet the bulk of the task force was devoted to the question of what constituted a referral from the public sector to the private sector. The department complained that the voluntary sector was turning down large

    32. Agenda for Group for Action Planning (GAP) policy group meeting of 2 December 1976, ICHAS, Council for Community Services File.
    33. "Gap Conference Results," 28–29 September 1977, ICHAS, Council for Community Services File.

numbers of children, and the voluntary sector complained that the referrals they were receiving were not "properly" or "adequately" prepared. While some agreement was reached on referrals, the task force report noted that the issue of the scarcity of homes for black infants "essentially remains unsolved."[34]

The general tenor of the organization was apparent even to some of its own members. In 1978, the minutes of a GAP meeting recorded that "it appears GAP has become a mini child care association"[35]—that is, a lobbying group. Two years later, a senior staff person in a member agency remarked, "GAP is the fox talking about the chickens."[36]

Our description of some of the contemporary problems of serving troubled youth suggest that responsiveness is partly a matter of how an agency fits into a collective response. The nineteenth-century orphanage or child welfare agency was in many cases the only organization that was aware of, and able to respond to, the needs of the troubled families of its own ethnic and religious group. Today the growth of state responsibility and the increased specialization within the private sector make it likely that some children will pass through the hands of several agencies. In such cases an agency's responsiveness is a matter of how prepared it is to surrender a degree of autonomy to permit a collective response.

Conclusion

The examples of responsiveness we have described confirm the importance of responsiveness as a criterion to judge organized social service. Indeed, if responsiveness is defined broadly, not as mere innovation or the capacity to change, but as the characteristic that describes the relationship between a service and a problem, the centrality of responsiveness is tautologous. Responsiveness is the only thing to be judged, and the dialectic between response and need is the only problem. When,

34. Task Force on Foster Family Care, Report, 28 June 1979, ICHAS, GAP policy meeting file, 3.
35. Minutes of GAP Policy Group, 30 November 1978 in ICHAS Council for Community Services File.
36. Interview with Joseph Devereux, 3 August 1981.

however, the private sector claims as a special characteristic, and indeed a justifying characteristic, that it is more responsive than the public sector, it is claiming a narrower virtue—that it is more agile and better able to shape and change its work. The histories of the changes we have described suggest that this definition of what constitutes responsiveness is not adequate. It is not enough that an agency is able to move in a direction it wants to go. Responsiveness is not just action, or even professionally and organizationally good action, but action that is appropriate in the context of the problem.

The response of the Children's Home and Aid Society and of Marillac House to families in the most distressed part of the city illustrates the point. For the society, introducing skilled help— staff who understood the dynamics of parenting and of child development—was a major response. But the problems of parenthood in those communities is not an isolated phenomenon but the result of number of issues set in a particular physical place. To Marillac House, equally aware of the problems of parenthood, the issue was not troubled parents but troubled parents living in a battered community. To them the litmus test of their adequacy was the continuation of the tried, tested, unglamorous, and nontechnical responses of the settlement house. The settlement house as a shadow of a community, or as the closest approximation to a community the neighborhood could sustain, dealt in both practical and psychological problems but judged that the essence of the situation had not changed from the days when Jane Addams created a community for people estranged by emigration.

The point of this comparison is not that settlement houses are "good." This settlement house was appropriate in East Lawndale because of the wretched state of the neighborhood. Rather, the point is that the response must be deeply embedded in the context of the problem; because of its particular approach, Marillac House was more deeply embedded than the society.

The responsiveness that many problems demand is not the responsiveness of an organization or a profession. For these problems the proximate agent for helping distressed families is an individual who is often not even an employee of an agency.

Adoptive parents are the proximate agents for helping adoptable children, foster parents for foster children, families and neighbors for children living with their natural parents. In these examples an agency or a program is not the prime agent but a device for encouraging the instrumentality of others. The test of the agency's responsiveness is its capacity to act as the midwife of the capacities of the laity—a task that a professional organization, almost by definition, will find at odds with its sense of itself. In cases where the laity are crucial—these constitute the bulk of the problems of child welfare—the question should not be which agency is responsive but what or who can persuade the laity to be responsive. In the case of the adoption of black children, the power of persuasion rested, not in professional public or private social welfare organizations, but in a person who, as a black priest, was able to persuade by reference to ethnic sensibilities and religious responsibility.

In extreme cases the responsiveness of an agency can be destructive of the end of relieving need. Responsiveness can amount to interference, which destroys the laity's capacity to respond. Acting under its child abuse authority, the state's coercive intervention in families where children are not in clear and present danger can tilt the balance toward the breakup of families who were otherwise holding themselves together. The screening out of candidates for adoptive parenthood by criteria not crucial to adequate parenting negates the capacity of these candidates to help children without permanent homes. Passing over neighbors and friends as sources of surrogate care for neglected children sometimes results in children being removed from their communities when they need only to be removed from their parents. And the concentration of resources on surrogate care, rather than on strategies that help families under pressure to survive intact, damages natural parents' potential to respond to their own children.

The histories we have recounted also show that in the aggregate—that is, the relationship between the aggregate of help and the aggregate of need—the heterogeneity of those allowed to respond may be more important than the responsiveness of any one organization. The world of those who can usefully respond to distress is far broader than the world of social welfare agencies. It includes the lawyer who does pro bono law and who brings a due process view to social welfare; the adoptive parents who form coalitions to pressure states to increase the number of adoptions; and the town council that forms an organization to think about the problems of runaway children. To use an evolutionary term, the problems of distressed families are intractable enough to warrant an emphasis on the importance of variation in the sources of help. The enlargement of the universe of relevant actors in child welfare to anyone who has a contribution to make will increase the possiblity of discovering effective responses. An overemphasis on the comparative responsiveness of the public sector or the private sector will obscure the heterogeneity of need and the adaptiveness of encouraging a heterogeneity of responses.

4

Fairness and Discrimination: Race

Introduction

We defined *responsiveness* in the last chapter as acting in a manner appropriate to the scale of a problem, devising fresh solutions where old solutions had failed, acting with an understanding of the context of a problem, and acting in co-operation with others to accept responsibility for families who need help. For a long time, good practice has also meant choosing problems and distributing resources in a way that delivers a rough justice to those receiving help.

Rough justice has always included the provision of physical sustenance to preserve life, and it has also meant acting in ways that increase children's liberty. The attack on asylums in the mid-nineteenth century was made in the name of rescuing children from the horrors of incarceration and restoring to them some of the liberty enjoyed by children who live with their own families. In the New Deal rough justice was primarily about the provision of sustenance. But as evidence accumulated about the unequal distribution of medical services and services to handicapped children, rough justice came to include a concern for the equal distribution of those services. (The architects of these clauses were particularly interested in the fate of rural counties and areas of special economic need.) In the 1960s and 1970s the issues of rough justice included concerns about sustenance and poverty but were often expressed in terms of race. There was a long history of racial discrimination in social services, and in the 1960s, the equally long-standing attempts to modify that discrimination received a powerful boost.

This chapter addresses the contemporary debate about racial discrimination and equity. The debate, which is often couched in terms of the equal distribution of services by race, looks at the racial record of public and private agencies. We start with this way of framing the question and set the current record in a historical perspective. Our broader purpose is to examine the assumptions of these definitions of racial justice and to suggest some other ways of constructing the question. Fairness that is concerned just with services is incomplete if only because of the discontinuities between service and need. It is also incomplete because the end is a served person. But our end is the expansion of citizenship and that is quite different. The benchmark of fairness must be that goal, not the fallible and changing ways of meeting it.

Historical Patterns of Discrimination

The principle that organizations providing federally funded social services should not discriminate on the basis of race was affirmed in Title VI of the Civil Rights Act of 1964. Concern at the lack of provision for black children in the social welfare system has a longer history. Much of the detail of the discrimination and the concern were shaped by local history, and that is where we will concentrate our attention.

The early history of child welfare services in metropolitan Chicago is a history of independent civic groups gradually persuading public authorities to provide services for black children that white sectarian and nonsectarian agencies, with a few notable exceptions, were unwilling to provide.[1] Although black private welfare agencies provided some care to dependent and

1. This history is taken from Malcolm Bush and Mark Testa, "Racial Bias in Child Welfare Services" (Paper presented at the National Association of Social Workers Minority Issues Conference, "Color in a White Society," Los Angeles, California, 9–12 June 1982).

neglected children—the first black-run institution for black children in Chicago was founded in 1899[2]—they never developed the capacity to serve a significant proportion of their community. Black agencies were unable to attain the financial stability that their white counterparts derived from endowment, fundraising auxiliaries, and access to community chests and other federated charities.

The first formal public declaration of concern for the condition of black dependent children came in 1913 when the "Committee to Consider Ways and Means for the Better Care of Dependent Colored Children" described the problem. Virtually no black children were accepted for placement in public or private institutions for dependent or neglected children. In contrast, they were overrepresented in detention and correctional facilities. The committee responded by issuing a clear call for nondiscrimination:

> It is the sense of this Committee that all children wards of the Court are equal and all institutions and organizations receiving public money for the care of dependent and neglected children should be compelled to receive and care for without discrimination as to race or color, assignments of the juvenile court.[3]

Private agencies' resistance to black children, as well as opposition by some reformers to institutional care for any children, prevented any concerted action until 1919. In that year the Illinois Children's Home and Aid Society (ICHAS), working with a coalition of black and white civic leaders and philanthropists, established as an auxiliary to the organization the Bureau for Dependent Colored Children. By the end of 1926, almost 200 of ICHAS's Cook County charges were black. No other private organization, however, exhibited the same concern for black

2. Sandra Stehno, "Social Services Provision to Black Children and Youth in the City of Chicago" (Preliminary dissertation proposal, School of Social Service Administration, University of Chicago, 1981).
3. Report of the Meeting to consider ways and means for better care to dependent black children, 11 January 1913, Illinois Children's Home and Aid Society mss. University of Illinois at Chicago Circle, quoted in Sandra M. Stehno, "Foster Care for Dependent Black Children in Chicago, 1899–1934" (Ph.D. diss., School of Social Service Administration, University of Chicago, April 1985).

children. By the end of that decade ICHAS's capacity to accept black children seemed clearly limited. Apparently the only solution lay in public action.

Public responsibility for the care of black children in Chicago was first demonstrated in 1928 by the Joint Service Bureau's Division of Child Placing for Negro Children. The division was specifically organized to relieve the pressure on the Cook County Juvenile Court for the placement of dependent and neglected black children, and to protect black children from incarceration.[4] The need was clear. In 1931, for example, the population of the Cook County Juvenile Detention Center was 21 percent black, and the population of the State Training School for Girls was 26 percent black.[5] At the time black children constituted only 4 percent of the total state population under twenty-one and 10 percent of the urban population.

Most of the black children the division accepted responsibility for were finally placed in foster homes financed by County Board funds. The success of the division's work is shown by the increasing number of black children supported by those funds. Between 1929 and 1931, the proportion of county-financed foster care for black children increased from 9 percent of all such foster care to 30 percent.[6]

The pattern of placing black children in public foster homes and white children in private institutional care persisted for several decades. With the expansion of public authority for the provision of foster care as an adjunct of poor relief—in 1934 the Cook County Department of Public Aid and the Cook County Relief Administration established children's divisions for the care of dependent children—larger numbers of black children

4. While the agency itself was private, the pressure for its establishment in 1922 and this expansion in 1928 were public, as was its purpose. The division's main task was placing black children in foster boarding homes that were paid for from Cook County boarding funds. The work of the division is described in Merton Julius Trast, "A Study of the Joint Service Bureau of the Protestant and Non-sectarian Child Caring Agencies of Chicago," (M.A. thesis, School of Social Service Administration, University of Chicago, 1934).

5. Council of Social Agencies of Chicago, *The South Side Survey: A Survey of Social and Philanthropic Agencies Available for Negroes in Chicago* (Chicago: Council of Social Agencies and the School of Social Service Administration, University of Chicago, June 1931).

6. Ibid.

came into substitute care. By 1938, some 10 percent of the dependent and neglected children in surrogate placements were black. This figure matched the overall percentage of black children in the state's urban population.[7] To some degree, therefore, the public authorities had done their work. But in that same year, 60 percent of the white children in substitute care were placed in child care institutions—compared to only 8 percent of black children in care.[8]

During the next twenty years civic concern over the treatment of minority children increased. In 1945, the Chicago Council for Social Agencies reported that 71 percent of the 1,573 black children in foster homes were placed under the public auspices of the Chicago Welfare Administration.[9] The previous year the Chicago Urban League issued a report that highlighted the extreme reluctance of private as well as public child welfare institutions to accept black children. The report described the reasons for this reluctance: "From representatives of private agencies whose attitude is known there is the recurrent phrase that Negro children 'will not be happy when integrated with non-Negro children.' It is difficult to know just how sincere this expression is."[10] In 1954, the Welfare Council of Metropolitan Chicago set up a committee for opening child care institutions to children of all races.[11] Two years later, however, the council doubted that the committee had achieved anything. The council had reason to be concerned. In 1960, only 2 percent of the children in private institutions were black.[12]

The resistance of private agencies to accepting significant

7. John Kahlert, *Child Dependency in Illinois* (Springfield, Ill.: Illinois Department of Public Aid, Division of Child Welfare, 1940).

8. Ibid., 43.

9. Council of Social Agencies of Chicago, Department of Statistics and Research, *Survey of Resources for Negro Children* (Chicago: Council of Social Agencies of Chicago, 1945), 4.

10. F.T. Lane, *A Study of the Need of Facilities for Negro Children under the Supervision of the Juvenile Court of Cook County* (Chicago: Chicago Urban League, 1944). 2.

11. Welfare Council of Metropolitan Chicago, *Report of the Committee on Institutional Care* (Chicago: Welfare Council of Metropolitan Chicago, 1956.)

12. Welfare Council of Metropolitan Chicago, Research Department, *Selected Data for the Committee on Institutional Care of Children* (Chicago: Welfare Council of Metropolitan Chicago, July 1960).

numbers of minority children placed additional pressures on public authorities to expand the public provision of foster care. In
1954, the Citizen's Committee for the Left-Out Child—a group
especially concerned with minority children—was formed to
press for a division of child welfare in the Cook County Department of Public Aid. That division was established the following
year. However, the demographic explosion of the early 1960s
and the steady immigration of black families from the South
continued to strain the service and fiscal capacity of local govern-
ments. Finally, in 1964, Illinois established a state Department of
Children and Family Services to provide and fund child welfare
services. As we have already seen, a precondition of the establishment of the department was the consent of the private sector.
That consent was given partly because of the increasing numbers
of black children in the Cook County caseload. It was clear to the
civic groups who discussed the establishment of a state agency
that the private sector's reluctance to serve minority children was
the public sector's opportunity and duty. The report of the Illinois Commission on Children is full of references to equal services "regardless of economic status, race, religion, geographic
location, veteran status of their parent or nature of their problem."[13] The report was specific about the public responsibility for
minority children: "A special effort should be made to provide
adoptive and foster homes for child [sic] of minority or mixed
groups. This should be primarily the responsibility of the state
child welfare service."[14]

The 1960s saw two other major changes affecting the provision of foster care services to minority children. The first change
was the legal pressure for equal treatment, which was boosted
by the civil rights movement. In an order that represented the
most unequivocal statement to date about racial discrimination,
the Cook County Department of Public Aid declared in 1962
that the department would not subsidize the placement of any
child in any private institution that discriminated against non-

13. Illinois Commission on Children, *Report of a Committee for a Comprehensive Family and Child Welfare Program in Illinois* (Springfield, Ill.: Illinois
Commission on Children, October 1962), 21.
14. Ibid., 22.

white children.[15] Two years later the Community Fund of Metropolitan Chicago issued a nondiscrimination order to all its member agencies.[16]

The second major change was the increase in federal funds for child welfare programs. This action helped to change private agencies' attitudes toward minority children. The 1962 Social Security amendments extended the definition of public services eligible for federal reimbursement under AFDC-foster care to include services contracted from a nonprofit agency by a public authority. Although the change was not made to encourage private agencies to accept minorities—race was barely mentioned in the Congressional hearings—it did create fiscal incentives for the private agencies to integrate their caseloads.

The expansion of state authority and the increased public subsidies for foster placements in private agencies had the desired effect of partially integrating the foster care population serviced by private agencies. There was a parallel increase in the number of white children in foster care whose care was paid for with public funds. In 1960, only 19 percent of the children receiving publicly financed child welfare services in Cook County were white. By 1969, the percentage had moved up to 28 percent white; by 1976, it was 42 percent white.[17] By the mid-1970s, the earlier patterns—virtually no institutional or other private sector care for black children, and few public sector services for white children—had changed considerably.

Current Patterns of Racial Differences

The greater quantity of data available for analysis in the late 1970s reveals that remnants of the earlier patterns of racial differences still exist. Significant variations by race persist in the two central services of institutional and foster home care and in

15. Corinne H. Brown, Acting Director, Cook County Department of Public Aid, Memorandum, 19 March 1962.

16. Stehno, "Social Services Provision," 13.

17. Illinois Department of Children and Family Services, *Statistical Handbook: Available Data 1949 through 1969* (Springfield, Ill.: State of Illinois, June 1970); and Department of Children and Family Services, unpublished data, 1978.

other services. We examine these patterns both in general and in individual agencies. Our analysis concentrates on Chicago and the metropolitan region, where there is a much larger minority population than in the rest of the state.

The percentage of black and white children in all child welfare placements provides a starting point for the more detailed figures. Between 1977 and 1979, about 30 percent of all the children placed for the first time in both Chicago and the metropolitan area were white; 70 percent were black. (At that time Hispanic children were not counted separately and were erratically placed in either the black or white categories.) Table 7 shows that white children, particularly those under the age of four, are much more likely to be placed in privately sponsored foster homes than their black counterparts. In institutional care, which in the virtual absence of publicly run facilities is a privately sponsored service in Illinois, the old patterns of discrimination persist in reduced, but still strong, form. In the age range from ten to nineteen, the period when institutional care is most likely to be used, the number of white children in institutions as a percentage of all white children placed exceeds the same black ratio by a margin of two to one. When institutional care is broken down into group home care and institutional care, a further pattern emerges. Table 8 shows that, while there are more whites than blacks in both types of facility, the white predominance is more marked in group homes—the professionally preferred option—than in institutional care. The differential placement of whites and blacks has an additional significance. Since institutional care is more expensive than other forms of care, older white children in Chicago have considerably more spent on them on a per diem basis than their black counterparts.

There are some clues as to the disposition of black children who seem to merit institutional care in the child welfare system and yet do not receive it. Specialized foster care, a recent development, is a way of establishing home care for children who, because of the extent of their problems, would normally be placed in institutions. The foster parents are specially picked, paid more than twice as much as regular foster parents, expected not to hold other employment, and are given special

City of Chicago, July 1976 to June 1979
(Number of children and youth placed into publicly supported foster care and percentage distribution by type of service and agency auspices)

Age at Placement Race of Child	Number in Foster Care Total	Percentage Distribution			
		Foster Homes		Specialized Foster Homes	Private Institutions
		Public	Private		
Under 1 Year					
White	109	51.7	43.8	4.5	—
Black	471	75.7	16.6	7.2	.4
1 to 4 Years					
White	136	61.2	28.4	9.5	.9
Black	408	78.0	11.0	10.1	.8
5 to 9 Years					
White	98	54.5	13.6	8.0	23.9
Black	325	71.6	10.3	10.7	7.3
10 to 14 Years					
White	219	28.9	3.0	7.0	61.1
Black	491	56.2	2.9	12.2	28.6
15 to 19 Years					
White	192	16.1	1.1	12.6	70.1
Black	354	37.0	.7	18.2	44.2

SOURCE: National Opinion Research Center, Children's Policy Research Project, Census of the Illinois Child Welfare Population, FY 1977–79, 1983.

Table 8   Children[a] in Chicago Area Private Agency Placements,[b] First Placed July 1976 to June 1979 by Race and Type of Service

	Group Homes	Insti-tutions	Foster Care	Specialized Foster Care	Independent Living Arrangement
Total	340	742	760	375	112
Black	125	360	467	269	80
White	215	382	293	106	32
Percent Black	37%	48%	61%	72%	71%

SOURCE: National Opinion Research Center, Children's Policy Research Project, Census of the Illinois Child Welfare Population, FY 1977–79, 1983.

[a]Children = child placements. Children may be counted several times as they move between placements.

[b]Forty-five agencies providing one or more services are represented in this table.

training and extra casework support. Tables 7 and 8 indicate that placement in a specialized foster home is a more likely option for older black children than it is for older white children. But the higher percentage of black children in specialized foster care accounts for only a small part of the difference between black and white institutional placement rates. Another part of that difference may be accounted for by patterns of placement in the juvenile detention system. Between October 1980 and May 1981, the Illinois Department of Corrections received nearly 400 juveniles from Cook County on delinquency petitions. Approximately two-thirds were black, one quarter were majority white, and one-tenth were Hispanics and Native Americans.[18] The contrast between these ratios and the ratios for placement in child welfare institutions suggests that some black children, who if they were white would be placed in child welfare institutions, are being sent to the correctional system. If

18. Illinois Department of Corrections, "Population and Capacity Report," in *Illinois Human Services Data Report*, vol. 3, pt. 1, sec. 1, 1982; quoted in Bush and Testa, "Racial Bias," 6.

this is so, it is a repetition of the pattern we noted in the 1920s and a very serious form of racial bias.[19]

Table 8 shows that the public sector provides more than four times as much foster care as the private sector. (This information and the following data come from a census of all child welfare placements in Illinois for children who first came into care between 1977 and 1979.)[20] The table also shows that black children are underrepresented in private agency foster care. If, however, the experience of foster care is roughly the same in homes sponsored by the public department and the private sector (there is very little evidence on this point), black underrepresentation in private agency foster care is not nearly as significant as black underrepresentation in institutional care, which is almost entirely privately sponsored.

These figures are totals for all private agencies. There remains the question of the distribution of minority children among private agencies. An analysis of the individual agencies shows that most agencies are integrated, but that only a few of them serve percentages of black children that mirror the racial composition of the entire system. Our census lists forty-five agencies in Cook County providing placement services for children; six of these agencies are black by origin. Twenty-eight of the agencies, or 62 percent of the total, provided at least one placement service whose clientele was 50 percent or more black. The forty-five agencies provided at total of eighty placement programs; half of these programs served 50 percent or more black clients. As we discussed earlier, black children were a higher percentage of foster home placements than of institutional or group home placements. Some 56 percent of all the children provided with placements by these forty-five agencies were black.

19. The difficulties of demonstrating that blacks and whites with roughly similar case histories have different chances of being placed in the child welfare and correctional systems are substantial. The chief problem is that many adolescents who come before the court have exhibited a range of behaviors from the nondelinquent to delinquent, and the court has the discretion to pick on the more or the less serious as the basis for its adjudication. A comparison of the relationship between adjudications and dispositions for black and white children, therefore, would not necessarily reveal fundamental disparities of treatment.

20. Children's Policy Research Project, Social Policy Research Center, *Census of Illinois Children First Placed into Care between 1977 and 1979* (Chicago: National Opinion Research Center, University of Chicago, 1983).

In more qualitative terms a few of these agencies served a largely black or a largely white clientele. The black agencies were black by design, mainly established since the late 1960s to serve the black community. Most of the small group of essentially white agencies were located in white suburbs and established to serve that population. The old-line sectarian agencies, established by predominantly white churches, and the nonsectarian agencies, governed by predominantly white boards of trustees, show substantial proportions of black clients. For example, among clients of the Catholic organization (which in 1963 supported the establishment of a public agency because the child welfare population was becoming "too black"), over 65 percent of foster children and 35 percent of children in institutions were black according to our census. The change reflected the church leadership's commitment to racial justice, but it also reflected the possibility that the church agencies could maintain their size and increase their government subsidies by changing their clientele. The same bureaucratic incentive existed for all private agencies. It is not a coincidence that the Child Care Association of Illinois, 70 percent of whose agency members operate institutions, offered to do a survey of the racial composition of its members' clients in 1983 when severe economic crisis produced large cuts in purchase-of-service contracts and when the Department of Children and Family Services was particularly concerned with the comparative lack of institutional resources for its black clients.[21]

Differences and Discrimination

This brief analysis shows the great distance that the white agencies have traveled toward racially equitable services in the last twenty years, as well as the persistence of racial differences in some services. However, the current racial differences in children's services do not necessarily indicate conscious discrimination.

21. Personal communications from Roxille Glasco and Harold Goldman, February and April 1983.

The assumption that a differential pattern of service is a sign of discrimination has several drawbacks. The first is conceptual. Black children, partly because they are overrepresented among poor children, are also overrepresented in child welfare systems. They are also almost four times more likely than white children to come from families that, by census definitions, are single-parent families. Different background might be responsible for different patterns of service. A second problem is that a blanket commitment to similar patterns of service ignores the tactical issue that some differences in service are likely to be more important than others. This hierarchy could exist because some differences in service in turn trigger other problems, or simply because some differences have more serious consequences. Different access to day care, for example, might be partly responsible for the differences between troubled families who finally cope and those who do not cope.

Another problem with the assumption that differences in service patterns are inherently unfair has to do with the ambiguous nature of outcomes. A placement service in child welfare is a means to an end—a decent independence. The relation between that placement and the characteristics of the adult who experienced that placement as a child turns out to be at best problematic and at worst completely opaque. This lack of connection is not just a problem of measurement. It is also a reflection of the role that one aspect of a person's childhood actually plays in the development of that person's adult life. Even if black children and white children receive different services, the black children may not necessarily be worse off by any long-term criterion.

We shall start this discussion with a description of the different backgrounds of black and white children. Simple population statistics indicate a different set of life chances for black and white children. A recent study of children in Illinois showed that: (1) five out of every ten black children lived in families with incomes below the poverty line compared to one out of every ten white children; (2) the risks of low birth weight and infant death for blacks were twice as high as for white children; (3) one-quarter of all black infants were born to teenage mothers compared to one-tenth of all white infants; and (4) one-half of all black children lived in single-parent families compared to one-tenth of all white children.[22]

These massive differences in life circumstances are reflected in the rates at which black and white children come into substitute care. In the city of Chicago the rate of initial placement into publicly supported foster care between July 1976 and June 1979 was 3.4 per 1,000 black children compared to 1.3 per 1,000 white children.[23] A 1983 census shows very similar percentages for the entire state.[24] Table 9 shows that for females in the zero to four age group this 2½:1 ratio of black to white placement increases to almost 5:1. The table shows that the difference persists across age groups (although it narrows in high age groups) and that it is greater in suburban communities than in the city.

Age is one clue to the difference between black and white placement rates as illustrated in Table 10. While for every group except white females a greater percentage of children come into care in the youngest category, this trend is more marked for black children. White children, on the other hand, come into care at higher rates than black children in the thirteen to fifteen and sixteen to twenty-one age groups. The reason why black and white children come into care at different ages is explained in Table 11. This table shows that, controlling for gender, black and white children come into care for different reasons. Black children of both sexes are much more likely than white children to come into care via an abuse petition, and black children are somewhat more likely than whites to be the subject of a dependency and neglect petition. White children, on the other hand, are twice as likely as black children to come into the child welfare system for reasons having to do with their own behavior. The different patterns of dispositions fit with the different age patterns. Older children are more likely to come into care for reasons related to their own behavior, while younger children are more likely to come into care for reasons related to their parents' behavior.

22. Mark Testa and Edward Lawlor, *The State of the Child: 1985* (Chicago: Chapin Hall Center for Children at the University of Chicago, 1985).

23. Bush and Testa, "Racial Bias," 3.

24. Testa and Lawlor, *State of the Child*, 48.

Table 9 *Children and Youth Placed in Foster Care, by Sex, Age, and Race of Child and Residence of Parents: Metropolitan Chicago, July 1976 to June 1979*

(Number of children and youth placed into publicly supported foster care. Rates are calculated using 1978 population estimates adjusted for three-year intervals.)

Age at Placement Race of Child	Central City				Suburban Ring			
	Males		Females		Males		Females	
	No.	Rate	No.	Rate	No.	Rate	No.	Rate
Birth to 4 Years								
White	178	1.67	119	1.21	211	1.12	171	.98
Black	574	6.69	504	6.01	102	6.81	83	5.69
5 to 9 Years								
White	77	.96	52	.65	93	.43	78	.38
Black	230	2.79	184	2.17	34	2.42	44	3.14
10 to 14 Years								
White	143	2.00	104	1.41	157	.60	165	.63
Black	285	3.19	273	2.92	56	3.93	41	2.79
15 to 19 Years								
White	79	.96	125	1.60	119	.40	183	.65
Black	153	1.67	224	2.33	29	1.95	24	1.53

SOURCES: National Opinion Research Center, Children's Policy Research Project, 1983; Kenneth E. Hinze, Donald J. Bogue, and Pierre de Vise, *Population Projections: City of Chicago and Suburban Ring, 1970–2000*, University of Chicago, Community and Family Study Center, 1978.

Table 10   Age of Children at Case Opening by Race and Sex for
Children Placed in Surrogate Care: Chicago Region, Fiscal Years
1977-79

	Age				Total[a]
Race and Sex	4 and under	5-12	13-15	16-21	by Race and Sex
White males	323 34.43 15.00	302 32.20 17.99	233 24.84 20.02	80 8.53 17.73	938 100%
Black males	855 45.12 39.69	647 34.14 38.53	296 15.62 25.43	97 5.12 21.51	1,895 100%
White females	238 28.20 11.05	208 24.65 12.39	274 32.46 23.54	124 14.69 27.49	844 100%
Black females	738 41.67 34.26	522 29.48 31.09	361 20.38 31.01	150 8.47 33.26	1,771 100%
Total by Age	2,154 100%	1,679 100%	1,164 100%	451 100%	5,448

SOURCE: National Opinion Research Center, Children's Policy Research Project, University of Chicago, 1983.
[a]Adjusted totals; cases with missing values are omitted.

The figures contain ambiguities. The higher admission rates
for whites aged thirteen to eighteen might be because black
children of that age are more likely to be steered toward the
correctional system, or because more affluent white communities have a lower tolerance for disruptive adolescent behavior
than poor black communities. Some people suggest that the
higher rates of child abuse in black families is partly the result of
different reporting patterns. Black children with injuries are
more likely to be treated at the outpatient clinics of large city
hospitals, which, in turn, are more likely to report suspected

Table 11 Reason for Child Placements by Race and Sex: Chicago Region, Fiscal Years 1977–79 (Unduplicated Child Count)

Race and Sex	Reason for Case Opening							Total by Race and Sex[a]
	Child's Behavior	Abused Child	Dependent/ Neglected	Unmarried Mother	Adoption	Caretaker Absent	Other and Not Reported	
White males	228 24.33 23.90	233 24.87 12.45	259 27.64 16.34	6 0.64 8.22	92 9.82 24.73	96 10.25 20.34	23 2.44 19.49	937 100%
Black males	251 13.25 26.31	693 36.59 37.02	616 32.52 38.86	17 0.90 23.29	112 5.91 30.11	160 8.45 33.90	45 2.38 38.14	1,894 100%
White females	238 28.20 24.95	238 28.20 12.71	212 25.12 13.38	11 1.30 15.07	64 7.58 17.20	68 8.06 14.41	13 1.54 11.02	844 100%
Black females	237 13.38 24.84	708 39.98 37.82	498 28.12 31.42	39 2.20 53.42	104 5.87 27.96	148 8.36 31.53	37 2.09 31.35	1,771 100%
Total by Case Type	954 100%	1,872 100%	1,585 100%	73 100%	372 100%	472 100%	118 100%	5,446

SOURCE: Children's Policy Research Project, Social Policy Research Center, National Opinion Research Center, University of Chicago, 1983.
[a]Adjusted totals, cases with missing values are omitted.

cases of abuse than physicians with a private practice or small suburban hospitals.

These finer distinctions do not alter the basic distinction: blacks are more likely to enter the system for reasons related to their early upbringing and whites for adolescent disruptive behavior. To put it another way, black children are more likely to come into care because of the conditions their families face and their parents' reactions to those conditions. The conditions include younger motherhood, single parenthood, and poverty.

The differences in background and in the reasons for coming into care do not, however, explain the different patterns of institutional placement. The majority of children placed in institutions in recent years came into care for reasons having to do with their own behavior. Table 11 shows that the total numbers (as opposed to the percentages) of black and white children who came into care on account of their behavior are very similar. This fact—together with the facts that some children graduate to institutions having initially come into care for other reasons and that blacks outnumber whites in the Cook County child welfare population by almost three to one—suggests a disparity between the needs of black children and the rate at which they are placed in institutions.

Several characteristics of institutional care help to explain the racial imbalances as something other than conscious discrimination. Child welfare agencies in Chicago have informal geographical boundaries that partly determine the clients they can serve. Most of the private institutions were built on the city's north side, and many were in place before the large immigration of blacks in the 1940s and 1950s. But the majority of the city's new black residents settled on the city's south and west sides. Consequently, in an era of child welfare thinking that emphasizes the importance of geographical proximity to maintain family ties, most institutional resources may be cut off from blacks simply because the facilities are physically distant from the major concentration of black families.

Another explanation of racial disparities is the large number of institutional beds provided by sectarian agencies. In a city where over 70 percent of the population of dependent and neglected children is black, a white sectarian agency that admits equal numbers of white and black clients is contributing to racial imbalance in the aggregate delivery of child welfare services. On the other hand, if the parent church is largely white and the agency admits black and white clients in a strict 2:1 ratio, the agency might well weaken its identity with its church members, reduce its ability to retain the support of contributors, and shake its sense of purpose.

The conclusion seems to be that the private sectarian agencies have made reasonable efforts to serve minority children but that the system as a whole is still discriminating against those children. This conclusion holds whatever one's view of the efficacy of institutional care.

Redefining Fairness

The problem that prompted the establishment of the Division of Child Placing for Negro Children in 1928 was larger than the refusal of private institutions to accept black children. The private agencies who ran the private institutions were the center of the social welfare world. Their refusal of help cut off the black population from most of the other forms of help for troubled families. It put black children in the same position that white children had been before the establishment of child welfare institutions: it left them, in extreme circumstances, with the choice of no care or the contemporary equivalent of the asylum—the correctional center. Refusing access to child welfare institutions, therefore, was merely one manifestation of refusing access to most forms of helping. And that is why the story of discrimination is important.

But as our history has shown, the social welfare world is now crisscrossed with organizations of helping, and the degree of discrimination in placement services is far less than it once was. Discrimination by one agency or group of agencies still leaves other opportunities for getting help. Access to service remains an issue in some fields—getting regular, affordable medical care is a prime example. But the explosive growth of service organizations changes the context in which the question of fairness is set.

The case of institutional care can serve as a starting point for reformulating the issue. In the 1920s, black children were de-

nied access to institutional care. Yet, according to current thinking, institutional care is the most coercive form of care at the
disposal of child welfare organizations. It is least like the care
that children receive in their own homes, and for almost a hundred years its detractors have asserted that it might actually be
harmful. Is it sensible to worry about racial imbalance in the
delivery of a service that may itself be harmful to some clients?
While agencies with institutions have been captured by the need
to maintain them, we need not follow their example.

There is another problem. As the number of services available to families in trouble has multiplied, so has our capacity to
analyze how those services are delivered to people of different
races. Yet it is simply not possible to pursue all the examples of
racial differences in the distribution of those services in the
name of racial justice; many may be simply irrelevant.

One way around these problems would be to draw up criteria
for ranking services and then concentrate on racial differences
in the services at the top of the list. For example, one criterion
could be the coerciveness of the service. This approach would
allow us to worry more about the distribution of noncoercive
services than the distribution of institutional care.

From the civic perspective that underlies this book, however,
raising the issue of fairness in the context of coercive or noncoercive services threatens the very meaning of fairness or justice.
Whether these services are good services or bad, or the best of
the available bad options, is not the crucial issue in a democracy. Equity is an attribute of citizenship, not clienthood. Its
primary concern should be equal protection from the wrongs of
society and equal access to its benefits.

This premise suggests a different criterion for thinking about
fairness. The focus of justice should be on opportunities that
promote citizenship and reduce clienthood. Clienthood threatens two critical characteristics of citizenship. The first is the
autonomy to determine one's own ends. The second is mutuality in one's relationships with the key people in one's life—that
is, the opportunity to deal with and be dealt with by them in
some reciprocal way.

If citizenship is the goal, the fairness of agencies and the fair
distribution of services can only be a secondary concern. It is

very easy to slip from a concern with fairness for people in trouble to a concern about the fairness of agencies. But, to return to another theme of the book, the relationship between the response to need and the need itself is rarely straightforward. We must judge the issue of justice first against our primary goals, rather than against the methods we use to attain those goals. Fairness of the method may still be important but only because we judge that method a useful vehicle for reaching a primary goal.

Fairness: Goals and Methods

We return to the goals we mentioned at the beginning of this chapter: life and liberty. The first goal takes us away from delivery-of-service statistics and back to the census.

An exemplary issue is infant mortality, which illustrates the importance of focusing on goals. For much of this century the infant mortality rates for white and black infants declined sharply. The black rates were, however, considerably higher than the white rates in every time period. In the 1980s, the rate of decline slowed down, and in some states the infant mortality rate actually increased. The rate of infant mortality for black infants is now about 20 per 1,000 live births, or twice the white rate.

Infant mortality exemplifies the shortcoming of focusing on one solution at the expense of examining the broader problem. In one sense black infants who are at risk receive good services. If they are born in large cities with good postnatal care units, they will receive, courtesy of Medicaid, the most advanced treatment. But the disproportionate allocation of funds to that care is a massive disservice to black families. A large proportion of low-weight births (the key indicator of infant distress) can be avoided by adequate prenatal care and diet at a much lower cost than the cost of intensive care. A 1978 study calculated that the average cost of neonatal intensive care was $13,616 per patient, compared with $350 for prenatal care.[25] But while the institutional

25. Peter Budetti, Office of Technological Assessment, quoted in C. Arden Miller, "Infant Mortality in the U.S." *Scientific American* 253, no. 1 (July 1985): 31–37.

imperatives of distinguished medical schools maintain the expensive intensive care programs, the political decisions of a conservative national administration eat away at the much cheaper preventive strategies. The effect of those decisions was magnified by the recession of 1981–82. "The states hardest hit by the recession reported a decline in the participation of pregnant women in prenatal care, consistent with the loss of Medicaid and insurance benefits and with the curtailment of support for public clinics."[26] In this case the distribution of resources functions to maintain a medical subspecialty practicing in major medical schools. It is not a distribution aimed at the equitable goal of maximizing the health of minority infants.

The protection of liberty is a recurring theme for families in trouble. Sometimes the threat is dramatic, as with the overrepresentation of nondelinquent black youths in correctional facilities that occurred earlier this century. Sometimes it is much less dramatic and consequently less visible. The maintenance of families to prevent the placement of children is such an issue. It is less dramatic than the issue of incarceration, because foster care is regarded as a service, not a punishment. But it is a service that is used after the failure of the family. In a democratic society it is not the first choice. If family sustenance rather than good foster care were the primary objective of child welfare systems, there would be a different distribution of resources. Such a distribution would especially benefit black families, whose children tend to enter the child welfare system at a young age because their families have problems coping. But just as the institutional imperatives in the large hospitals diverted funds from the prevention of neonatal distress to its treatment, so the imperatives of traditional child welfare agencies do the same for troubled families.

The working out of these pressures are quite straightforward. When the Illinois Department of Children and Family Services was established in 1963, one of the aims of its civic (as opposed to private agency) supporters was to redress the balance between child placement and family sustenance in favor of the latter. The history of child welfare as a placement operation

26. Ibid., 37.

was, however, deeply entrenched in the organization of services. The early success of the department in establishing family support programs was quickly curtailed. Well-established private agencies whose primary (and most expensive) tasks were the provision of institutional and foster care placements would simply not allow the diversion of significant portions of the child welfare budget to such directly family-sustaining services as day care and homemaker services. From the mid-1970s, the day care and homemaker lines of the department's budget were actually used as reserves for the placement lines, which, in turn, were overspent each year. In the same decade, while the daily population of child welfare institutions declined by half, the institutional line of the budget remained a constant 20 percent of the entire child welfare budget.

In these two examples reflections on the central problem of maintaining the citizenship of troubled families would suggest different service strategies than currently employed. But the issue of fairness is a much bigger issue than the selection and equal distribution of the most appropriate services. It is more fundamentally a matter of respecting the citizenship of people in trouble. For minorities that has always included the issue of fair judgments—the assessment of problems in a way that was unbiased by race. Fair judgments are still an issue. Unfair judgments put people at risk of inappropriate or even harmful treatment. For example, Chicago has three times as many students enrolled in programs for the mildly mentally retarded as any other school system in the United States. A 1982 study suggested that as many as 7,000 of the Chicago Public Schools' 12,000 students in such programs are misclassified.[27] These children are being denied an appropriate education. Minority parents and students in poor inner-city neighborhoods have little power to negotiate their interactions with large public or private organizations. The result is that there is little check on the common organizational tactic of selecting client categories that maximize the convenience of the organization.

Fair judgments depend on the adequate presentation of differ-

27. Designs for Change, *Caught in the Web: Misplaced Children in Chicago's Classes for the Mentally Retarded* (Chicago: Designs for Change, 1982).

ent views. The comparative weakness of political power in poor minority communities produces a separation between those who perceive a problem because it is their problem and those who have the power to act on the problem. White agencies who have minority clients and minority staff still act in a white context in the sense that they are more likely to use their political power first for the preservation of their agencies. They are less likely to use it to address what are perceived to be largely minority problems. The lack of attention paid to any constructive reform of the welfare system is an example of this.

There are several ways of reducing this powerlessness. We can redefine fair practice for traditional agencies to include the task of addressing public policy issues that differentially affect their minority clients. By accepting public money, private agencies accept a civic responsibility that is fulfilled only when they use their political power for minority as well as white clients. Another strategy is to empower poor, minority communities to voice the broad range of community concerns. Fair definitions of problems and solutions cannot be constructed in the absence of the voices of the people who know the problems and their contexts, because the problems are theirs.

Conclusion

Fairness is a matter of how people are treated in a particular context. One could apply the notion to political prisoners or to the subjects of an empire. Both groups can be treated fairly or unfairly according to the rules of those in authority. But both these contexts are, by a broader standard, unfair. The point of campaigns against racial discrimination is often to broaden the context in which the treatment of racial minorities is judged. But to judge the condition of black clients against the condition of white clients and to compare the services they receive is still to judge fairness in a restrictive and demeaning context. The only context that satisfies the demands of a free society is that of the body of citizens. Equal treatment is attention that maximizes everyone's chance to escape clienthood and attain citizenship.

5

Fairness and Discrimination: Difficult Children

Introduction

In the face of racial discrimination, we argued in the last chapter, our primary goal should be the restoration and preservation of citizenship. Services are means, not ends, and should not usurp the primacy of the ends. In this chapter we examine the situation of the small group of children for whom the child welfare system is the only source of help standing between them and state mental hospitals, prisons, or the streets. These children cannot, on the face of it, expect the independence associated with full citizenship. For them good service appears to be a reasonable goal; it is potentially more sustaining and less coercive than any of their other options.

This chapter examines the problem of these children. They are "difficult" in the view of the service system because taking care of them is unusually taxing. We look at the problem first in the language of the day-to-day debate about these children. Then we reexamine the premises of that debate.

The problem of difficult children is interesting partly because it appears to challenge our premise that the appropriate goal for children in trouble is a decent independence. But there are also other reasons to look at their situation. In every social welfare system difficult clients—those who tax the resources of the system—symbolize, define, and shape those systems way beyond their numerical importance. They affect, therefore, everyone else in those systems. In child welfare the small group of serious abuse cases diverts attention from the much larger category of neglect. The most dangerous adult convicts affect the character of the rest of the prison system. The care of coronary bypass patients influences the distribution of resources in the medical system and helps to determine attitudes about what constitutes appropriate medical intervention.

Difficult clients in the deviant social welfare systems (this excludes the heart patient) are also important because the average organization does not want to serve them and because they are hard to ignore. This situation has two consequences. For us, they are a constant nuisance. For themselves, they risk being moved into more coercive systems as less coercive systems give up on them. Difficult children thus offer a superb window into the operation of the helping enterprise. More importantly, we shall discover that their "difficultness" is as much a matter of the organizations' reactions to them as of the children's behavior. For that reason their condition depends on the way the organizations and the average citizen regard them.

Before we examine the way the system handles difficult children, we should give some account of the children who fall into this category.

Definitions of Difficult Children

The official child welfare system in Illinois, the juvenile court and the Department of Children and Family Services, has six official designations for children: abused, neglected, dependent, delinquent, the new "minor requiring authoritative intervention" (which replaces the former "minor in need of supervision"), and addicted minors. While within each category there may be children who are in greater or lesser danger or need, the terms themselves can be set in a hierarchy according to how difficult each set of children is likely to be for surrogate parents. "Difficult" here simply means difficult to control, cope with, or live with. Dependent children who are in care because they have no parents or guardian or because their parents or guardian are unable to care for them are likely to be least difficult in this sense; delinquent children are likely to be most difficult. Minors in need of authoritative intervention are likely to be more difficult than neglected children. To some degree these categories are correlated with age; dependent children and abused children are younger, the children in the other categories are older. Another characteristic divides children in the same way: children who come to the state's attention by reason of their parents' behavior and children who come by reason of their own behavior. Youth services personnel have a more colloquial way of expressing similar divisions. They distinguish between home kids, street kids, delinquent kids, and psychotic kids.

It is easy to see who the private sector regards as difficult because their views on the matter are enshrined in the contracts they negotiate with the state. The agencies sign a separate contract for each service they provide and they place in each contract a list of exclusions—that is, a list of children they will not serve. In the 1980 Department of Children and Family Services contract book four categories of child accounted for the majority of exclusions in the institutional contracts, the foster care contracts, and the counseling contracts. These were aggressive children, psychotic children, retarded children, and children involved in substance abuse. In each contract different adjectives were used to qualify the behavior—to determine degrees of the behavior that were unacceptable—but the four basic categories were the same.

We are still, however, dealing with official categories that are poor substitutes for the children themselves. One example of children who represent the irreducibly hard cases in the child welfare system are those children who become the concern of what is known in Illinois as the Governor's Initiative. We can get closer to these children because they were the objects of considerable attention. In 1979, a program was set up inside the Governor's Office—and therefore outside the jurisdiction of the regular social service departments—to find placements for children who were being bounced not only from one placement to another but also from the jurisdiction of one department to another. The story is very much like the story that led to the Joint Service Project for Adolescents, which we described in chapter 3. In 1979, the same judge, Judge Joseph Schneider, in the case of *David B. and Daniel C.,*[1] ordered the Department of Mental Health and the Department of Children and Family Services to cooperate in providing adequate care for the two boys named in the suit and for all children in a like situation.[2] As in the Joint Service Project case, the children were considered not appropriate for the mental health system and too difficult for the child welfare system. Eager to avoid having the court instruct them in the minutiae of their own business, the Department of Children and Family Services devised a scheme whereby the final responsibility for these children would rest with a specially designed unit in the Governor's Office. The point of this scheme was to shift the responsibility for decisions the departments were unable to make to a body with the power to compel the departments to accept a particular decision.

Some fifteen months after the project commenced an independent consulting company described the first twenty-nine children who entered the project as follows: 75 percent of them were male and 55 percent were between thirteen and eighteen years old. According to court records, seventeen of the young people's mothers and six of their fathers still expressed an interest in their children; only five children had other relatives who were said to be interested in them.[3] All but one of the children were deemed to be in need of special education classes, and 40 percent had been classified as learning disabled. Of the total, 70

1. *In Re David B. and Daniel C.,* Circuit Court of Cook County, 78 Co 1520.
2. For an early account and history of the Governor's Initiative, see Seth I. Hirshorn and Jean Covington, "Evaluation of the Governor's Cook County Court Project, Final Report (First Draft), Vols. 1 and 2." SIH Inc., Ann Arbor, Mich., December 1980. Photocopy.
3. It is the experience of social workers who make a special effort to find family members who are interested in playing a role in the lives of troubled children that official records always underestimate the possibility of finding such people. One agency director said about the difficult adolescents he tried to place in foster homes after they had spent time in institutions: "The Department's attitude is that they don't have families. Then we discover in the first two phone calls they make that the first is to a girlfriend and the second is to a sister or a mother. And the number has been in the kid's head for ten years and this is the first opportunity they've had to call. Over a third of our kids go home and that's to families where DCFS said there wasn't any family." Interview with John Halsey, Director, Youth Enrichment Services, 16 July 1980.

percent were said to need a program for the emotionally disturbed, and 45 percent were considered socially maladjusted. Some two-thirds of the group were described as being physically assaultive to other people and 40 percent were reckoned dangerous to themselves—that is, capable of inflicting physical harm on themselves (although in the majority of cases that behavior fell far short of being suicidal). Two-thirds of them had delinquency petitions preferred against them.

Two quick sketches of individual children provide a flavor of the people who ended up in the Initiative. They are examples, not typical cases (although their behavior is not exceptional within this group); the average characteristics used to describe the Initiative's population hide as many differences as the similarities they display.

One seventeen-year-old boy first came to the attention of the juvenile court on a delinquency petition in which it was alleged that he had been involved in four instances of burglary, robbery, and theft.[4] He was said to have an IQ of 86, classified as in the dull average range. He was a frequent truant. By the time he reached the Initiative, he had been excluded from the Chicago public school system. His mother said he was ungovernable at home, and he had once threatened to shoot his brother. He was said to bully and con younger children, and he was frequently involved in fighting and drug abuse. In just over a year the boy had spent time in three state placements and in the homes of three relatives. At the time of his admission to the Initiative six institutions who regularly contracted with the Department of Children and Family Services had declined to accept him.

The second person is a girl who was seventeen at the time we saw her records. She had come to the attention of the juvenile court at the age of two on a neglect petition. Her father had, in fact, thrown her out of a window. She stayed in a single Department of Children and Family Services foster home until she was nine and then returned to the court on a minor-in-need-of-

4. The case histories were extracted from the Governor's Initiative case files to which we were kindly granted access by the director of the Initiative. This access was granted on the condition that we would take every precaution to maintain the confidentiality of the records. Consequently, we extracted no names from the records.

supervision petition at the request of her mother, who found her uncontrollable. That same year she had been raped by two youths in a local park. Between that year and the time she came to the attention of the Initiative, she lived in eight different placements. She ran away from most of them. She also had a baby and came back to the juvenile court on a child abuse charge when her child suffered a broken leg. The girl was said to have an IQ of 63 and was characterized as being mildly retarded with a strong will; this combination was said to be the cause of her troubles. She had engaged in shoplifting, prostitution, and arson. At the time of her referral to the Initiative she had been turned down by sixteen different agencies.

While these two cases (and indeed the entire subsample) evade any tight etiology, several people involved with the children saw a relationship between their experiences in placement and their subsequent behavior. The children tended to ask for help by behaving badly, while the average placement refused to consider keeping a child who displayed any such behavior. The director of an agency that accepted children like the Initiative's children in its foster home program put it this way:

> The bulk of the cases are very angry kids who have ten placements and the last placement was strictly an institution. Finally they got violent and they attacked the staff. We say to our foster parents, "Kids who get violent get violent because they are afraid no one is going to listen to them. . . ." Most private agencies pride their possessions and their staff and if you start to mess with either of those you're out.[5]

The problem of difficult children, however, is not just the degree of difficult behavior. It is also a problem of how many of them exist and what proportion of the child welfare population they represent. The persistence with which the private agency contracts exclude a priori certain types of children suggests that they are numerous enough to be a constant danger to organizations trying to stay on an even keel. In fact, that perception of the incidence of difficult children is exaggerated. The Governor's Initiative was one of several projects designed

5. Interview with John Halsey, 16 July 1980.

to care for difficult children, so its caseload is not the total caseload of such children in the state. But the estimates made of the number of difficult children in the state before the project started and the number of children referred to the project, albeit by a very careful screening process,[6] show a large discrepancy between the uninformed professional view and the reality. Announcing the establishment of the project, the *Chicago Tribune* reported:

> [Judge] Schneider indicated in court that eighty-six children fall into the category to be served by the plan. However, Kiley [the Governor's special assistant for social services] said Department of Mental Health statistics show that there could be as many as 10,000 youths in the state who would be eligible.[7]

The director of the Initiative, commenting on those early estimates, said that some of the child welfare professionals he canvassed put the figure as high as 80,000 children.

One set of figures with which these estimates can be compared is the total number of children in publicly financed care in the year the project opened—1979. In that year there were about 4,500 mentally handicapped or developmentally disabled children in residential facilities in Illinois and about 13,000 children in child welfare placements. In addition, about 1,000 children were committed by the juvenile court to the Department of Corrections. The high estimate of children who, by definition, were so troublesome that they could not fit into the existing systems was over four times the total number of children in those systems. The Governor's Office estimate was over 50 percent of those children. By contrast, the judge's estimate was 0.4 percent of the children in the existing systems.

Another comparison are the children actually served by the Initiative. By 1981, the Initiative was receiving about seventy

---

6. The rules governing the referral of children to the Initiative by the juvenile court (the only body empowered to refer to the project) were that a referral could take place only when: (1) all available resources for securing services had been tried without success; (2) disagreement existed between two or more state agencies over accepting placement, treatment, or funding responsibilities for a child; and (3) disagreement existed between the court and a state agency over the specific service plan for a child.

7. *Chicago Tribune*, 12 July 1979, sec. 3, p. 1.

referrals a year and at any one time was handling about twenty active cases.[8] It was obliged to accept all the cases referred to it (referrals were made by the juvenile court). The Initiative could not control either the number of referrals or the number of acceptances. Apparently, therefore, the profession's view of the incidence of "difficultness" was grossly exaggerated.

By other ways of counting, difficult children are not a high percentage of children in the child welfare system. A mental or a physical handicap, to take another example, was recorded for 4.6 percent of all the children in the Illinois child welfare census between 1977 and 1979.[9]

Parent behavior still accounts for most of the problems that bring children into the child welfare system. The same census showed that, of the 6,000 placements made in the Chicago area between 1977 and 1979, 80 percent involved children who were in care primarily for reasons having to do with their parents' circumstances and behavior, and 17 percent were in care for reasons of their own behavior. This comparison is not to suggest that the 80 percent of cases did not contain problems or complexities. But the problems most discussed by agencies who feel burdened are the problems of how to deal with a child whose behavior causes trouble. The reason for this emphasis is straightforward. A difficult child abuse case can be dealt with by disengagement—that is, by moving the child out of the natural home and by ceasing to bother about the problem of returning the child to that home. Given the ambiguity of the situation, the powerlessness of abusive parents, and a lack of data about agencies' comparative success in maintaining children in abusive homes, such a disengagement will go unnoticed. When a child who is a ward of the state causes problems in a placement and either runs away or is removed because his or her surrogate parents cannot cope, the situation cannot be ignored. The child has to be found another home, and this constitutes much more

8. Barry Berzy, "The Governor's Cook County Court Project: Presentation and Analysis of Selected Issues" (M.A. thesis, School of Social Service Administration, University of Chicago, June 1981).

9. Fred Wulczyn, "Analysis of the Census of All Children Entering the Illinois Department of Children and Family Services' Caseload between 1977 and 1979," Children's Policy Research Project, National Opinion Research Center, University of Chicago, November 1982.

of a burden. Thus difficulty is not a function of how hard it is to achieve the system's official goals but a function of the effort needed to cope with a child on a day-to-day basis. The same is true in medicine. A difficult patient is not so much a patient whose condition is difficult to cure as a patient whose behavior impedes the smooth running of the hospital.

The fear of difficult children has another source, and that source leads us to a critical component of the phenomenon. The debate about who takes difficult children has become more urgent with the perception that children in care have become more difficult. It is perhaps inevitable that one generation of workers thinks its task more difficult than that of the last. But this perception, as a description of what has changed in the last ten years, has some validity. Difficult behaviors, gang membership, drug addiction, and prostitution have become more common in middle and even early adolescence. They can no longer be regarded as the prerogative of older adolescents, and agencies accustomed to the less disruptive behavior of younger adolescents are taken aback when confronted with difficult behavior in this age group. Another reason is that the distribution of children between various public departments has changed in a way that makes the job of the child welfare department and its contractees more difficult. The pressure to place children in less coercive environments meant that, beginning in the 1970s, some children who would formerly have been placed in mental health or correctional systems moved into the child welfare system. The same impetus altered the distribution of children within the child welfare system, as children formerly placed in institutions were treated in less coercive ways. Consequently, agencies were faced with the task of placing in foster homes children whom they would previously have considered too difficult for that option.

These changes are a reminder that the difficulty a case presents is not totally determined by the behavior of a child. Rather it is determined by the behavior of a child in a particular context. A disturbed child who is under sedation in a back ward may not be difficult to handle. The difficulty (which from the child's perspective is an opportunity) is caused by placing the child further up the continuum to normal care.

Who Looks After Difficult Children?

The charge of discrimination by some behavioral characteristic of a client is a twofold charge. First, some agencies are being treated unfairly because they are required to admit more than their reasonable share of difficult clients. Second, in consequence, the clients in the agencies that shoulder an unequal burden are also the subject of discrimination.

In the last chapter we noted the progression from a concern with fairness to a client to a concern about the equal distribution of services, and from that to a concern about fairness by, and then to, an agency. That progression gradually transforms the object of attention from a person, the client, to an organization, the agency. In the case of difficult clients the issue of the distribution of clients in the child welfare system is a good starting point because the difficult client who fails to secure help in this system will be faced with worse options. It is also an issue commonly discussed in terms of the roles of public and private agencies, and that is where we start our discussion.

The charge that agencies who do not take their fair share of difficult clients are being unfair has been spelt out in several ways. The English social welfare theorist Richard Titmuss argued that wherever there were private and public services operating together difficult clients would be disproportionately steered toward the public system while resources would be disproportionately steered toward the private system.[10] Titmuss had in mind situations where a market system of service operated alongside a public welfare system of service. The accuracy of this charge is most dramatically seen in communities in the United States where private and public hospitals operate side by side.

The situation in a purchase-of-service system, such as the child welfare system we are describing, is somewhat different. Here all the clients are public clients, and most of the money that supports them is public money; the clientele, however, is divided between public and not-for-profit private agencies. Moreover, since most of the money in both parts of the system

10. See, for example, Richard Titmuss, "Choice and 'The Welfare State,' " in *Commitment to Welfare* (London: Allen and Unwin, 1976), 138–52.

is public money, it is distributed by a public body, which should in theory be able to prevent a lopsided distribution of resources between the two types of agency. The public sector complains, however, that the private sector consistently refuses to take its appropriate share of difficult clients, so that the public sector has become the sector of last resort. This situation is considered to be particularly unfair because it appears to contradict the private sector claim that it is the specialized service sector for children who need special attention.

The evidence suggests that the private sector in a purchase-of-service system does select its clients on the basis of degree of "difficulty." People from both sides of the dispute agree that such selection takes place. A contract officer for a Chicago area office of the Department of Children and Family Services remarked, "I only have teenagers and black babies and they [the private agencies] send me sheets and sheets of homes I can't use because they will only take young kids and white kids."[11] The director of a highly regarded private agency said the same thing with a different emphasis. "The voluntary sectors can provide better services now than the state because they [the voluntary sector] can limit intake. I don't have to take a fire setter when I don't have 24-hour coverage."[12] Several independent analyses confirm these statements. In 1974, the Children's Home and Aid Society conducted a survey of its own and four other agencies' operations preparatory to discussions of a possible merger of the five agencies. The society discovered that the agencies' rate of acceptance of referrals from the Department of Children and Family Services ranged from 29 percent to 67 percent, with an average acceptance rate of 45 percent. The average decline rate then was 55 percent.[13] In 1976, the Group for Action Planning surveyed its members and found, for the thirteen responding agencies, an acceptance rate of about 60 percent.[14] In 1980, a private consulting firm working for the department deter-

11. Interview with Susan Demaree, 31 July 1980.
12. Harold Goldman's report of an interview with Donna Pressma, Director of the Jewish Children's Bureau of Chicago, 1982.
13. Minutes of ICHAS program heads meeting, 7 October 1974, 3.
14. Document for discussion at a GAP policy group meeting, 2 December 1976. ICHAS GAP files.

Table 12   Reason for Placement of Child by Child's Placement in Public or Private Foster Home Care: State of Illinois, Fiscal Years 1977–79

Reason for Placement	Number in Public Foster Care	Percent of Public Foster Care	Number in Private Foster Care	Percent of Private Foster Care
Child's Behavior	671	11.5	64	10.2
Abused Child	1,735	29.6	211	33.8
Dependent/ Neglected Child	3,457	58.9	350	56.0
Totals	5,863	100	625	100

SOURCE; Fred Wulczyn, Selected Characteristics of Board Placements: Fiscal Years 1977–79, Census of Illinois Department of Children and Family Services Clients, November 1982, Children's Policy Research Project, National Opinion Research Center, the University of Chicago.

mined that the rejection rate of department referrals to private agencies was 53 percent.[15]

It is more difficult to determine which clients the agencies are accepting and which they are rejecting. We know from the previous chapter that private agencies, as part of a weakening historical trend, serve a smaller percentage of minority clients than the department. Table 12 shows that for the gross categories of child behavior—abused child, and dependent and neglected child—there is little difference in the composition of public and private foster agency caseloads. There is a difference, however, by age. Table 13 shows that private foster care accommodates a decreasing proportion of foster children at each age level that children enter care. This measure, which correlates with chronological age, is a useful indication of how easily a child adapts to surrogate care. The later the child is placed, the more difficult the child is likely to find that event. Whereas private agencies

15. Arthur Young and Company, *Report to the Department of Children and Family Services: Review of Current Operations in Cook County Region*, (Chicago: Arthur Young and Company, October 1980), 49. The number of rejections and referrals were counted for four months in all the Chicago area offices except the specialized intake units.

Table 13   Difficult Children? The Age of Entry of Children in Public and Private Foster Family Care in Cook County, Fiscal Years 1977–79

Auspices	Age at Entry						Total
	0	1–4	5–12	13–15	16–21		
Public Placements							
Number	770	902	1,076	681	205		3,634
Percent of all Public Placements	21.2	24.8	29.6	18.7	5.6		100
Percent of all Placements Public and Private	75.8	76.9	84.0	95.0	97.0		
Private Placements							
Number	246	271	203	36	7		763
Percent of all Private Placements	32.2	35.5	26.6	4.7	0.9		100
Percent of all Placements Public and Private	24.2	23.1	16.0	5.0	3.0		
Totals	1,016	1,173	1,279	717	212		4,397

SOURCE: National Opinion Research Center, Children's Policy Research Project, 1983.

provided almost 24 percent of the foster care placements for babies, the corresponding percentage for thirteen- to fifteen-year-olds was 5 percent.

This figure does not mean that private agencies turn their backs on adolescents. Private agencies provide most of the institutional care in the state, and institutional care is now mainly used to house older children. What the totals do mean is that the public sector is more willing than the private sector to serve older children in less coercive settings. That is a more "difficult" task for a social worker, simply because it increases the possibility that the placement will be disrupted and require attention.

Differences and Discrimination

It is one thing to demonstrate that the private sector chooses its clients, rejecting as many as half of those it is offered. It is a separate question whether this pattern is discriminatory or inappropriate. Detailed arguments between the Department of Children and Family Services and the providers center around the issue of "no-decline" contracts—contracts where the providers agree to serve a specified number of a certain kind of child and within those limits agree to accept every child referred to them. Such a contract is open to dispute because the criteria are open to interpretation. There is, however, a prior dispute—whether a no-decline contract is ever reasonable. Most private agencies, particularly well-established ones, resist such contracts. The department pursues them because of the private sector rejection rate and the enormous amount of time and energy it takes to find placements for difficult children.

The arguments in favor of allowing the contracting agencies to select their clients emphasize two points: (1) the possibility of a precise match between a child with a particular set of needs and a particular service, and (2) the need to control the disruption caused by difficult children so that a reasonable standard of caring or treatment can be maintained for other children in the same setting. The lobbyist for two of the largest private agencies in the state denied that the issue was about "difficulty."

"When you package a service, you define it. You say, 'we serve this type of kid.' Because of advances in social welfare work, we can make that differentiation. It's not really a matter of easy or difficult. It is a question of the program and the kid."[16] The director of the Child Care Association put it in different terms: "The private agencies are voluntary and they stand for a certain ideology. Some of them are sectarian and some have other ideologies, and as such they have a right to pick and choose."[17]

The last statement is somewhat misleading. There is not a dispute today about sectarian agencies serving their own kind. That right is preserved in the Juvenile Court Act. The issue is their selection of clients who are not of their own kind—clients that the agencies take in order to maintain their size in an era when the needs of the agencies' own kind of clients do not exhaust the agencies' capacities.

The issue of difficulty is usually not about a private agency's refusal to take *any* difficult children but about the number of difficult children the agency will take. Thoughtful people in the Department of Children and Family Services admit that, once they find a program that will take difficult children, they will overload that program. Individual state workers also admit that they minimize a child's problems in order to get the child placed. This practice is partly responsible for the private agencies' insistence that they should be allowed to diagnose children themselves before deciding whether to admit them.

The department's procedures create another disincentive for private agencies to serve difficult children. As the department took on a new, more difficult clientele during the 1970s, it tried to persuade private agencies to establish additional programs for such children. It encountered little enthusiasm among the traditional agencies, partly because it was department policy not to provide capital costs for new institutions, and partly because a private agency had no guarantee that the department would renew its contract for the service of such children for any reasonable length of time. Department contracts run for one year; in theory an agency that had gone to the expense of setting up a

16. Interview with Tom Nolan, Lobbyist for Catholic Charities of the Chicago Archdiocese, 23 September 1980.

17. Interview with Bob Ralls, Executive Director, Child Care Association of Illinois, 20 August 1980.

program could suddenly find itself without clients. According to the private agency lobbyist quoted earlier:

> You only have a guarantee for twelve months and you have no capital costs. So you're setting up the program out of your own pocket. You have laborious negotiations about licensing and your program, and then you don't end up with full costs. Then your board will say to you, "These kids are the state's responsibility." Why am I messing up my organization by pulling their chestnuts out of the fire?[18]

The Department of Children and Family Services partly solved this problem by persuading individuals to create new agencies to serve difficult children. In many cases these agencies were organized by people who had once worked in the public sector, were concerned with the overcoercive treatment of difficult children, and were confident enough of their own understanding of what the public sector wanted and how it operated to take the risk.

The major arguments against the private sector's demand for the right to select clients are that selection is a cover for discrimination and that the level of specificity needed to make a good match between child and program is easily exaggerated. There are certainly important distinctions between programs designed for younger and older children, or for "home kids" and "delinquent kids." A few children who exhibit uncontrolled bizarre behavior may need programs with the capacity to administer psychotropic drugs if they are to stay in relatively uncoercive settings. Beyond that, the capacity of a program may have less to do with the exactness of a certain therapeutic approach than the intangible capacity of some program directors to extract the best from children with turbulent histories. Just as program capacity defies precise definition, so too does the condition of a child. Whenever diagnostic reports move from descriptions of a child's behavior to overall assessment and formal diagnosis, the opinions of different consulting experts vary significantly.[19]

Diagnosis itself can be used as a weapon in the battle of

18. Interview with Tom Nolan, 23 September 1980.
19. See, for example, Berzy, "Governor's Cook County Court Project," 1981.

referrals. The insistence on private sector diagnoses as supplements to whatever diagnoses the department has completed has been used as a device to find a temporary home for a child to whom no one will offer a permanent home. An analysis of one program for difficult children showed that prior to the commencement of the program one child had received five "diagnostic evaluation" admissions to psychiatric hospitals in less than two months; another child, four in under five months; and a third child, twelve such admissions in less than two and a half years.[20]

In some instances the refusal of a client on the basis that the client has not received an adequate diagnosis is a clear case of ignoring the basic needs of the client. For example, such a judgment could be made of the private sector's refusal to take children who need shelter care without the paraphernalia of diagnosis and assessment. *Shelter care* is a term used to describe a program for children who, because of an emergency, have literally no place to spend the night and need a shelter for a few nights until more permanent arrangements can be made. The insistence on the regularities of diagnosis and evaluation in these cases makes them a weapon to defend an agency against the inconvenience of finding room at short notice for clients it would prefer not to take.

There remains the argument of the agency director we quoted earlier, who said that she could provide better services to the children she chose to serve because she was able to turn down, for example, fire setters who need enormous amounts of attention. In certain situations energy devoted to some clients means less energy devoted to others. A public sector caseworker with seventy or eighty cases to handle faces this dilemma constantly. Such forced choosing is an inevitable accompaniment of life in street-level bureaucracies.[21] But it is important that this dilemma is dealt with on its merits, not concealed behind implausible claims. It is not appropriate for the private sector to claim that the right to select less difficult clients allows them to develop innovative

20. Ibid., 5.
21. The point is made most vividly and sympathetically by Michael Lipsky in *Street Level Bureaucracy: Dilemmas of the Individual in Public Services* (New York: Russell Sage Foundation, 1980).

approaches to the problems of distressed families. The difficult clients, not the less difficult, are the ones who need the imaginative help of the most experienced workers. Moreover, solutions that work in an artificially calm environment will not survive the pressured and untidy demands the average social service agency experiences.

Nor is it convincing to assert that selection allows for a significant improvement in the quality of the service provided to the remaining clients. The director who made the statement was the head of a children's agency that prided itself on its skilled, professional service. The assumption behind the claim was that the better the service, the better off the client. That seeming truism, however, is misleading. If a neglected or disturbed child's essential need is a supportive environment in which to grow up, a range of contexts will probably be adequate. There is no guarantee that one context that is better than a second still adequate context will actually be more beneficial for the particular child. The assumption about the relation between context and child outcome (above a certain level of adequate care) begs the question of the causal relationship between the two. It also begs the question of what a "better outcome" is—above the level where a child becomes a lawful, self-supporting citizen. None of this argument denies the possibility that a badly organized agency recruiting grossly inadequate surrogate caretakers is a threat to the well-being of dependent children. But the reader should treat with caution the claim that there is a better than adequate care that can be obtained if some agencies are allowed the conditions to hone their special skills.

This skepticism about the private sector's defense of selection, also does not deny that there are more and less satisfactory ways of distributing the task of helping demanding children. Nor does it imply that the public sector's record is unblemished. All bureaucracies select clients and tasks to maintain a level of equilibrium within the organization. The Department of Children and Family Services selects by keeping out or expelling clients that it thinks belong in mental health or correctional facilities. There is, however, a difference between an organization that has a legal responsibility to find homes for distressed children and an organization that conceives of its professional

responsibility as providing the best care. The Abused and Neglected Child Reporting Act states that the Department of Children and Family Services *shall* protect the best interests of the
children who come to its attention under the provisions of the
act and *shall* protect those children from further harm.[22] That
requirement, of course, means all such children, no matter what
the resources at the department's disposal. The inevitable tension between minimal but universal protection and the best service is both exacerbated and disguised by the fact that the public
and the private sectors pay attention to opposite sides of that
tension.

As we will see later in this chapter, the care of difficult children
is a much broader issue than the comparative roles of public and
private agencies. But to sum up this part of the analysis, we
should note that in this, as in other characteristics, the private
sector is not homogeneous. There are considerable differences
among agencies as to how willing they are to accept difficult
children. A few agencies regard difficult children as central to
their purpose and that, as we will see later, is one reason for their
success. In some respects the public sector is handicapped in
caring for these children. The care of difficult children requires
flexibility, determination, and a willingness to take risks that are
not naturally present in a large, centralized bureaucracy. On the
other hand, the extra attention demanded by difficult children
means extra costs, and virtually no private agency can afford
those costs without a heavy reliance on public money.

The reluctance of some private agencies to take difficult children does raise a crucial question about the definition of "private." When it allows an agency to accept public money while
shunning responsibility for those who most need help, privateness is reduced to the protection of a comfortable existence. At
the extreme it becomes an exercise in self-gratification. The
client exists to make the helper feel good; clients who cannot
perform that role are rejected. At this point privateness loses all
trace of civic responsibility and wears its most offensive face—
the protection of privilege, or the privilege of enjoying the role
of helper while ignoring those who need the most help.

22. The Abused and Neglected Child Reporting Act, P.A. 81–1077, sec. 2.

Difficult Children and the Fair Distribution
of Resources

The reluctance of some public and private agencies to take difficult children is based on the realistic assessment that such children require the expenditure of more resources than less disturbed children. The question of what constitutes an appropriate distribution of resources for demanding children is difficult in every social welfare field. We will engage the issue for our population by returning to the Governor's Initiative.

The Governor's Initiative demonstrated that in the aggregate it was possible to deal with difficult children without either shifting them from placement to placement or moving them to coercive placements. By a variety of measures the program was a success. The children's placements after they had been referred to the Initiative were more stable than they had been before that referral, lasting an average of seventy-eight days, compared to an average of fifty-eight days.[23] The most frequently used pre-Initiative placements were state and private psychiatric hospitals. The most frequently used placements for children in the Initiative were specialized treatment centers and residential schools. These facilities have their roots in the child welfare system, not the mental hospital system, and are generally less coercive. The children had received an average of eight refusals even from such facilities before their referral to the Initiative.

The reasons for the Initiative's success at this aggregate level are straightforward. The state, represented by the Governor's Office, was determined to avoid the embarrassment of judicial intervention in state bureaucracies and put pressure on the departments to cooperate more than they usually would. At the same time the Initiative, operating on its own, placed some difficult children out of state and negotiated per diems for residential treatment centers that were significantly higher than the prevailing rates. Private agencies seemed to cooperate more with the Initiative. Since the Initiative staff had low caseloads

23. This description of the outcomes of the Initiative is taken from Berzy, "Governor's Cook County Court Project," and Hirshorn, "Evaluation of the Governor's Cook County Court Project."

(about twenty cases compared to the usual fifty to a hundred cases), the agencies could get advice, help, answers to questions, and payment of bills in a way that was not possible outside the Initiative.

The state was thus able to respond effectively to its most difficult charges by an unusual outlay of energy and resources. The strategy, however, had two problems: (1) demands from the Departments of Mental Health and Children and Family Services that the Initiative no longer be allowed to operate under special conditions, and (2) demands from private providers that they start receiving such special contracts for more of their clients.

Efforts like the Initiative are by their nature temporary. No Governor's Office wants to maintain a caseload function indefinitely, nor is any likely to want such intimate acquaintance with the work. This project was no exception. Its functions were eased back into the child welfare department. The effort leaves a question, however, about the size of the effort that difficult children justify.

In some cases the Governor's Initiative contracts were so high that they appeared to include a bonus for taking the children. For example, one child, who in 1981 was being taken care of for $197 per day (almost $72,000 a year), had in his contract provisions for one-on-one supervision from seven in the morning to eleven at night, twenty hours of individual vocational counseling per week, twenty hours of individual academic counseling per week, a twice-a-week session with a behavioral consultant, and a social worker whenever needed.

Money clearly works as an incentive in the world of institutional care. The Children's Home and Aid Society agreed to build an institution for very disturbed youngsters partly because all its costs were guaranteed. Some residential centers that had refused to accept children from the Department of Mental Health or the Department of Children and Family Services accepted them at the higher rates the Initiative was able to offer. Money is also an incentive in foster care. Specialized foster parents take difficult children into their own homes in return for higher than normal payments.

At the level of the person providing care, the individual house parent or foster parent, one might argue that it is better to find people motivated by personal and professional rewards rather than higher payments. A few successful institutions ignore the regular profession's demand for skilled workers and hire young, untrained workers, capitalizing for a few years on their enthusiasm, common touch, and altruism. The foster parent system has always been worried by the possibility that money rather than empathy for children might be the motivation for signing up. Yet the most difficult children in the system might not need heartfelt, pure devotion as much as decent, affectionate care from people who might also appreciate or need the financial rewards. One agency director, who paid his foster parents $6,000 a year per child and had some of them caring for four children (thus providing a salary rather than an allowance), argued the opposite. The payment of more money lowered the emotional temperature enough to prevent the young people from panicking that they were being forced into a lifelong relationship and the caretakers from demanding as their reward the total devotion of their charges. As he expressed it:

> If you don't pay families enough, you have to appeal to their altruism and in return the families want control. They say if you are costing me all this extra you are mine. So the families want the reward of their loyalties. The kid is caught in a real bind. The foster parents say to them if you call the mother one more time you can pack your bags. You have to balance altruism with money.[24]

This point of view does not argue the overriding importance of financial reward. The same director said that most of the people who signed up to be specialized foster parents were motivated by religious conviction or a personal experience of the child welfare system. Nor does it argue that young people merely wanted a hostel, or that this kind of arrangement is suitable for all children in the system. There is evidence that younger children do want from surrogate parents the love and commitment they think natural parents should provide, and that

24. Halsey, 16 July 1980.

some of them are dismayed when they learn of the financial side of the arrangement.[25] Troubled older children at the very least need a decent person who will listen to them. Between the end points of decent, affectionate care and a natural parent-child relationship, the calculus will be different for different children.

The issue of reasonable distribution of resources must also be raised in relation to children who have exhausted the wisdom and imagination of all parts of the system. A fair economics might include a prescription that at some point expensive care be terminated. The Department of Children and Family Services does that now by refusing to support young people once they reach the age of eighteen. Critics of that policy point to examples of children who would benefit enormously from some extra help. But even some of those critics agree that the arbitrary cutoff concentrates the mind wonderfully on the problem of how to increase a young person's practical capacity to live an unsheltered life, and that the longest stay in care will not improve the chances of some young people.

This problem is common to many helping services: the difficulty of living with the ambiguity that some clients can be helped and that some cannot. An associate director of the department compared the situation of troubled youth to that of abused children:

> The big problem is that we refuse to see that there are some kids who we can't help. That's not to say that we shouldn't try but we should realize at some point that we can't help them and those kids are screwing up the whole system. . . . Look at child abuse advertisements that we have now: we say, "you call us and we will help." The fact of the matter is that we may not be able to help. Look at those four or five kids in Chicago several years ago who we were paying half a million dollars a year for to a group called Child Psychiatry Associates who are now out of business. If you tell someone on the streets that you are paying out $200 a day for a kid and if I were on the streets I would say, "Hell, I'll take five of those kids." What will anyone do with them except

25. Andrew Gordon, Margo Gordon, John McKnight, and Malcolm Bush, "Experiences of Wardship: Interim Report II to the Office of Child Development, U.S. Department of Health, Education and Welfare," Center for Urban Affairs, Northwestern University, Evanston, Ill., 1975.

shoot them full of thorazine? We should try to help everyone, but there is a limit.[26]

The lessons of difficult children from an administrative perspective is that there are limits to resources. Denying that those limits exist will merely conceal the decision that is bound to be made about who will or will not get help. But this administrative perspective does not get to the heart of the matter—the daily attempt to care for difficult children in a way that increases their chances of coping. That is our next topic.

Strategies for Helping Difficult Children

The bureaucratic response was not the most interesting lesson of the Governor's Initiative. Most bureaucracies under enough pressure can produce special responses for a limited period of time. The unusual aspect of the Initiative was the way in which individual agencies managed to cope with difficult children. One such agency that took difficult children under both regular contracts with the Department of Children and Family Services and under contracts with the Initiative was an agency called Kaleidoscope. The agency had a reputation for taking difficult children whom no one else would take, holding on to them without coercion, and doing reasonably well with them— that is, setting a fair proportion of them back on the road to a more normal life.[27] This agency was self-consciously different from other agencies in a number of ways and was convinced that these differences accounted for its ability to help difficult children. Its senior staff, although professionally trained, thought that a psychologically therapeutic view of difficult children too often led to categorizations that prevented sensitivity to their individual situations and problems. While formal therapy might be useful for some children under certain conditions, imaginative commonsense talk was the most useful day-to-day language.

26. Interview with William Ryan, Associate Director of the Illinois Department of Children and Family Services, 20 August 1980.
27. Information about Kaleidoscope came from a number of sources including an interview with its director, Mel Breed, and several of his senior staff on 26 August 1981, and from contract officials in the department.

Kaleidoscope also displayed a tolerance for deviant behavior. This tolerance was expressed in several ways. There was a conscious effort to persuade the staff that some behavior they found deviant should be regarded as normal. According to a senior staff member:

> Two years ago, every one of our black staff thought that if someone masturbated past a certain age, they were going to be gay. If women did it, they would be lesbians. We have to take these issues as part of our staff development.[28]

There was also a tolerance for partial success—a recognition that the states of being normal and abnormal were not dichotomous but a continuum and that moving a person one or two steps toward the normal was worthwhile.

> We handled a kid with an IQ of 50 who was in the back wards eating sheets. We had the kid for six years. The kid is now out on public aid, had a baby, is doing okay. That's a success. But for the Department that's a failure.[29]

> If a kid is stealing ten times a month, and if after a few months here he's down to eight times a month, that's a success. We had a transvestite here. Success was to get him into a good relationship and not wearing eye shadow. That's a success. But DCFS [the Department of Children and Family Services] says it's a failure because he's still wearing women's clothes.[30]

The acceptance of deviance finally meant a recognition that some disturbed children were going to fail mightily, and that some failures of that kind were inevitable. Kaleidoscope deeply regretted the failures but realized that, if it was to continue to take difficult children, such incidents were inevitable. The immediate problem was preventing a less realistic (and much more remote public) from using those incidents to close the organization down. The director of another organization that took difficult children, Virginia House in Chicago, expressed the issue of failures succinctly. The director recounted the story of how a sixteen-year-old girl who used to make herself sick by snorting

28. Ibid.
29. Ibid.
30. Ibid.

spray deodorants had landed herself in the hospital and then had come to Virginia House. In an attempt to help her all the girls had agreed to stop using such deodorants. One night the director came downstairs after hearing a crash to find the girl dying on the floor with a cellophane bag over her head and a spray deodorant nearby.

> I got the reputation of being a rock that time. But I wasn't a rock. It's just that I accepted it. When the girl died, I just knew that that's the way it had to be. The only time I felt strong emotion was when the priest was here praying over her, and that's because I knew it was out of my hands. . . . Some things in life we must accept without question. I don't mean dogma; I mean things we can't do anything about. If a child is not using her potential, in the end it's not our fault. . . . You give them a bottom line—you teach them to think, to reason, and you give them some kind of God—and then you let them go.[31]

Kaleidoscope was also different because it argued that unusual settings produced unusual behavior, and that unusual children needed settings that were as close as possible to the normal. The organization insisted, therefore, that the house parents of its small group homes cook and clean like ordinary parents, and that the group homes be mixed by sex and age; the organization further maintained that single-sex, single-age homes were ready-made gangs. It similarly insisted that its foster parents go to work like normal parents. That private families could take children so difficult that institutions had turned them down was itself a major discovery.

Finally, what enabled the staff and foster parents to cope with the hazard of difficult children was the sense that that was the central nature of the job. Difficult children were not the price they paid for the fact that the bulk of the children they took were not difficult; instead such children were precisely the population they wished to serve. So strong was this conviction that the staff regarded refusing a referral as an admission of failure.

Overall Kaleidoscope viewed its charges as varieties (ex-

---

31. Quoted in Mary O'Connell, "Mother Johnson's House of Good Repute," *Salt* (July–August 1981): 16.

treme perhaps) of ordinary people, not as examples of client types. In our language the organization was insisting on the young people's citizenship. The answer to their problems was not specialized treatment in special separate places but the mining of reserves of energy and imagination in staff and surrogate parents to allow the children to live in as normal places as possible. Abnormal behavior was to be discouraged and reduced, but it was not allowed to become the total definition of the child.

Conclusion: Redefining Difficultness

We can now return to the issue of definition. The history of the organized response to troubled families allows us to redefine *difficult,* not solely in terms of the characteristics of a particular child, but in terms of that child in a variety of contexts. *Difficult* analyzed from this perspective has a variety of meanings.

The accepted meaning of the term *difficult* as it is applied to these children is that no one knows how to deal with them or handle them because of their behavior. But a child's behavior always interacts with the child's context to produce the degree of difficulty a surrogate parent has in handling that child. Children might be sedated in psychiatric hospitals and cause their custodians very little effort. The same unsedated children receiving very little attention in a large institution might become violent as a way of attracting attention. And the experience of specialized foster care suggests that a child who is violent in the context of an institution might not be violent in the context of a foster home, where the adults were primed to expect difficult behavior. (We should remember that in some circumstances— for example, a prisoner of war camp—to behave badly in an institution of questionable legitimacy is to behave honorably.) By ignoring the context in which treatment is carried out we reduce the number of options for helping children.

Another sense of the term *difficult* is that, although the child is manageable, the costs of that management are high and the rewards low. The rewards and costs may or may not be monetary. One important reward in any professional-client relationship is the "success" of the client as described in the profession-al's terms. Success, which in child welfare very often means normal development, will be more likely with dependent chil-dren than it will be with troubled adolescents and more likely with adoptable babies than with abusive mothers. Success, as well as being a function of expectations, is itself a function of context. So for the staff members of an institution, success may be the adaptation that may reduce the child's capacity to live outside of institutions.

Rewards will also be high in situations where professionals sense that they can exercise their special skills. Hence for some social workers residential treatment centers are good places to be, while shelter care is a poor option. As a Department of Children and Family Services contracting officer who had tried in vain to persuade private agencies to provide shelter care (emer-gency care while more permanent arrangements are made) put it, "In shelter care there are very few rewards for the practitioners. There are no programs. The kids are on the lam."[32]

Rewards will be low in contexts different from those in which the worker is used to working. It will be difficult for white social workers to keep in touch with natural parents who live in poor black or Hispanic sections of a large city, not only because of the physical danger, but also because the psychological environ-ment (the way in which people interact with each other) is differ-ent. By contrast, a black aide who lives in that part of the city, while possibly objecting to the physical danger and to the de-pressing physical environment, will not find that environment "difficult" because it is strange. Settlement house workers fall between the points of natural familiarity and strangeness by habituating themselves through residence and by creating an environment of their own inside the settlement house.

The professional helper's personal assessment of the costs and rewards of helping is thus a crucial part of the context that defines a client's difficultness. Where helpers find costs so high and rewards so low that the task is labeled "difficult," the cli-ent's interests might be better served by searching for other helpers who do not add up those sums in the same way.

---

32. Interview with Sonia Read, Illinois Department of Children and Family Services Contracting Unit, 16 September 1980.

A group of children may also be difficult because of a disjunction between changing situations and an unchanging norm. In rural communities in eighteenth- and nineteenth-century America, an able-bodied dependent youth was not a problem but an opportunity. As late as 1899, it was still possible to report that there was "generally a demand for boys and girls from twelve to fourteen years of age. The main difficulty is to find homes for children from seven to eleven years of age."[33] That situation changed when younger children became valued as surrogate family members and when older children, who were too restive to play that role, lost their work value. In a large city that had passed through the first industrial revolution, dependent youth were transformed from opportunities into a potential mob. As expectations about the length of the passage to adulthood changed and high school started to fill the gap, the problem was reduced.

The contemporary equivalent of these situations may well be the condition of young unmarried mothers. Many teenage mothers today are refusing to take the once customary routes of either marriage or adoption as a way out. While the fertility rate of fifteen- to nineteen-year-olds in Illinois was 40 percent lower in 1983 than it was in 1960, the percentage of those births to *unmarried* teenagers increased from 17 percent to over 66 percent.[34] In this situation the dysfunction is created as the clients refuse the once-accepted solution to their condition. The problem then changes from one of how to regularize the position of unmarried mothers (by either getting them married or taking away their mothering responsibilities) to one of how to improve the life chances of a single mother and her children, whose condition may well be the new norm among her family and neighbors.

The last form of difficulty is the one most relevant to the children caught up in programs like the Governor's Initiative. It is the difficulty caused by children who need tending rather than

33. T. M. Mulry, "Report of the Committee on Neglected and Dependent Children." Proceedings of the National Conference of Charities and Corrections, 1899; quoted in Robert H. Bremner, ed., *Children and Youth in America: A Documentary History*, vol. 2 (Cambridge, Mass.: Harvard University Press, 1967–74), 300.

34. Mark Testa and Edward Lawlor, *The State of the Child: 1985* (Chicago: Chapin Hall Center for Children, University of Chicago, 1985), 30.

treating, but who live in a world where treating is the goal. We use the word *treat* here in the sense of an action designed to produce the outcome "cure" or the return to a "normal state." In this context *tend* refers to a sense of watching out for, bestowing attention on, and fostering. The difference between *treating* and *tending* is most obvious in those branches of medicine where an intervention aimed at cure is continued in a situation where a dying patient needs care, or in medical terminology, palliative care.[35]

In the case of troubled children the issue is, not the recognition of death, but the recognition that between normal and grossly abnormal behavior lie a number of conditions that can be distinguished as better or worse. (Such a recognition is, of course, also relevant to medicine for some nonterminal patients.) The decision that the relevant states are the in-between states, not the dichotomous states of cure and noncure, very often means that the milder tending interventions are more appropriate than the harsher strategies aimed at rooting out the causes. To repeat an earlier example, a youth given to transvestism might respond to untrained surrogate parents, who try to persuade him that the trouble caused by the more obvious of his transvestite behaviors might not be worth the price, rather than to a psychiatrist, who tries to exorcise the transvestism entirely by curing some antecedent psychic trauma.

Choosing tending rather than treating means accepting as improvements states of being that are still regarded as abnormal by the rest of the world. It involves the renunciation of outcomes that would attract the applause of peers. Tending means accepting the risk of choosing lower expectations when there is some slight chance that "cure" is possible. It also requires patience—the patience that permits watching and waiting when that seems appropriate. Tending, in short, requires a tolerance for ambiguity, the recognition that some problems are insoluble, some distressed conditions can be altered, and some clients of the social welfare system inhabit a grey world in between— but are very much aware of the differences in shades of grey.

35. On this point, see Haydn Bush, "Cure," *Science 84* (September 1984): 34–35.

This analysis of the care of difficult children suggests that the prerequisite for their citizenship is an honest recognition of the variety of the human condition. Such a recognition does not require denial that their behavior can make it difficult for them to cope with the ordinary world, or that the behavior may be damaging to themselves or to others. But if we concentrate only on their weakness and place them in situations that do not sustain them—and would not sustain us—we deny their humanity in the name of a tidy and sanitized vision of the human condition. Or, if we pretend that they are exactly like the rest of us, or could be made so, we may be disappointed by their "refusal to respond" and be tempted to put them out of sight.

The "we" in this last paragraph refers to all of us, not just professional helpers. The helpers, as our surrogates, reflect our discomfort with difficult people as much as their own. We help determine the context difficult children inhabit, and by virtue of that, we help determine their condition.

6

Quality as Right Judgment

Introduction

The last two chapters were about equal treatment. The issue of equal treatment is often raised by supporters of the public sector. The public sector justifies its massive expansion on the basis of providing equal treatment to the previously unserved or underserved, and the drive for equity is a real part of the esprit de corps of the active and engaged public social service staff. Similarly, quality is the watchword of private sector agencies. It justifies their separate existence and their attempts to choose their clients. For those who think the public–private distinction is important, the criterion "quality" is the tie-breaking test—the test that should settle the debate about which sector ought to be the center of the social welfare enterprise.

This chapter argues that the nature of quality in services for troubled families is ambiguous; that quality is not reducible to quantifiable outcome measure, or even to a group of such measures; that the central issue is appropriate judgments; and that the appropriateness of a judgment has to do with who makes the judgment and how it is made. Whether the agency that makes judgments is organized under public or private auspices is not very important.

This conclusion is at odds with the usual way of thinking about quality. There is an expectation in the professional world of service that interventions, or the reactions to trouble, can be shaped with increasing finesse. Combined with this expectation is the idea that finely tuned measurements will demonstrate the positive effects of these interventions on the lives of clients. These rising expectations for the efficacy of interventions are paralleled by increasing hopes for the clients themselves.

Such rising expectations are of recent origin. In Charles Loring Brace's nineteenth-century account of service to the children of New York the dominant quality is decency. The task of charity for him was removing children from circumstances so terrible that only a handful would survive unharmed, and placing them in a setting that was decent—one that would give the children a reasonable chance of growing up independent and respectable. The agencies of the child and the Almighty were strong enough to achieve worthy citizenship, if only the child was given a chance in a clean environment, free from corruption, and filled instead with the influence of good people.

The contemporary notion of quality service has much more to it than that of providing a decent environment for a child. The pseudo-scientific faith in the relationship between the minutiae of parenting and the details of an adult's character leads to the expectation that minor variations in practice will produce different outcomes for the child. Organizations interested in quality must, therefore, be cognizant of quite small details of the care of a child. A salvationist strand in the social work ethos reinforces this tendency with the belief that individuals can be made over through the agency of skilled practitioners. As the contemporary concern with a fulfilled psyche is added to the "lesser" goal of sufficiency and respectability, the criterion "quality" finally obscures what is actually possible. Another strand of rhetoric leads in the same direction—that of client as customer and service as goods. Under this rhetoric the state has the duty to purchase the best that the client would choose if the client had the means.

This dramatic change in expectations stems partly from tangible changes in the condition of clients. The ability to do what Brace dreamed of doing—putting a roof over the head of homeless children and providing food for their stomachs—leads to a quest to go one better. Moreover, we are more aware than Brace was of the average condition of our clients as they come into the service system. We are beginning to be able to track their progress through that system. We also know that there are orderly and less orderly organizations. Thus we are aware that we can do more than relieve destitution, that we can detect with more statistical finesse the condition of our clients, and evaluate—at least according to management standards—the quality of social welfare agencies.

The long-term improvement in the condition of children and our more detailed sense of what it is we are doing can, however, produce a misleadingly mechanistic understanding of the relationship between the child welfare system and children's welfare. Better systems will not necessarily produce better outcomes because the context of children's lives relevant to their well-being is far broader than the most comprehensive child welfare system. Once we have provided hungry children with food and homeless children with shelter, the nature of interventions and outcomes become much more complicated. We start this analysis of quality with those complexities.

The Difficulties of Choosing and Measuring Outcomes

The difficulties in choosing, and then in measuring, the effects of the actions of service bureaucracies are now part of the social welfare debate.[1] The first problem is that the statement of public purpose and intent is often couched in idealized language. Such language cannot be the touchstone for evaluating actual events. The act that created the Illinois Department of Children and Family Services directs that agency to provide services for the purposes of "protecting and promoting the welfare of children" and "preventing or remedying or assisting in the solution of problems which may result in the neglect, abuse, exploitation or delinquency of children."[2] Of these words, *assist* is the verb that best describes the possibilities for formal intervention. The other verbs speak of actions that on many occasions may be outside the

1. See, for example, Michael Lipsky, "Goals and Performance Measures," chap. 4 in *Street Level Bureaucracy* (New York: Russell Sage Foundation, 1980), 40–53.
2. An Act Creating the Department of Children and Family Services, Illinois Revised Statutes.

competence of any organization. Moreover, by not specifying the actions with any degree of concreteness, the verbs place no limit on the theoretical possibilities. The lack of concreteness means that another level of specification must be constructed before the attempt can be made to judge the effect of the interventions.

The level of specification that is avoided in the statute would have provided enough clarity and detail to engender conflict. Conflicting goals, either at the margins or closer to the center of the enterprise, are a constant of publicly mandated services. Very often those conflicts represent legitimate political disagreements. Such disagreements are not only about the desirability of certain goals but also about whether the goals are achievable, how the goals should be achieved, and whether it is appropriate for the state to attempt to achieve them.

One conflict about the range of possible goals translates into the problem of the good (or even the adequate) versus the best. For some people the provision of adequate physical sustenance is a worthy goal. For others the attempt to restructure the psyche of their clients is the ultimate test of social services. For these people that is also the minimum goal, since in this belief system nothing else will be achieved without this restructuring. At another pole is the legal activist who, intent on a client's due process or liberty rights, is concerned more with protecting a client from a service system than considering the client's present condition. In many situations physical necessities, psychic health, and freedom from interference compete as legitimate goals.

The estimation of what is possible not only influences judgments about the appropriate goals but also influences the definition of the problem; in circular fashion this definition will itself affect the choice of goals. The fifteen-year-old neglected child who is partly out of the control of his parents and has committed some delinquent acts is, in the eyes of the crusading states-attorney, a threat to the community. For this official the goal is social control through incarceration. Less coercive alternatives have failed and will fail. To other actors the child may well be a noncriminal who is merely having a rough adolescence, and for whom the appropriate goal is skillful guardianship. Such help will give him a reasonable chance of staying out of trouble and making the most of his potential.

This example points to a conflict beyond the conflict of reasonable expectations. The youth's right to a fair chance in his home community may conflict with the community's assessment of its right to protection from incivility, disturbance, or crime. There are other examples of the clash of interests, or more extremely, the clash of rights. The decision to move children away from their parents is taken in the name of the children's best interests. On any particular occasion that decision may indeed be in their best interests. But at the same time such actions rob parents of their children and thwart their interest in maintaining their family.

The last set of difficulties about what judgments should count has to do with the ambiguity about whether goals have been achieved and the relationship between the means and the apparent ends. The vaguer the goals, the more difficult to determine whether they have been achieved. Vague goals, as well as goals that are not vague but are difficult to observe, require proxies; if those surrogates are ill-chosen, the relationship between them and the actual goals may be tenuous. The placement of a child in a foster home or the return of a child to his or her natural home is often considered a success if the arrangement endures. But the fact that a child does not run away from a home or that a natural or surrogate parent does not request the removal of a child is a crude indication of whether the child is receiving adequate care.

Even quite concrete goals can harbor an ambiguity about what led to their accomplishment. If a youth who has been delinquent does not turn into an adult criminal, a variety of alternative explanations are available—not just the conclusion that some state intervention was responsible for the good outcome. The longer the time that elapses between the intervention and the judging of the outcome, the more difficult it is to pin down the causal relationships. The mere passage of time during which the youth matures might explain the good outcome. Other significant events may have been crucial, and some of those may have been fortuitous. The act of being accounted a criminal adult is itself a constructed process, dependent on a set of considerations and actions over and above the criminal act.

What this recital of difficulties emphasizes is that judgments about outcomes are indeed judgments, not measurements. The critical questions about judgments are not what events or data should be used—the answer is the best available—but who should make the judgments and in what manner. The first question needs one modification: the issue is who should make judgments in a democratic society, a society where the right to judge flows upward from the citizen, not downward from a centralized authority.

This modification only increases in importance as we make judgments on the basis of increasingly diverse criteria about what constitutes an adequate family. One person's sustenance is another person's deprivation, and there are a wide variety of views of what constitutes decent citizenship. More and better data do not solve the problem because people with different interpretations of sustenance and citizenship will look for different evidence. This conclusion does not mean that data are unimportant, or that an anarchy of judgments is the best we can hope for. Most of us will share a belief in some of the key attributes of sustenance and citizenship, and where we disagree there will be patterns to the disagreements. The existence of disagreements, however, means that judgments at some point call for negotiation and choice. The fact that negotiation is the means by which judgments are made permits a further refinement to our question: who should make judgments and in what manner should they be made?[3]

This approach to the issue of quality rests on the premise that sustenance is critical to children in troubled families, and that someone knows what aspects of sustenance are important. Children themselves can be explicit about what sustains them, and our emphasis on sustenance relies on the perspective of some children in the child welfare system. The views of a large group of wards of the state of Illinois who were interviewed about their placements coalesced on several elements of sustenance: the children wanted to feel trusted, cared about, wanted, and— depending on their age—either loved or cared for affection-

3. The centrality of the problem of judgment in a pluralistic society is described in Michael Denny, "The Privilege of Ourselves: Hannah Arendt on Judgement," in *Hannah Arendt: The Recovery of the Public World,* ed. Melvyn A. Hill (New York: St. Martin's Press, 1979), 245–74.

ately.[4] The same children could rate different types of place-ment according to these characteristics; in general, they agreed that such sustenance could be found in the homes of relatives and some foster parents, but not in institutions. These judgments about sustenance are more sensitive than the judgments any outsider could make, though fallible like anyone else's judgments. The issue of good care for these children may rest, not so much on other people's assessment of their long-term success, but on whether the children's judgments about sustenance are taken into consideration.

The difficulty of choosing goals and assessing outcomes does not prevent some description of what the enterprise is about. Before we look at the process of judgment, we should describe what is to be judged.

Defining the Task and Identifying the Actors

What is it that is to be done well? Beyond the recent beliefs that particular finely tuned services will produce particular finely tuned outcomes is the older reality that child welfare is about decent care and sustenance for children who lack them. Those are the end goals—end goals in the sense that they make a direct difference to the lives of children and are worthwhile in themselves. From these goals we can make a critical deduction about child welfare systems. They cannot, themselves, achieve the goals. No child welfare program, service, or social worker provides the decent care and sustenance that children ask for and that we all think children require. A child welfare system may aid people who are providing that sustenance. It might arrange for sustenance to be provided by people other than a child's natural parents when those parents do not provide it. Or the system may provide an imitation of that sustenance in an

4. For a comprehensive description of the research project, see Andrew C. Gordon, Margo T. Gordon, John McKnight, and Malcolm Bush, "Experiences of Wardship: Interim Report II to the Office of Child Development, U.S. Department of Health, Education and Welfare," Center for Urban Affairs, Northwestern University, Evanston, Ill., 1975. For a detailed description of the children's view of sustenance, see Malcolm Bush, "Institutions for Dependent and Neglected Children: A Therapeutic Option of Choice or a Last Resort?" *American Journal of Orthopsychiatry* 50 (February 1980): 239–55.

institutional setting when all else fails. But it does not provide the sustenance itself. Sustenance is provided by natural parents, relatives, friends, adoptive parents, and surrogate parents.

The system, which is broadly defined as the organized activity to improve the welfare of children and families in trouble, does other things. It makes decisions. A social welfare system in the guise of a court and a social welfare agency makes the decision whether children who have been brought to its attention need more or better care and attention. The court makes the decision whether such care can be provided in the children's natural homes. If care cannot be provided in the natural home, a social welfare agency will then make a decision that a particular child should be placed in a particular surrogate home. At a later date the agency, together with the court, will make a decision that the child will stay in the surrogate home, be moved to another surrogate home, or returned to the natural parents.

The second group of activities the child welfare system performs are actions to improve the care children receive. This group includes collecting and distributing resources, recruiting adoptive and foster parents, and helping families in trouble through mediation—negotiating with landlords, police, and schools on behalf of the family. The category also includes actions aimed at changing the clients' behavior through advice, sympathy, coercion, or formal psychological manipulations. Lastly, these activities include actions to reduce the strains of the context in which the children live. Such actions might include trying to control gang violence or reducing unemployment. In general, social service agencies do not accept special responsibility for this last group of actions and very often regard these problems as outside their province.

The last group of activities in which the system engages can be labeled bureaucratic processes. These actions record and direct the sustaining, the decision making, and the helping. They range from paperwork (recording situations prior to decision making, and filling in forms required for federal reimbursement of local services) to supervising the caretakers of the children in placement. The decision making, some of the practical helping, and the bureaucratic processes can be conceptualized in another way. Formal organizations exist because some children are not being sustained in their natural homes. The job of the formal organizations is to recognize those situations and to set in motion processes that will provide sustenance. While they cannot sustain, such organizations can recognize children whose network of family and friends leave them wanting, and they can connect the children with adults who are able to care for them.

This account of organizational actions allows us to construct a list of people who perform the actions and whose performance is to be judged. Decisions in social welfare systems are a two-step process: the construction of a story and the negotiation of a decision.[5] To different degrees the children, their parents, friends, neighbors, school teachers, doctors, social workers, the juvenile court judge, and other court personnel are involved in both the construction of the story and the negotiation of the decision. The contributions differ according to formal and informal rules, the particular case, the particular set of actors, and the particular distribution of skill and power among them.

The practical helping at the level of the individual client family is also performed by a variety of different people: friends, neighbors, grandparents, other relatives, and social workers. This dispersion of effort is true for both the trouble-shooting variety of helping and the advice-coercion-sympathy aimed at getting the families themselves to stay out of trouble. The practical helping that is aimed at relieving the strains of the context that troubled families inhabit is the province of the entire political system.

The subset of helping activities most removed from the child— bureaucratic processes—involves a much smaller group of actors. It is performed by the office employees of social welfare agencies.

This recital, which serves as a preamble to a discussion of quality, identifies the work that is to be done and identifies the doers. The mere listing of the activities and the actors begins to balance the perspective that a service is a discrete entity, performed by designated, professional actors, which can be ex-

---

5. This is an epistemological statement. For a description of how the negotiation of a client's status or guilt works in a related field, see Aaron V. Cicourel, *The Social Organization of Juvenile Delinquency* (New York: John Wiley, 1968).

pected to have a discrete and discernible end. This account demonstrates that there is a broad array of actors, and that organized service is not the end product but a means of helping the sustainers do their sustaining. Analyses, evaluations, and bureaucratic reforms that concentrate on the organized process will miss this crucial part of the picture.

While it did not put the problem into these words, the permanency movement (the attempt to find children secure, legally permanent homes outside the guardianship of the child welfare system) recognized this situation. The movement was a recognition that the de jure sharing of responsibility and sustenance between an organization and a surrogate parent did not work, because it produced a situation where no one had or exercised real responsibility.

These discussions of outcome measures and organizational tasks point to judgments as the heart of the organized response to troubled families. Discussions of quality usually focus on outcomes—good management and good professional practice. These are important, but they hide the reality that the heart of organized child welfare is the exercise of state authority, delegated to a variety of organizations, to make decisions about family life and to watch or monitor the carrying out of those decisions. Our discussion of quality will concentrate on those central functions. We start with formal and informal decisions and then move to the guardianship function of monitoring.

Making Judgments: The Courts

Public judgments about publicly sanctioned actions are generally taken by surrogates for the public—the court and the public agency. These two entities, in a combination that depends on the division of the *parens patriae* authority in a particular state, make daily decisions about the adequacy of the attention paid to children who need help. They are the judges of other people's actions, and they take actions themselves that are open to each other's scrutiny. On occasions the public judgments take the form of public comment in the media or legislative action, and these can be triggered by an unusual case or by special investigations or reports.

The fact that the courts and agencies are surrogates of the public is an inevitable consequence of the structure of advanced societies. Since they are surrogates, however, and since they do not derive their authority from themselves, we must ask whether they reflect the general view of good judgments. In a democracy we assume one element of a good judgment is the adequate consideration of all the relevant views.

The juvenile court, the place where the judgment is made on behalf of the public that the state needs to intervene in the life of a family, conducts its business in a manner that limits the possibilities of making good judgments. A study of the court in Cook County showed that the court acted in a way that seriously diminished its roles as public servant and as a body capable of making reasoned judgments that reflected the views of all the interested parties.[6]

This study's characterization of the inadequacy of court decisions is straightforward. In the first place the time allotted to cases was not appropriate. Hearings that could determine whether a young person would be allowed to stay with his or her parents lasted an average of five minutes. For the short time that a case was discusssed, the language prevented a fair consideration of the story. The constant use of legal terms made the hearings opaque to anyone except the court employees or other legally trained participants. Consequently, among those exluded were the subjects of the hearing and members of the public (court watchers representing civic groups) who were present.

The subjects, the young people and their families, were disenfranchised before the judgments were made. (There are, of course, no legal grounds for treating them as other than citizens even after the judgments are made, except in the respect that parents might lose the custody or guardianship of their children.) The study monitored 777 proceedings in the court. In only 70 of the proceedings did an official of the court consult a minor in a substantive fashion, and in only 38 cases was a parent consulted. The minor was invited to tell the court his or her version of the story on just two occasions. These were not criminal trials; they

6. Janice Linn, Kim Zalent, William Geller, and Harris Meyer, *Minors in Need: A Study of Status Offenders at the Juvenile Court of Cook County* (Chicago: Chicago Law Enforcement Study Group, 1979).

were proceedings to determine whether, in the best interests of the child, the child needed to be placed for a period of time outside the parental home. Although the story hinged on the relationship between the parents and the children, and on the children's lives in their homes, their accounts were not heard. When the parents broke their silence to protest a particular version of the story, they were silenced by calls for "order in the court." Substituting for the actual story of these key actors was very often hearsay, sometimes strings of hearsay: "The truant officer was told by the teacher who had spoken to the mother about her efforts with the police to find the youth. All this reported by a caseworker."[7]

In other cases not even the events as told by nonparticipants served as the basis for judgment. Despite the law, the legal staff set out their judgments or conclusions about these cases without benefit of anybody's version of the facts.

The juvenile code has long recognized that in a court hearing the deck would be stacked against the subjects' accounts if they did not have, in addition to their own voice, someone familiar with the language and the ways of the court. The code provides for two such representatives, a guardian ad litem and a public defender. The job of the former is to foster the best interests of the child and that of the latter to further "lawful objectives of his client through all reasonable means permitted by law."[8] Despite the clear difference in function (which recognizes the possibility of a difference between the best interests of the child and the child's lawful objectives), the guardian ad litem agreed to accept both roles in the same hearing in 128 of the 777 proceedings monitored.

The court also recognizes the possibility of faulty judgments by providing for an appeal. The right to appeal in juvenile cases (other than delinquency hearings) is governed by the rules of civil proceedings rather than criminal proceedings. This distinction means that the court is not required to inform minors of their right to appeal nor to provide them with free counsel or

7. Ibid., 80.
8. *ABA Code of Professional Responsibility and Code of Judicial Conduct* (Chicago: American Bar Association), DRT-/101(A), 1975, amended August 1978; quoted in Linn et al., *Minors in Need*, 89.

transcripts if they are indigent. The study we have cited could find only four appeals brought on behalf of minors in need of supervision in the history of that category in the entire state. The opportunity for a second judgment was not a reality.

Making Judgments: The Social Welfare Bureaucracy

The activities of the court constitute, at least in theory, a public judgment about a family's story and the possibility of state action. Within the social welfare bureaucracy another kind of judgment takes place either as the result of deliberate action or as a result of deliberate (or unintentional) nonaction. This judgment—about whether the child who is the subject of state action is being adequately sustained—emerges from a process very different from the one taking place in the court. Most of the time it is a judgment made by a single person, the caseworker, and the process is invisible to other people. That invisibility is a matter of practice, not a matter of theory. The judgment the worker makes is, in theory, inspected by a supervisor and open at any time to court review. We have already seen how the court operates in making its decisions, and we shall discuss its new attempts at monitoring agencies later in this chapter. The general consensus about public agencies and indeed about many private agencies is that supervision is done by people who were trained (or, in many cases, not trained) to be caseworkers and who, when promoted, have very little sense of the nature of the supervisor's job and of ways to perform it. The sternest independent critics suggest that supervision does not in fact occur. That means in many situations there is no orderly, routine inspection of the actions and non-actions of caseworkers.[9]

---

9. For criticisms of the Illinois Department of Children and Family Services, see American Humane Society, "Evaluation and Consultation. Cook County, Illinois Child Protective Services," Supplemental Report to the Illinois Department of Children and Family Services, 25 May 1977; Better Government Association of Chicago, *The State and the Child in Need: A White Paper Prepared by the Advocacy Project of the Better Government Association* (Chicago: Better Government Association, December 1979); and Arthur Young and Company, *Report to DCFS: Guidelines for the Implementation of Case Management and Case Monitoring Procedures in the Cook County Region* (Chicago: Arthur Young and Company, December 1980).

Not only is there no inspection of the decision there is also no witness to the failure to make a decision. Not making decisions—leaving in place whatever emergency arrangements were made at the time the state assumed guardianship, or not deciding whether long-term arrangements are still sustaining—has as powerful an effect as making a decision. The revelations of the consequences of this common indecision in the 1970s—the breakup of children's relationships with their families, and the high percentage of children who wandered from one temporary placement to another—led to the establishment of a federally mandated system of inspection. (This system is discussed later in this chapter in the section "Monitoring Decisions.")

But even if the internal system worked as it was designed, it would be incapable of producing decisions that reflected the public responsibility of social welfare agencies. Supervisory systems are hierarchical. A solitary decision is inspected by another person acting on his or her own. The ambiguity that surrounds many child welfare cases and the often contradictory principles that govern their administration require instead open discussion that recognizes that conflicting interpretations, prognoses, and decisions are inherent in the events themselves. The recognition of these conflicts in debate is more likely to achieve reasonable decisions.

A bureaucratic system may define its work in terms of process particularly when, as is the case in child welfare, the specification and measurement of goals are difficult. But the language of process is different from the language of goals hammered out by debate. The concentration on process takes time and energy away from the goals that are the justification for the process. A hierarchical system that works exactly to specification could still operate in a way that ignores the reality of the problems as the families in trouble experience them.

The solitariness of the process also affects the kind of information used to make judgments. Once a child enters the custody of the state, the parents run the risk of becoming lost to the child-care system and, therefore, incapable of presenting their version of the story. This danger is not an isolated risk. A report prepared in the late 1970s showed that, for 47 percent of the population of children in Cook County who had been in surrogate care for over two years and were still under the age of thirteen, there was no record of any contact between the Department of Children and Family Services and the parents after the child had been placed away from home.[10] For these families, the parents' changing circumstances, their problems, and their capabilities could not be a part of the information that was used to make decisions about their children's lives.

The absence of critical knowledge obviously detracts from the judgments made about crucial events in children's lives. But even when such critical knowledge is available, it can be structured in ways that make it less authentic. Social welfare agencies rely heavily on written records. These agencies are required to use such records for funding purposes by statutes concerned with the progress of children in state guardianship and by the principles of their professional training. The importance of these records is magnified in agencies that may experience staff turnovers as high as 40 percent a year. In these agencies (and such figures occur in both the public and the private sector) the records are surrogates for the memory and knowledge of individual caseworkers who have live contact with the children in their caseloads.

The sociological literature on case records stresses that their content is context-specific—the content depends not only on the actuality of the lives they describe but on the structure and belief systems of the organizations for whom and in which they are written.[11] One major consequence of this emphasis is that records are written partly to demonstrate that "good practice" as officially described is being carried out. This is not just a matter of professional and bureaucratic self-advertisement; it is a way of coping with ambiguity so that action can be taken. "In the interests of . . . making situations sensible, and of facilitating interactions, actors explicitly define the relation between their questionable conduct and prevailing norms."[12]

    10. Carole J. Alexander, "An Analysis of Cook County Children in Foster Care Two Years or More, Under the Age of Thirteen," Illinois Department of Children and Family Services, October 1978.
    11. See Harold Garfinkel, " 'Good' Organizational Reasons for 'Bad' Case Records," in *Ethnomethodology,* ed. Roy Turner (Harmondsworth, Middlesex, England: Penguin Education, 1975), 109–27.
    12. John Hewitt and Randall Stokes, "Disclaimers," *American Sociological Review* 40, no. 1 (1975): 11.

One definition of authentic knowledge in a social welfare situation might be that it embraces the understandings of all the relevant actors—of the families themselves, their relatives and friends, as well as the various professional actors. By this definition case records are not authentic. They represent only one side of the story. The official perspective would be more useful if it was constructed according to rules that allowed people who did not share that perspective to evaluate and challenge the conclusions the records contained. These rules would be rules about the handling of evidence, the demonstration of assertions, and the accuracy of factual data. Social work case records, however, can flout these standards.[13] The public records in Cook County showed that frequently critical evidence about assertions was lacking, evidence that was used was not evaluated, old evidence was repeated as if it were recent evidence, and—where contradictory evidence existed—the contradictions were ignored as one version was asserted. One internal departmental study even demonstrated that in over 60 percent of case records some of the vital facts about a child and family were erroneous.[14] Most critically, the records were in practice not open to inspection by anyone except the writer. Thus there was no institutional expectation that the story on which a judgment was to be made (perhaps by a second, third, or even more distant generation of caseworker than the one who started the story) would be inspected or even challenged by a person other than the writer.

These characteristics of the information used to make decisions cast doubt on their quality. The language in which they are composed also challenges their authenticity. Since the mid-1950s, the central language of clinical social work has been a language that in direct and indirect descent had its origin in the vocabulary of Freudian psychology. The line of descent underwent a major shift in the development of ego psychology in the 1930s, and the Freudian inheritance has since been joined by the language of behaviorism. More recently there have been attempts to name problems in a more ordinary language common

13. Malcolm Bush, "The Public and Private Purposes of Case Records," *Children and Youth Services Review* 6, no. 1 (1984): 1–18.

14. Executive Summary, Region 2B CWS Case Inventory, Illinois Department of Children and Family Services, January 1981.

to helpers and helped. But in case records the critical events of a story and the critical recommendation for help are often couched in a language deriving from Freud. It is the language of impulses, ego strengths, oedipal conflicts, castration fears, transference, acting out, adjustments, repression, and hostility. In its pure form the language presents the challenge of having changed the way we look at ourselves and our lives but at the same time not giving us concepts that are tightly enough defined to allow their validity to be tested. Moreover, the more one moves away from the events Freud taught us to notice to the theoretical structures that are supposed to connect these events, the less the language commands common agreement.[15] In case records, though, we are not dealing with the language in its pure form. Most caseworkers have a severely limited command of the formal structure of the theory; they use the vocabulary they do possess in an undisciplined and, as previously observed, unchecked fashion.[16] By using words pregnant with unspecified meaning, caseworkers can avoid responsibility for the relationship between fact and interpretation. Such lack of clarity, of course, also prevents the records from being the instruments of a public judgment about conflicting stories.

Judgments and Expert Knowledge

This discussion of the professional language of social work brings to the surface the issue that has been hiding in this argument—the role of expert knowledge in the process of judgment. If expert knowledge is required to perform the central tasks involved in helping troubled families, then the criteria appropriate to judging those actions must be criteria about the adequate performance of expert tasks. As a corollary, experts must be at least partly involved in making those judgments. The expert role in judging becomes larger as the actions become too esoteric to be read by nonexperts.

15. See Alisdair MacIntyre, "Psychoanalysis: The Future of an Illusion?" in *Against the Self Images of the Age: Essays on Ideology and Philosophy* (Notre Dame, Ind.: University of Notre Dame Press, 1978).
16. Bush, "Public and Private Purposes."

Implicit in our argument about judgment has been the idea that substantial parts of the process should be open to non-experts. We now argue explicitly that much of the other work of the social welfare enterprise is not expert in the sense that it is, or should be, esoteric. If the heart of the social welfare enterprise for troubled families is the provision of sustenance, and if sustenance itself can be provided only by natural parents and their surrogates, the heart of the enterprise does not require expert knowledge. Some pieces of expert knowledge in the areas of health and child development have become part of the commonsense knowledge of the laity in their role as parents. But the center of the enterprise is not an expert matter.

The tasks of the outsiders involved in a family's welfare are to notice when a family's troubles threaten the child's well-being and to act to remove that threat. These tasks involve two sets of interactions, both of which might require professional knowledge: interaction with the children and their families, and interaction with the courts and the social welfare agencies.

There is no doubt that navigating the child welfare bureaucracies requires knowledge. This knowledge can be gained both by education—the process of other people leading a novice through the system either in the classroom or in the workplace—and by experience that provides either a tacit or an articulated knowledge. There is a large difference in the effectiveness of people who are, or are not, skilled at manipulating the bureaucracy. But the interaction and its outcomes are not esoteric. It does not require a set of cognitive skills that can be gained only by years of specialized study.

The second set of interactions is more problematic simply because there is a sharp division of opinion as to whether it requires expert understanding. That is the interaction that in the language of the profession of social work is called casework. Casework is the interaction between the individual representatives of the social welfare system and the individual client family. In chapter 8 we will look at the variety of psychological theories that inform casework. For now we will raise the issue about the expertness of casework in relation to its psychoanalytic roots. Our purpose is merely to show that fundamental questions can be raised about the premises of the esoteric theories that underlie casework.

A major reason why expert psychological knowledge—as opposed to vigorous common sense informed by experience and some psychological knowledge—may not be the key to understanding troubled families' reactions to the world around them is that the mainstream of casework has an exaggerated interest in etiology. The adherents of psychoanalytic casework have failed to demonstrate that a person's remote past affects his or her present in a precise fashion, and even if they could, there is no guarantee that the explanation would be of any use in devising some relief for the present distress. The problem with this emphasis is stated forcefully by one of the most subtle and careful users of Freudian theory, Erik Erikson, in his work on Mahatma Gandhi:

> In case histories we have learned to trace the beginnings of human conflict further and further back into childhood and I have characterized as originology the habitual effort to find the "causes" of a man's whole development in his childhood conflicts. By this I mean to say that beginnings do not explain complex developments much better than do the ends, and originology can be as great a fallacy as teleology.[17]

Erikson went on to point out the political consequences of this approach; in Gandhi's case these consequences were the opposite of what they would be for social welfare clients, though just as harmful.

> I consider any attempt to reduce a leader of Gandhi's stature to earlier as well as bigger and better childhood traumata both wrong in method and evil in influence—and this precisely because I can foresee a time when man will have to come to grips with his need to personify and surrender to "greatness."[18]

The opposite case of social welfare clients is the temptation for nonclients to depersonify and dominate troubled people. Pseudo-scientific explanations grounded in the "inevitability" of

17. Erik Erikson, *Gandhi's Truth: On the Origins of Militant Nonviolence* (New York: Norton, 1969), 98.
18. Ibid., 99.

the consequences of unpromising childhoods will serve this purpose just as well as they serve the deification Erikson feared.

Even if there were no doubts about the premises and postulates of the mainstream psychological theories, their role in informing judgments about clients would still be questionable. These are "ideal" methods in the context of social work because the conditions they require (the time, the expertise, and the cooperation of clients) are lacking in the bulk of social welfare encounters. The absence of these conditions is an inescapable fact of a system whose central characteristic is, and always will be, scarce resources.

The condition of expert knowledge about troubled families does not, therefore, warrant its elevation to a predominant role in making judgments about those families. Nor does it justify limiting the families' accounts of their situation to the expert's translation of those chronicles. A good judgment, which respects the citizenship of the people whose lives are being judged, requires their firsthand participation.

We turn now from the judgments themselves to the various devices that have been established to monitor the process of making decisions.

Monitoring Decisions: Traditional Strategies

The shortcomings that we have observed in social welfare organizations are not the result of a lack of concern. There have always been critics of the inadequacy of the system's decisions and actions. These concerns have at times resulted in mechanisms for more routine inspection of organized helping. The introduction in the mid-nineteenth century of licensing rules and skeleton oversight organizations to enforce them are one example. So are the recent attempts to use program evaluation to watch the effects of what is being done for children.

Such processes have legitimate purposes apart from, or in addition to, watching over judgment; they ask questions other than whether the response to a particular child is an appropriate response. The question we shall ask of them, however, reflects our concerns. We wish to discover what strategies for making and monitoring decisions encourage sustenance. In the language of a different enterprise, what processes will accomplish quality control? Other questions are prompted by the processes that actually exist: how closely do processes designed to promote sustenance approach that goal, and are the processes fairly executed? We reiterate the centrality of sustenance because some of the processes were not designed for that purpose, and because those that were dealt with the difficulties of capturing that phenomenon by the substitution of proxies.

There are important differences among the various processes that exist today—differences that coincide with the different times the processes were introduced. The dividing line is the passage of the Federal Child Welfare and Adoption Assistance Law of 1980. Before the implementation of that act there were three major strategies for watching over the child welfare enterprise. The first strategy includes the variety of activities designed to monitor public and private agencies. It includes fiscal monitoring, the evaluation of management practices, and licensing—the process whereby the state asks whether it can reasonably entrust children to an agency's care.

The state monitors the fiscal activities of its subagencies and contracting agencies because it is required to by law. Organizations like the United Way spend a great deal of time monitoring the fiscal practices of their member agencies because their funds are raised in the corporate world, which demands such accounting (and because otherwise good agencies can collapse through inadequate fiscal management). The United Way also uses the experience of the corporate world to improve the general management skills of private agency staff. The state occasionally follows suit by hiring prestigious management consulting firms. This step is sometimes taken in response to crises or scandals and sometimes at the behest of senior staff who wish to get their unwieldy ships in order.

The second major set of watching activities involves the collection of aggregate information and the attempt to discover patterns of events in the lives of state wards. In the last decade this form of watching has been crucial in discovering the patterns of children's lives in care—the large numbers who do not return home and who move in apparently aimless fashion from placement to placement. This activity has received a massive boost from the computerization of records and from the development of techniques for analyzing those data.

The third activity, program evaluation, takes particular programs as the level of analysis in an attempt to distinguish those that produce desired outcomes from those that do not. This endeavor has forced the specification of inputs and outcomes in situations where previously good outcomes were assumed. In some fields it has produced important information. In social welfare its contribution has been less spectacular, partly because it has proved difficult to demonstrate the effectiveness of social casework and partly because program evaluation is a more powerful instrument in situations where inputs and outcomes can properly (rather than artificially) be reduced to discrete, noninteracting phenomena. As we said earlier, social service programs do not sustain children, and with the exception of income redistribution programs, they constitute a small part of the lives of adults who do sustain children.

The key feature of these strategies in terms of our question is that they are all to some degree removed from the lives of individual children. Moreover, when attempts have been made to move from this kind of watching to the watching of individual children, the attempts have been beaten back. In late 1975, for example, the United Way of Metropolitan Chicago made the decision to follow up the examination of aggregate data from its member agencies with the inspection of individual case files and interviews with selected clients. The director of the Illinois Children's Home and Aid Society told his staff in February 1976:

> Despite our objections, the Community Fund will audit our files. We are vulnerable if we have terminated cases not (officially) closed. It is possible that people will be calling our clients to ask if they are receiving care, when they were last seen, and if present service is satisfactory.[19]

The director was clearly concerned about outsiders comparing the image of clients in the files to the reality of the clients in person. His concern and that of other directors resulted in a

---

19. Illinois Children's Home and Aid Society, Minutes Program Heads' Meeting, 2 February 1976.

successful veto of the United Way initiative. He reported to his program directors four months later:

> The Community Fund has wanted to audit statistics which would mean direct involvement with the clients. That plan was abandoned because of our protest and instead they will follow through the system by which the statistics are gathered. It is a system audit.[20]

What the director avoided by this pressure was not only an audit that compared the reported services totals with the count in the files but also a comparison of the file representation of clients with the clients themselves.

Similarly the state in the mid-1970s attempted to develop and maintain an institutional evaluation unit to visit institutions and collect information from children themselves. The unit was founded by a director committed to the notion of inspecting the day-to-day reality of children's lives. It was disbanded under pressure from the institutions when a director without that commitment took office.[21] The notion of inspecting state institutions in Illinois goes back to the establishment of the Board of State Commissioners of Public Charities in 1869. But the notion of using these inspections to fathom the situation of individual children is still resisted.

In the absence of a specific determination to judge the "quality" of a child's care, the organizations fall back on strategies that are appropriate to their original, limited purposes but that fall far short of this broader goal. An associate director of the Department of Children and Family Services who had wrestled with the problem admitted the shortcomings of the substitutes:

---

20. Illinois Children's Home and Aid Society, Minutes Program Heads' Meeting, 7 June 1976.

21. The story is more complicated than this as observers in both the public and private sector complained that the logic of the evaluation process was never worked out, and the evaluations were at one period badly conceptualized and organized. It remains true, however, that part of the private sector's objections was due to professional horror at the prospect of other professionals, or nonprofessionals, talking to "their" children. I am indebted to Harold Goldman, formerly Legal Counsel to the Illinois Department of Children and Family Services, for an account of this episode.

Case monitoring and supervision in the state leaves a lot to be desired. The real problem is that no one has figured out how to do it. . . . The issue in monitoring is monitor what? . . . What we can monitor is where the kid is, how long he's been there, what kind of services he's getting provided, the number of homes he has visited. We can tell of course whether a kid has been adopted. . . . A lot of people try to monitor process and quality and it really can't be done.[22]

The departmental contract officer also retreated to measures at a distance from the children while admitting their inadequacy:

During the year, I analyze their quarterly report. I ask, "Are expenditures matching up to services? Do you have the salaries for five social workers? Why are you paying your foster parents so little? Why is there so much money for object expenses?" Then I look at the utilization rate. "Why are you delivering seventy-five units of service to one family when we agreed on fifty-five?" Accountability is very limited. It's just building a contract in such a way that we get what we are paying for. Maybe we should have a case by case monitoring by liaisons.[23]

And from the private sector, the watching seemed even more irrelevant to the lives of individual children. To repeat a quotation we used earlier, an agency director explained:

I think the Department should have a tough monitoring system for service and that it should think about outcome measures and feedback from clients and follow-up studies of effectiveness. They don't do that. They only notice whether supplies are necessary. Is a coffee pot an allowable expense when you are doing therapy with alcoholics?[24]

This comment takes us back to the problem of surrogate or proxy criteria. When there is such distance between the central measure—a child's well-being—and its proxy, the proxy sheds

22. Interview with William Ryan, Associate Director, Illinois Department of Children and Family Services, 20 August 1980.

23. Interview with Sonia Read, contracting unit, Illinois Department of Children and Family Services, 6 August 1981.

24. Interview with Ann Brown, Director, Associates in Crisis Therapy, 17 July 1981.

no light on the phenomenon it is representing. Even when the two are closer, the proxy has to be interpreted or have meaning added to it to represent the real event. The collection of aggregate data about the number of children returned to their own homes, placed in adoptive homes, or living with relatives was instituted in the reasonable belief that these outcomes were better situations for children than placements in foster homes. But in the absence of understandings of what each option meant for an individual child, those data ignored situations where the general judgment was wrong or even harmful for a particular child.[25] Some of the meaning needed to interpret the proxy can come only from the children themselves.

The inadequacies of proxies is an increasingly urgent issue in the face of recent changes in the social services. The enthusiasm for management skills in social welfare agencies (justified by evidence of poor practice) spills over into an enthusiasm for computerized management accounting systems. Computer programs are now being designed to "track" the progress of clients. The dangers of such routinization (with their attendant proxies and simplifications) is suggested by a comment from the very different world of corporations. Calling for American industry to recognize the importance of flexible responses and product quality in the modern world market, an observer argues:

> As the bureaucratic gap between executives and production workers continues to widen, the enterprise becomes more dependent on "hard" quantifiable data, and less sensitive to qualitative information. Professional managers concentrate on month-to-month profit figures, data on growth sales, and return on investment. "Softer," less quantifiable information—about product quality, worker morale, and customer satisfaction—may be at least as important to the firm's long term success. But such information cannot be conveyed efficiently upward through the layers of staff. Even if such qualitative information occasionally works its way to senior executives without becoming too distorted in the process, it is often still ignored. Information like this does not

---

25. For a discussion of specific examples of the inadequacy of the "best" outcomes for children, see Malcolm Bush and Harold Goldman, "The Psychological Parenting and Permanency Principles in Child Welfare," *American Journal of Orthopsychiatry* 52, no. 2 (April 1982): 223–35.

invite quick decisions and crisp directives. Professional managers have come to preside over a symbolic economy.[26]

The danger of using such systems to watch over the lives of children is that the symbolic children of the computer printout may be the most real embodiment of those children in the imaginations of people who make the decisions about their lives. This has nothing to do with the good or bad intentions of the managers. It has to do with the fact that good management has traditionally meant reducing diversity to allow for productive, routinized procedures.[27] In the manufacture of widgets the routinization allows for a scale of production unknown to preassembly line manufacturing. The reduction of diversity in child welfare—represented, for example, by a one-dimensional description of two or three preferred outcomes for all children—robs the individual child of the crucial details of his or her individual situation. The symbolic child aggregated in summary statistics is still enormously useful for discussing patterns of careers in the child welfare system. But that symbolic child will be of limited use in making decisions about any one real child.

The last problem of relying on aggregate data is that, as the data become the basis for distributing resources, the temptation will increase to manipulate the data for the advantage of the organizations seeking funds. When the data are not audited against the units of which they are made up—events in lives of individual children—deception will be easy. A program director of a highly respected agency said about the intensive and comprehensive United Way schemes: "Did you know we were inflating our adoption figures by one-third to the United Way when I came here? They don't know and they don't care."[28]

26. Robert Reich, "The Next American Frontier," *Atlantic Monthly*, March 1983, 51. In Reich's version of the symbolic economy, the issue is incompetence. When people are represented by their case files, the problem is much graver. Talking about life in postoccupation Czechoslovakia, the novelist Milan Kundera explained, "In the bureaucratic universe of Kafkaesque social life, the institutional dossier operates as a platonic ideal: it, rather than physical existence, represents reality. The human being is only a pale shadow of what his dossier contains." Milan Kundera, quoted in Fred Misurella, "Not Silent, But in Exile and with Cunning," *Partisan Review* 52, no. 2 (1985): 88–89.

27. I am indebted to John McKnight for this idea.

28. Interview with Marjorie Topps, Director of Adoption Services, Illinois Children's Home and Aid Society, 22 July 1980.

A similar incident of much more massive proportions occurred in the mid-1970s over the work of the Chicago Area Council of the Boy Scouts. In January 1974, the Community Fund of Chicago accepted the council's estimate that in the 1973–74 fiscal year the Scouts would have served 89,000 children.[29] In June of that year, the *Chicago Tribune* reported that professional scout staff had told their reporters of "widespread cheating to meet the Boy Scout quotas imposed on them,"[30] and in January 1975, the *New York Times* noted that the new membership figures showed a drop of 40,000 for 1974. "A principal reason for the drop was the decision to put 'more stringent requirements on staff members in registering boys.'"[31] There are two points to notice about these stories. The first point is that they were not detected by the regular mechanisms of accounting—in this case the United Way's elaborate system. The second point is that, although the press was prepared to dig out and run the second story, and conceivably might have done the same for the first, the story was about fiscal integrity and the scandal of dishonesty. The scandal was newsworthy because of the size of the deceit and because the Boy Scouts' many claims to virtue make them a good target. Press scrutiny will also follow the individual child where the outcome is scandalous, but it will not exist for the average case where a decision causes no scandal but merely makes it difficult for a child to reach an adequate independence.

Monitoring Decisions: Bureaucratic Reform

The attempts at watching that we have just described indicate that the child welfare system is very much aware of the problem and consequences of not watching. In 1980, after years of lobbying and negotiating, a diverse coalition of people successfully pushed for federal legislation that mandated (for the

29. Chicago Community Fund Archives, University of Illinois at Chicago, Boy Scouts, 80–122, Box 1.

30. *Chicago Tribune,* 10 June 1974, reported in Chicago Community Fund Archives.

31. *New York Times,* 26 January 1975, reported in Chicago Community Fund Archives.

receipt of certain federal monies) a watching system that differed from earlier systems in crucial respects. The Adoption
Assistance and Child Welfare Act of 1980 enjoined on partici-
pating states a two-pronged individual case review system.[32]
The law provided that the case of each child be reviewed every
six months to determine whether each child had a case plan
"designed to achieve placement in the least restrictive (most
family like) setting available" and that progress was being made
toward the goals set out in the plan.[33] In addition, each case was
to be reviewed every eighteen months to determine whether the
child should be retained in the child welfare system or returned
to his or her parents. The first review was to be conducted by a
court or by administrative review process, which meant "review
open to the participation of the parents of the child, conducted
by a panel of appropriate persons at least one of whom is not
responsible for the case management of, or the delivery of services to, either the child or the parents who are the subject of
the review."[34] The second review was to be conducted by the
relevant court or an administrative body appointed or approved
by the court.

This statute was a landmark in child welfare legislation because it imposed goals on the states for child welfare interventions and established processes for monitoring the achievement
of those goals. The legislation reflected widespread dissatisfaction with current procedures. It also reflected the belief that the
states would not set up such strict watching procedures themselves. The question remains, however, whether the practices
set up in the states to implement the legislation contain the
essential elements of the process of judgment.

The state of Illinois adopted the letter and spirit of the law
with speed and vigor. While the publication of regulations under the law was delayed by the change of national administration in 1980, the Department of Children and Family Services
quickly introduced procedures for the six-month reviews that
included, and in some significant respects surpassed, the federal

32. Adoption Assistance and Child Welfare Act of 1980, P.L. 96–272.
33. Ibid., sec. 475 (5).
34. Ibid., sec. 475 (6).

requirements.[35] These new procedures brought the public department much closer to the goal of making open and, therefore, fair judgments about its wards. The major feature of the change was that decisions about cases, instead of being the private preserve of caseworkers, were formally and regularly examined by a case review administrator in the presence of other parties to the case. An independent evaluation of the department's case reviews ascertained that the department was conducting reviews of close to 90 percent of those of its wards whose care had been contracted out to private agencies.[36] Moreover, the department was having some success in securing the attendance of parents (whose right to attend was guaranteed in the federal statute) and of children, thirteen years of age or older, whose right to attend was set out in the state regulations. It was having somewhat less success securing the attendance of foster parents whose legal status at the hearings was also mandated in the state regulations. To observers inside and outside the public bureaucracy, this large-scale good faith effort by the Department of Children and Family Services was an improvement of massive proportions. The effort meant that the department now had an operating supervisory system that it had lacked. It also meant that the supervisory system contained a critical element of the process of judgment—the possibility of the decision makers hearing the story as told by the key actors.

A close examination of the department's efforts, however, reveals a tension between ordinary bureaucratic practice and the larger claims of judgment. To be fair, that judgment must be made after the competing claims of all the actors, particularly the claims of those whose lives are affected, are heard. There was no doubt in the minds of observers that the department's case reviews were being conducted by fair-minded, competent people. But the shortcomings of the process tended to erode the public purpose of stating and adjusting conflicting claims in favor of practices that supported the bureaucratic purpose. The

35. Illinois Department of Children and Family Services, Procedures Memorandum on Client Service Planning, 27 July 1981; and the Illinois Register, 21 November 1980.

36. Illinois Action for Foster Children, *The Report of the Monitoring Project of P.L. 96–272, State of Illinois,* Glencoe, Ill., May 1983.

array of persons at the hearings was such that there was no effective counterweight to this tendency. When people were missing from the hearings, they were not the case reviewer or the department's caseworker but the private agency caseworker who, for a purchase of service client, knew much more about the child than the public agency caseworker. Outsiders reported occasions when the case reviewer dissuaded legal aid attorneys from appearing at hearings and likewise dissuaded the client's private attorneys from taking part. Despite the guarantee in the department's guidelines that parents could be accompanied by a friend, relative, advocate, or legal counsel, legal counsel tended not to complain about the exclusion for fear of alienating the case reviewer. These absences could only diminish the client's voice.

In similar fashion, although the department's regulations guaranteed an appeal in the form of a staffing to be attended by a number of public and private agency staff, in practice private agency personnel were reluctant to use the procedure. One private sector caseworker commenting on her reluctance to use the appeal system even in the few cases where she thought the review had been badly handled, said: "It doesn't win you any friends."[37] A legal aid attorney commented that the parents' interpretations of the brisk, official notes they received about the hearing (which, she said, parents felt were threatening and nonexplanatory) made the process seem a punitive exercise in bureaucratic power.[38] When a major child advocacy group (representing the national Children's Defense Fund) requested permission to interview public sector caseworkers about the hearings, the department replied, "In our view, additional staff interviews on the implementation process would not be productive."[39] Lastly, private agencies saw instances where the department was using the reviews as a tool of fiscal policy. The agencies argued that the

37. Interview with Mary Pat Clemmons, Association House, 20 September 1984.

38. Interview with Patricia Connell, Legal Assistance Foundation, 14 September 1984.

39. Letter dated 29 December 1982, from Mary Ann Kren, Chief, Office of Rules and Procedures, Illinois Department of Children and Family Services, to the Illinois Action for Foster Children, quoted in Illinois Action for Foster Children, *Report of the Monitoring Project*, 7.

department denied particular goals for children in order to re-
trench in those service areas.

It is important to be clear about the drift of this criticism. The
review process represented a massive improvement in the department's work. According to a range of observers, the department was making strenuous efforts to ensure the participation
of natural parents, foster parents, and older children, which was
a major change from previous department practice. But a crucial aspect of good judgment was lacking. Although the key
actors were often present, the process was essentially an internal bureaucratic process. The decision-making power and the
power to dictate the process were in the hands of the organization whose actions were the subject of the review. It is perfectly
proper, of course, for a large organization to have such a procedure. But an internal process cannot satisfy the public purpose
of holding those bureaucracies responsible for the decisions
they make about the children the public entrusts to their care.
This is not a matter of "good" or "bad," "reformed" or "unre-
formed" bureaucracies. It is a simple matter of the likely behavior of the best bureaucracies in situations where powerless individuals are challenging the organization's decisions.

There is another issue about internal review—whether judgments, once made, are executed. Administrative case reviews
are a recent phenomena, and there is only slight evidence about
their effectiveness. A coherent case review system probably
does change the pattern of decision-making in organizations
that previously relied on inadequate supervisory systems. The
associate director of Human Services in the state of California
reported to a U.S. Senate hearing on the Adoption Assistance
and Child Welfare Bill that, within two years of implementing
an administrative review process, Los Angeles County reduced
its foster caseload from over 11,000 children to fewer than
9,000.[40]

Case reviews, however, also produce other kinds of judgments—judgments about systemic problems in child welfare
that adversely affect the lives of a significant number of chil-

40. U.S. Senate hearings on H.R. 3434, September 1979, Statement of
Ronald F. Gibbs, Associate Director for Human Resources on Behalf of the
National Association of Counties, 307.

dren. Case reviews do uncover important systematic problems, but the people who conduct reviews are powerless to do anything except draw attention to those problems. Case reviews do not affect internal problems because they are conducted by midlevel staff who have little power to change policy at higher levels. They do not affect problems external to the organization because of the nature of relationships between equally powerful organizations.

In Illinois, for example, the case reviews showed up a serious problem in the work of the juvenile court and the Department of Children and Family Services. The permanent planning for a child, and hence the case review system, was arranged to start from the moment a child became a ward of the state. But the decision to move from temporary custody (which did not trigger permanency planning) to regular custody was taking the courts up to two and a half years to make. In this long period of time the child was officially in limbo, going back to court only to have the temporary custody order renewed in the face of a series of continuances of adjudication and dispositional hearings. The problem had partly to do with the court and partly to do with the information the department was giving the court. But the case reviewers who witnessed the unwarranted renewals of temporary custody orders were powerless to act.

These shortcomings of an improved system may mark the limits of internal reform. There are, however, possibilities outside the bureaucracies and we turn to these next.

Monitoring Decisions: The Citizen Role

The concern and inventiveness of the last few years have produced another way of monitoring and judging what is happening to children in the state's custody. The proponents of this other system, citizens review boards, foresaw the problems of even adequate internal review and devised a mechanism they thought was capable of producing fair and effective judgments. The process differed slightly in each of the thirteen states that had established such boards by 1980, but the common element was the use of trained citizen volunteers who were independent of the child welfare system. These citizens were to examine the decisions made about individual children and the progress being made toward the implementation of those decisions.

The procedures were similar to the procedures the state of Illinois adopted in response to the 1980 federal law. The essential difference was the bestowal of some measure of authority and responsibility on citizens. These citizens were interested enough in child welfare to get involved but did not have memberships in organizations that had bureaucratic interests in the outcome of child welfare decisions.

Some observers of the development of citizens review boards argued that they were superfluous, that a good internal review system would accomplish all that the external boards could do, and that there was a limit to the number of effective monitoring systems that could be set up inside or outside the child welfare system. Our question about the boards is more precise. Do they exhibit the characteristics of good judgment lacking in the internal review systems?

The evidence suggests that they do.[41] In the first place they represent a broader range of legitimate interests. The most important aspect is that children, natural parents, and surrogate parents have the same status at the hearings as the staff of the child welfare agencies. They are all informants and petitioners since the process is controlled by people not beholden to any particular institutional interest. Observers in Arizona said that natural parents and other interested parties now feel "that there is a non-adversarial forum in which to express their concerns. It gives them a feeling of not being 'trapped' in the system."[42] As one foster parent said, "Finally there is somebody willing to listen." Judicial personnel in Maryland thought that the review open to all parties brought the rights of natural parents to the forefront of the discussion. That opportunity highlighted both the rights and responsibilities of parents: a judge in Arizona commented that the open discussion helped parents who other-

41. Much of the information for this analysis comes from Jon R. Conte, Shirley M. Buttrick, and Gaylord Gieske, "A Qualitative Evaluation of Citizens Review Boards in Four States," Center for Social Policy and Research, University of Illinois at Chicago Circle and the League of Women Voters of Illinois, Chicago, January 1981.
42. Ibid., 55.

wise could not face the fact that they were not adequately caring for their children.

This broader representation of interests had advantages in addition to legitimizing the voice of the natural parents. Some observers noted that the people serving on boards were able to suggest alternatives and resources overlooked by the professional staffs. Additionally, they brought the broad interest and judgment of the community to bear on the decision. Commenting on the New Jersey system, a report on citizen review boards in four states noted:

> Every layer of the court system interviewed was impressed with the perspective that local citizens bring from their various experiences to the discussion of what is in the best interest of the child. The variety of experiences, expertise and knowledge of their communities is combined with a level of concern for the welfare of the child.[43]

In addition to creating a more legitimate setting for the making of judgments, citizens review boards created for the entire system what internal review created for the lower levels of the bureaucracies. One administrator put it quite candidly: "From a system's point of view, citizens looking over our shoulder is vital."[44] Another observer interviewed for a different study was even more explicit:

> These volunteers because they do not owe their jobs to the court system are able to criticize aspects of foster care that need scrutiny both in the court system and DYFS (Department of Youth and Family Services). The review act is creating advocates of children who can open up the locked doors of the juvenile court system and pave the way for improvements.[45]

We noted earlier that the Illinois case review system uncovered systemic problems in the organization of child welfare services but was unable to do more than bring them to the

43. Ibid., 86–87.
44. Ibid., 86.
45. Center for Analysis of Public Issues, "In Search of Paper Children: An Analysis of New Jersey's Foster Care Review Board, Summary and Conclusions," Princeton, N.J., n.d., 7.

attention of senior staff in the same organization. The 1983 official report of the State Foster Care Review Board to the Arizona Supreme Court not only gave recommendations for improvements but also listed the recommendations of prior annual reports and the degree to which those recommendations had been adopted in legislation and implemented.[46] This type of delineation put public pressure on the system and enlarged the public that was concerned and informed about state wards.

The argument for citizens review boards does not depend on a pessimistic view of bureaucracies. Nor does it assume the complete powerlessness of most clients. There is a dialectic of control in social systems that includes as one of its currents "the capability of the weak, in the regularized relations of autonomy and dependency that constitute social systems, to turn their weakness back against the powerful."[47] Some clients in some situations know how to work the system, and the bureaucracies we have been describing perform some part of the job they were set up to do. The issue is rather how can citizens who are clients challenge the benevolent actions of helping bureaucracies when they disagree with the judgment (or in some cases the non-judgment) of the helpers. Or to put it in more formal terms, "Where is the right to overrule the central judgment that a particular decision or distribution is equitable for you. . . . The issue is the presence of a dialogue between those whose equity (or good) is being chosen for them and the decision-makers."[48]

Nonclient citizens enter the picture as mediators who do not represent any of the organized systems of helping. They are necessary simply because citizens who are clients are not powerful actors in their own right. Nonclient citizens serving on citizens review boards may be as blind as anyone else to the relevant characteristics of a client's situation. But if they are chosen from among people who, either by habitation or imaginative

46. Arizona Supreme Court, State Foster Care Review Board Recommendations and Report, Phoenix, Ariz., January 1983.

47. Anthony Giddens, *Profiles and Critiques in Social Theory* (Berkeley and Los Angeles: University of California Press, 1979), 39.

48. John McKnight, remarks at the Center for Urban Affairs seminar, Northwestern University, 6 July 1982.

contact, know the place clients come from, they may be able to see when claims that are legitimate from an organization's perspective are not legitimate from the vantage point of those who come to the organization for help.

The opposition to citizens review boards is strong. In Illinois the lobbyist for the private child care association formally and successfully opposed legislation to set up review boards. He did this with the tacit approval of the Department of Children and Family Services, which did not wish to be seen opposing the boards publicly. In Massachusetts and Iowa, legislators voted against such legislation on the grounds that internal monitoring systems made the boards superfluous. A similar argument was used to oppose the extension of a small citizens review system in Delaware and to limit the system to two counties in Minnesota.[49]

In some cases the opposition to citizen boards is cynical and acknowledges the central issue of the distribution of power and control over the service system. The Illinois lobbyist who opposed the boards said at the time the legislation was being considered (he was the lobbyist for several private agencies): "Catholic Charities' public position is that it is a tricky issue. Privately its position is that it is a dumb idea. It will raise the cost to the agency. We will have to have someone massaging every citizens' review board."[50] In other cases opponents warned about the impact more criticism would have on an already beleaguered social work profession, and many people were genuinely concerned about the waste of duplicate controls.

The last criticism misses the distinction between systems set up to ensure that members of a bureaucracy perform within a given set of rules and a system set up to challenge those rules when they conflict with clients' interests. As to the other criticism, the evidence suggests that review boards have the opposite effect on worker morale. The presence of external reviewers has had the effect of encouraging better and more energetic work. In addition the review process gives workers an appeal

49. Personal communication, Mary Lee Allen of the Children's Defense Fund, Washington, D.C., 29 September 1984.

50. Interview with Tom Nolan, September 23, 1980.

system in cases where their decisions were turned down by superiors with less knowledge of the cases in question.[51]

The necessity for citizen involvement of the kind that the boards represent is a sign of the current state of the dialectic between need and response. Public and private social welfare agencies developed in response to the inability and the unwillingness of individual citizens to cope with certain kinds of trouble. This analysis of the quality of the work of organized social welfare suggests that we have reached the limits of that historic change. The delegation of more authority to more efficient and professional organizations may no longer improve the condition of the distressed. These organizations have changed the context of helping and the relationships between the helpers and the helped. Future improvements may depend on citizens reasserting their authority over the organizations to which they delegated their responsibility.

Conclusion

This chapter has stressed the claims of judgment over the claims of measurement. This is an unusual argument in an age when science, research, and accounting devices are invoked as the tools for improving the condition of all manner of social welfare problems. We should be clear about the premises on which the argument is made.

Historically, the central concerns of social welfare were events that were themselves the problem. The counting of the events was a count of the problem. The number of children without (natural or surrogate) parents, the number of children without homes, the number of infant deaths, and the number of children stunted by malnutrition were the problem and were the evidence of the problem. A reduction in these numbers was an improvement, a sign of the success of whatever had been done about the problems. There are always problems of inference, but the provision of shelters for the homeless and unadulterated milk for poor children were unambiguous improvements.

---

51. A number of examples of the positive effects review boards had on the work of caseworkers are described in Conte, Buttrick, and Gieske, "Qualitative Evaluation."

Some of these numbers are still clear evidence about the condition of children in trouble. But most of the children in child welfare systems in this country today are not in such extreme danger that their status can be determined by such counts. Instead we seek decent care for children who lack such care in the hopes that they will turn out to be responsible citizens.

There are several consequences of our concentration on less obvious manifestations of distress. The nature of the problem, the appropriate response, and the signs of the success of the response become less clear, more ambiguous, and more controversial. At the same time the possibility increases that the negative effects of the response outweigh the positive effects. In particular the response may be at odds with the client's sense of what is appropriate. A more mundane, practical consequence is that we are forced to rely on proxies to assess the problem and the client's condition after the response has been delivered.

There is another important historical trend. The organized response to need has developed to the stage where the agencies of helping include powerful bureaucracies, and where the definitions of need and response will affect the livelihoods of a vast army of professional helpers.

In these circumstances the accomplishment of good outcomes and the detection of good outcomes require effort in addition to the careful organization, monitoring, and analysis of service. Strategies for helping will be more useful if they recognize conflicting interests, and in particular recognize the legitimacy of the client's definition of the problem, of appropriate responses, and of "good" outcomes. These strategies are more likely to be successful if they are implemented in the knowledge that good outcomes require more than efficient organizations. They require the recognition that service organizations have legitimate beliefs, understandings, practices, and interests that will not always coincide with the best interests of their clients.

This conclusion takes us back to civic responsibility. The recognition of the client's legitimate (though like everyone else's, fallible) voice is recognition that the person in trouble is first a citizen. We designate certain organizations to tackle problems with which we cannot cope individually. If these organizations have shortcomings, we must remember that they are public servants, and at some level we, as citizens, are responsible for their actions. That responsibility cannot be fulfilled by relying on the mechanisms they devise for producing good work. We are finally the judges and the guarantors of that good work, and such responsibilities cannot be delegated.

III

THE BROADER CONTEXT OF TROUBLE AND SUSTENANCE

7

Family Distress and Poverty

Introduction

Much of this book has been about the service response to need. The purpose of the discussions has been to sketch out the ways in which families in trouble can be helped back on the road to a decent independence. We have analyzed some critical aspects of the work of social welfare organizations that help children whose situation has brought them to the attention of the public authorities. One of the critical family characteristics of these children is poverty. Poverty is connected with troubled families in two ways. Extreme poverty is trouble itself. It is debilitating, it can be life threatening, and it affects the life chances of the children who are raised in it. Poverty is also an issue because it is a frequent antecedent of other forms of family trouble: it very often accompanies the family incapacity that requires a service response.

These two connections suggest two issues. First, there is the issue of the extent of poverty; this issue is most fruitfully set, like most of our issues, in a historical context. That comparison gives us a perspective on contemporary patterns of poverty. The second issue is about the connection between poverty and other forms of trouble. This second issue leads us to the current debates about welfare. Aid to Dependent Children (ADC) was a response to the problem of the children of widowed mothers: its purpose was to keep them out of institutions by giving their mothers the means to raise them at home. Its successor, Aid to Families with Dependent Children (AFDC), is both a response and a problem. It is a response to the dependency of single, divorced, separated, and widowed mothers, and it is a problem because it is said to encourage the first three of these conditions. Single parenthood is no longer a condition to be alleviated; it is a problem to be prevented. The question is whether AFDC is so flawed a vehicle that its negative consequences outweigh its benefits. The proponents of the argument that AFDC is seriously flawed rest their case on a sometimes complicated analysis of a two-variable universe. According to this view, the fact that AFDC and single parenthood have expanded in tandom is no coincidence. The most recent critics of this view have embraced a three-variable universe and argue the case that unemployment explains some of the increase in single parenthood. That view also merits attention.

These discussions will not, however, satisfy the criteria set out in the introduction. Definitions are as crucial a part of the problem of need as an evaluation of the organized response. We should not allow AFDC to slip from the category of a major response to that of a major problem without considering whether the receipt of welfare is a useful defining characteristic of need. As a corollary we should ask whether single parenthood constitutes a satisfactory definition of a problem.

Patterns of Poverty

The two most striking trends in poverty in the last hundred years are the long-term trend in the reduction of poverty and the recent short-term trend in the slowing down and reversal of that improvement. Much of the change is related to the general economy. A smaller, though still very significant, part of the change is the result of cash transfer payments.

Two useful ways to describe the changes in family income caused by an expanding economy and increases in productivity are changes in real wages and changes in consumption patterns. Before 1947, when the Bureau of the Census started to report incomes from the much wider pool of people who had recently been required to file tax returns, national income figures were calculated from projections from small sets of data; they may contain wide margins of error. They give, however, some indication of the magnitude of the changes.

A variety of estimates of the trends in real wages (wages adjusted for inflation) for the years 1860–90 cluster around a 50 percent increase for those thirty years.[1] The trend is upward for the entire period except for the years of the Civil War and the immediate postwar period. Real wages exhibited little change between 1890 and 1915, but between 1915 and 1924, according to one study, real wages in the unionized manufacturing industries increased 25 percent, and in all manufacturing industries about 12 percent. At the same time the length of the average working week dropped from sixty to fifty hours.[2] Another study estimates a 60 percent increase in the per capita real wage for the entire nation between 1929 and 1945.[3] From 1947 to 1970, median family income (in 1967 dollars) went from $4,531 to $8,473.[4] In the next ten years to 1980, white median family income remained relatively stable in current dollars while black median family income fell about 5 percent.[5] Median income tells us little about the distribution of income among different groups, but other figures demonstrate that the group in which we are most interested, the poor, did not gain much relative to other groups. In 1947, the poorest fifth of white families received 5.4 percent of the nation's aggregate income, and in 1970 they received 5.8 percent.[6] The comparable figures for black

1. Clarence D. Long, *Wages and Earnings in the United States, 1860–1890* (Princeton, N.J.: Princeton University Press, 1960), 68.

2. Paul H. Douglas, *Real Wages in the United States, 1890–1926* (Boston: Houghton Mifflin, 1930), 128–131.

3. Richard Easterlin, "Interregional Differences in Per Capita Income, Population and Total Income, 1840–1950," in National Bureau of Economic Research, ed., *Trends in the American Economy in the Nineteenth Century: Studies in Income and Wealth*, vol. 24 (Princeton, N.J.: Princeton University Press, 1960), 30.

4. U.S. Bureau of the Census, *Historical Statistics of the United States. Bicentennial Edition: Colonial Times to 1970* (Washington, D.C.: Bureau of the Census, 1975), 297.

5. Andrew Hacker, ed., *U/S: A Statistical Portrait of the American People* (New York: Viking Press, 1983), 145.

6. U.S. Bureau of the Census, *Historical Statistics*, 293.

and other minority families were 4.3 percent and 4.5 percent. Since 1979, the share of total income going to people in the bottom half of the income scale has been declining.

The long-term trend in real income is unambiguous—it was an increase of massive proportions that affected all groups in society notwithstanding occasional reverses and slowdowns. The picture of consumption patterns is equally dramatic. In 1900, 3 percent of all American households had electricity; in 1976, 99 percent of all poor families had electric service.[7] In 1900, 1 percent of all families had central heating, a convenience enjoyed by 62 percent of all poor families in 1976. In 1900, 18 percent of American families had ice refrigerators. In 1976, 99 percent of all poor families had mechanical refrigeration, and by that same year 99 percent of all poor families had flush toilets, which only 15 percent of all families had possessed in 1900. The intent of this comparison is not to minimize the condition of the contemporary poor—it is by now a truism, not a political statement, to say that poverty is relative to time and place—but to point out that the condition of poor families has changed along with the condition of median income families.

Since 1935, the income-increasing efforts of economic growth have been accompanied by federal income transfer programs both contractual, as in Social Security old-age insurance, and noncontractual, as in Aid to Families with Dependent Children. While the latter helps poor children directly, the former, by adding to the economic security of those children's grandparents, has an indirect effect on the children's well-being. The trends in the noncontractual income programs and the in-kind programs (the most important of which are the food stamp program and Medicaid) show a slow initial growth with major increases in coverage in the 1960s. By 1981, on the eve of the Reagan cuts, 7.5 million children were benefiting from AFDC payments at a federal cost of about $7.6 billion, which was slightly more than half the total cost of the programs. In that year 12.2 percent of all children under eighteen benefited from

7. This and the following data on consumption patterns in the United States come from Stanley Lebergoh, *The American Economy: Income, Wealth and Want* (Princeton, N.J.: Princeton University Press, 1976).

the program. The comparative figure for 1960 was 3 percent. In 1981, the federal government incurred outlays of $10 billion on food stamps and $18 billion for Medicaid, much of which benefited children in poor families.

There are a variety of ways of characterizing the economic effect of these programs (and the general expansion of the economy) on poor families. One way is to chart the number of families below the poverty line, which is an artificial standard based on a multiple of food costs that are rated as minimally adequate for a temporary period. The official multiple is 3; the actual multiple—that is, the actual proportion of other costs to food costs—may be as high as 5. (The higher multiple and the several alternative indices of poverty produce larger estimates of poverty.) The national poverty level was 22.4 percent of the population when it was first calculated in 1959.[8] By the mid-1970s, as a result of the increased benefits derived from transfer programs and economic growth, it had dropped to between 11 and 12 percent. The poverty level for children in this period stayed above the overall poverty rate. It ranged from over 18 percent in the mid-1960s to a low of 14 percent in the early 1970s.

This long-term trend in the reduction of poverty came to at least a temporary halt in the 1970s. For our population, families with children, the last ten years has seen a significant increase in poverty. By 1983, 22 percent of American children were living in families whose income was below the poverty line. There are several reasons for this: the general state of the economy, an increase in the percent of children living in single-parent families, and budget cuts in transfer programs. We will discuss the first two later. The decreasing rate of spending on transfer payments starts in the middle 1970s but is most dramatic in President Reagan's first administration.

These policy changes—lower rates of expenditures and more stringent eligibility rules—show up in a number of different statistics. In 1980, 83 percent of children living in families below

8. This and the following information about the poverty level are taken from the American Public Welfare Association, "Poverty Reaches Highest Level Since 1965: Hits Young Hardest," *Washington Reports* 18, no.7 (September 1983): 1–7.

the poverty line received Medicaid. In 1982, the corresponding figure was 73 percent.[9] In 1974, 78 percent of children in poor families received AFDC grants. In 1980, that figure had declined to 67 percent and by 1982 to 52 percent. Accompanying the decline in the percentage of poor children receiving grants was a decline in their value. Between 1976 and 1983, the nationwide average grant declined in constant dollars by 12 percent. In some of the largest industrial states—New York, Pennsylvania, Illinois, New Jersey, and Ohio—the decline was between 20 and 30 percent.

Inequality among states and among different groups of poor children is still, as it was in 1935, a dramatic part of the problem. AFDC payments, like the Mothers' Pension payments that preceded them, vary widely from state to state, and the variations are far wider than variations in per capita income and the cost of living. For example, in 1980 Michigan paid $390 a month for a welfare family with one parent and two children.[10] The state of Texas provided a payment of $108. In 1982, the consumer price index average for all urban consumers was 283 points with Detroit scoring 279 and Dallas 293. In 1980, the state per capita income in Michigan was $9,950 and in Texas $9,545. Income, however, is just one part of the distribution equation; the other part is access to welfare payments. In 1980, 78 percent of single mothers in Michigan were receiving welfare payments compared to 20 percent of single mothers in Texas.

The other manifestation of this inequality is the different pattern of poverty by race. In 1983, 15 percent of white children were living in poor families. The same was true of 38 percent of Hispanic children and 47 percent of black children.

Poverty and Other Troubles

This description of poverty and poverty programs is the background for the issue of the relationship between poverty and other forms of family distress. Two forms of distress will

---

9. The data in this paragraph are taken from Children's Defense Fund, *American Children in Poverty* (Washington, D.C.: Children's Defense Fund, 1984).

10. These and the following data are taken from Hacker, *U/S*.

concern us here: the obvious and visible accompaniments of poverty, and the other troubles that trigger state attention toward individual families.

From Charles Loring Brace's day to the present, articulate observers have given us still-life pictures of conditions that the mainstream of the contemporary society would find intolerable. One of Brace's colleagues, reporting on a visit to a tenement house in New York in the 1860s, wrote:

> In a dark cellar filled with smoke, there sleep, all in one room, with no kind of partition dividing them, two men with their wives, a girl of thirteen or fourteen; two men and a large boy of about seventeen years of age; a mother with two more boys, one about ten years old, and one large boy of fifteen; another woman with two boys, nine and eleven years of age—in all fourteen persons.[11]

Brace added as a footnote that, while New York City's annual death rates were 28 per 1,000 and while the "clean" wards showed 15 per 1,000, "Our Sixth ward reaches 43, and 'Gotham Court' in Chevy Street, attains the horrible maximum of 195 per 1,000."[12]

Forty years later, in 1902, a medical inspector in New York City caught a scene in "Hell's Kitchen," which she recorded in her autobiography:

> I climbed stair after stair, knocked on door after door, met drunk after drunk, filthy mother after filthy mother and dying baby after dying baby. . . . It was an appalling summer too, with an average of fifteen hundred babies dying each week in the city; lean, miserable, wailing little souls carried off wholesale by dysentery.[13]

Almost seventy years after this scene was observed, when the poverty rate among children was lower than it had ever been

11. Charles Loring Brace, *The Dangerous Classes of New York and Twenty Years Work Among Them* (New York: Wynkoop and Hallenbeck, 1872). Reprint. Washington, D.C.: National Organization of Social Workers Classic Series, 1973, 54–55.

12. Ibid., 57.

13. S. Josephine Baker, *Fighting for Life* (New York: MacMillan, 1939); quoted in Robert H. Bremner, *Children and Youth in America: A Documentary History*, vol.2, pts.1–6, (Cambridge, Mass.: Harvard University Press, 1971), 17.

and lower than it has been since, an inquiry into rural hunger and malnutrition in Mississippi recorded the following testimony from witnesses:

> There are days without any food four or five at a time the parents go hungry and the child may live on powdered milk for a week at a time when we just "make do" and mix whatever we have with water and the end of the month when food stamps run out, commodities run out, the Headstart doctor refers to this as a time of discomfort.[14]

The same inquiry reported that the consequences of such scenes were substantial newborn deaths, irreversible brain damage due to protein deficiency, and nutritional anemia from protein and iron deficiency in between 30 and 70 percent of children from poor backgrounds.

These three examples, stretching over a hundred years, illustrate the poverty that causes death, the extreme manifestation of family distress, and the whole range of discomfort, pain, and despair that precedes such deaths. At least in the earliest account poverty was also one of the elements in the disintegration of poor families—as parents deserted children, and children slipped off to make their own way on the streets. The incidence of such scenes is much lower today than it was a hundred years ago. The poverty that demonstrates itself in large numbers of children without caretaking parents and roofs over their heads has disappeared from the United States. It has not disappeared from the large cities of other countries; in Brazil, for example, the estimates of street children range from 3 to 20 million out of a population of 120 million.

The common lot of the poor in the United States is much less dramatic. Carol Stack, a sympathetic observer of poor minority communities and a believer in the energy and effectiveness with which the poor cope with their poverty, checked off a different list of contemporary manifestations of poverty: small, rented frame houses in major need of repair (26 percent condemned as dilapidated in the community she studied and 13 percent listed as

---

14. Citizen's Board of Inquiry into Hunger and Malnutrition in the United States, *Hunger U.S.A.* (Boston: Beacon Press, 1968); quoted in Bremner, *Children and Youth*, vol. 3, pts. 5–7, 1335.

unfit); accommodations that were freezing in winter and overrun by insects in the summer; high unemployment rates with most employment opportunities being in low-paying service industries; overcrowding (her core family slept fourteen in a three-bedroom house); the absence of working cars and the consequent need to spend much of the day walking to shops, doctors' appointments, and welfare offices outside the neighborhood; clothes purchased secondhand from Goodwill or Salvation Army stores; neighborhoods with unpaved, broken streets; the swapping of necessities to avoid the deprivation caused by marginal incomes (hot cornbread and greens swapped for diapers and milk, second-hand sheets and towels swapped for a secondhand dress); the impossibility of building a cash surplus for emergencies both because of income levels, and because of the obligations of the swapping networks; and frequent evictions by landlords and condemnations of property.[15] Such poverty is still engrossing since it requires enormous exertions to keep children fed and clothed and offers little possibility of respite, much less of the comforts taken for granted by the rest of the population. Infant mortality figures show that it is still life-threatening.

But those infant mortality figures also illustrate the change in the condition of children. The average annual death rate among children under age two in New York State between 1909 and 1912 was 87 per 1,000 live births. In 1980, the nationwide death rate for children under age one was 13 per 1,000, and for ages one to four, 0.7 per 1,000. (In India in 1978, it was 125 per 1,000.) Improved sanitation, uncontaminated milk and water supplies, less crowded conditions, and antibiotics explain much of the difference. The persistent remnant of the poverty effect, however, is seen in the disparity between white and minority rates that we noted in chapter 4. In 1984, the infant mortality rate in Illinois for white infants was 9.4 per 1,000 and for minority infants 20.4 per 1,000. Nor, as we discovered in that chapter, can the improvement in infant mortality rates be taken for granted. Between 1981 and 1982, infant mortality rates actually increased in eleven states.

15. Carol Stack, *All Our Kin: Strategies for Survival in a Black Community* (New York: Harper and Row, 1975).

These figures represent the most obvious and the most serious accompaniments of child poverty. The next part of the issue is the relationship between poverty and the disintegration of poor families. If poverty is a strong antecedent of the family disintegration caused by abuse, neglect, and dependency, relief of poverty should be a family-maintaining strategy.

There is a strong relationship between poverty and the state taking guardianship of children. At the national level the data are highly suggestive; at the state level they are crystal clear. A high point in out-of-home placement of children in the child welfare system was reached in 1933 when 249,000 children were in care at a rate of 5.9 per 1,000 children.[16] In 1935, the passage of the Social Security Act advanced economic security through pensions, disability payments, unemployment insurance, and aid to dependent children. The 1933 high point in the number of placements was not recorded again until 1962, when the total number of children in care represented a placement rate of 3.8 per 1,000. While the placement rate increased after 1962, it did not reach 5.9 again. The 448,000 children in care in 1975 represented a rate of 5.0 per 1,000. While this evidence about the development of transfer programs and the decrease in placement rates is circumstantial, we should remember that the proponents of ADC were intent on precisely this change. They wanted to reduce the number of children who were cared for by the state because their mothers could not earn an income and care for their children at the same time.

The post-1962 national data raise something of a problem. Between the mid-1960s and the mid-1970s, the number of children living in poverty dropped from about 19 percent of the child population to 14 percent. At the same time the rate of children placed into surrogate care rose from about 4 per 1,000 to 5 per 1,000. These two trends do not necessarily point to a weakening of the relationship between poverty and the breakup of troubled families. There are other explanations. In the 1960s, the spread of state child abuse laws increased the probability

16. Bernice Boehm, "The Child in Foster Care," in *Foster Care in Question: A National Reassessment by Twenty-One Experts*, ed. Helen Stone (New York: Child Welfare League of America Inc., 1970), 270–77.

that children in trouble would be brought to the attention of the state. Moreover, the structure of the child welfare population began to change in this period as child welfare systems became increasingly responsible for delinquent and nuisance-causing youths; such children had previously been the responsibility of departments of correction.

The national picture is clear enough. State data provide an even clearer picture of the relationship. In 1982, the state of Wisconsin conducted a census of all children in child welfare placements in the state. The census revealed that 46 percent of the children's natural families were supported by AFDC payments and that 72 percent of the families had family incomes below $10,000.[17] A six-month study of all reported cases of child abuse in Cook County in Illinois suggested that 73 percent of the children came from families where the parents either received AFDC or were unemployed.[18] The majority of children in child welfare systems clearly come from poor families. Not all poor children, of course, end up in these systems. Only a few do. If we calculate statewide Illinois percentages from the Wisconsin numbers (the Cook County figures just quoted will not be representative of state statistics), some 4 percent of the Illinois AFDC population, at any point in time, have case files opened on them in the state department and about 1 percent are actually living in substitute care.[19] Thus poverty is a common, though not a sufficient, characteristic of families who come to the attention of the state.

Local data also show the details of the relationship between poverty and placement. In some cases the relationship is direct: the children were in placement because the parents literally had no money to buy food, pay the rent, or keep the house heated in winter. A New York City study of the reasons why some 27,000 children were placed in care showed that about 5 percent came

17. State of Wisconsin, Division of Community Services, "Alternate Case Inventory," 29 July 1983.

18. Frederick Brown, "Policies and Practices of the Child Protective Services System in Cook County," Jane Addams College of Social Work, University of Illinois at Chicago Circle, September 1979.

19. These somewhat tortuous calculations are necessary because Illinois did not have parental income figures in its computerized case records.

into care for the sole reason of lack of money.[20] A Cook County study showed about 6 percent coming into care solely for lack of money; about 18 percent cited money as one of several principal causes.[21]

The indirect consequences of poverty are much more frequent precursors of placement and also more difficult to estimate. The Wisconsin data demonstrate, however, some very suggestive patterns. Most children now coming into child welfare systems are labeled as either (or both) abused and neglected children. (The other major categories have to do with the children's behavior.) The Wisconsin study shows that whereas neglect is the largest single reason for placement in families with incomes under $10,000, it does not even appear as a category for families with incomes over $15,000. The realities behind these official categories are described in an analysis of all the abuse and neglect cases reported to the authorities in Cook County over a six-month period between July and December 1977. Of all the reported cases, 27 percent involved mild malnutrition, which was further described as irregular and poor feeding.[22] Another 13 percent of all the cases involved clothing neglect, and 11 percent of all the cases involved substandard housing. A strong relationship clearly exists between these phenomena and poverty.

The relationship between abuse and poverty is more complicated. First, plenty of evidence indicates that abuse of poor children is carefully and conscientiously reported by the emergency rooms of the city hospitals where poor children go for treatment. The same abuse is, however, underreported by private physicians who examine the children of the middle classes.

20. Trudy Lash and Heidi Sigal, *State of the Child: New York* (New York City: Foundation for Child Development, 1976), 176.

21. Andrew C. Gordon, Margo Gordon, John McKnight, and Malcolm Bush, "Experiences of Wardship: Interim Report II to the Office of Child Development, U.S. Department of Health, Education and Welfare," Center for Urban Affairs, Northwestern University, 1975.

22. H. Frederick Brown, "Policies and Practices," 5-2. I have recalculated Brown's percentages by excluding his category on sibling abuse as a reason for a child abuse and neglect report. This is because that reason obscures the nature of the act and does not describe the condition or treatment of the child about whom the report is being made. The category sibling abuse was the largest single category and hence distorted the true incidence of the real categories of abuse and neglect. The percentages in this report total more than 100 percent because every type of harm recorded in each case was included in the analysis.

Second, abuse comprises different kinds of activity with different relations to poverty. Somewhere between the neglect we have described and the imposition of physical damage to a child is the category of lack of supervision—children being left on their own—a category occurring in 34 percent of the Cook County cases. Lack of supervision probably includes inadequate care by virtue of a parent working, a parent having lost interest in a child, and a parent being overwhelmed by his or her situation. Physical abuse—which ranges from overuse of physical discipline with no visible injury noted to physical discipline resulting in bruises and welts—was reported in 17 and 26 percent of cases, respectively. The categories of severe physical harm, such as fractures, concussion, and poisoning, occurred in fractions of 1 percent except for burns and scalding, which occurred in 3 percent of cases. In each of these categories the stress and constraints imposed by poverty and substandard living conditions are likely to be one of the elements in the equation that produces the harm.

AFDC: A Solution or a Problem?

These consequences of poverty have always inspired the response of monetary relief. The monetary relief, in turn, has resulted in the counterresponse that charity, or more recently welfare, has its own problems. A hundred years ago some commentators feared that the distribution of charitable monies might unintentionally help to sustain an irresponsible and debauched life. Liquor figured dramatically in the scenes of dissolution that outdoor relief was reckoned to produce. The negative effect of cash relief most feared today is the establishment of single-parent families. The fear can be expressed in a variety of ways reflecting different attributions about motives. AFDC can be seen as a license for illicit sex and an incentive for the conception of additional children. A more sober concern is that the attachment of grants to single mothers constitutes an economic incentive for the creation and maintenance of a single-parent families; this circumstance in turn prolongs the poverty that is the condition for the grant. Then there is the political and anthropological argument that a multigenerational dependence on cash grants feeds on itself by creating a new norm—the norm that reliance on AFDC is a proper way to obtain an income. These notions are sometimes wrapped up in the culture of poverty argument: the social organization, expectations, and behavior of poor minority communities perpetuate, if they did not create, the poverty those communities experience.[23]

For the moment we will accept the assumptions that buttress these fears and examine the argument on its merits. The facts that have produced these beliefs and theories constitute a major demographic change. In 1960, there were 2.5 million American families with children that the United States' census labeled "female headed." In 1972, there were 4 million and in 1980, 8.5 million. In 1960, in Illinois 4.7 percent of white children and youth lived with their mothers only. In 1980, the percentage was 10.4. The comparative percentages for black children were 25.8 percent and 43 percent. By 1980, nationwide, 23.4 percent of all children aged seventeen or younger were living with one parent, another relative, or a nonrelative.

Just as the proportion of children living in single-parent families changed dramatically, so too did the reasons for that condition. A study of families in Philadelphia a hundred years ago showed that widowhood accounted for about three-quarters of female-headed families among blacks, Germans, Irish, and native American whites.[24] The 1980 census showed that widowhood accounted for less than 10 percent of black female-headed families and that single, separated, and divorced women made up the bulk of that population in roughly equal proportions. The recent increase in the rate of these changes is striking. Between 1970 and 1980, the number of black children growing up in fatherless families increased by 41 percent, and most of

23. For the formulation of the culture of poverty argument, see the works of Franklin E. Frazier and Oscar Lewis. The first major refutation of the theory is contained in Charles A. Valentine, *Culture and Poverty: Critique and Counter Proposal* (Chicago: University of Chicago Press, 1968).
24. F. F. Furstenburg Jr., T. Hershberg, and J. Modell, "The Origins of the Female-Headed Black Family: The Impact of the Urban Experience," *Journal of Interdisciplinary History* 6 (1975): 211–33; quoted in William Julius Wilson and Kathryn M. Neckerman, "Poverty and Family Structure: The Widening Gap Between Evidence and Public Policy Issues," Department of Sociology, University of Chicago, 1985.

that growth occurred in families in which the mother had never been married.[25] In contrast the increasing percentage of white children growing up in single-parent families was mainly due to an increase in separation and divorce.

These changes are connected to the issue of poverty because an increasing percent of single-parent families are poor, and an increasing percent of all poor families are single-parent families. In 1960, about 20 percent of poor white families and 30 percent of poor black families were headed by women. By 1982, those percentages had risen to 35 and 70 percent, respectively.

The extent of family poverty is made more significant by the duration of that poverty. While the bulk of families who ever experience poverty are poor for one or two years only, 60 percent of families who are poor at any one time remain poor for more than eight years.[26] This pattern, like the others we have described, affects black children more strongly than white children. As the researcher who calculated these trends put it, "the average poor black child today appears to be in the midst of a poverty spell which will last for almost two decades."[27]

There is then a correlation between single-parent families and poverty. The number of single-parent families has increased substantially over the last twenty years. So has the number of families receiving AFDC. These correlations and the ever-present fear of pauperism raise the question of whether the existence of AFDC encourages the formation of single-parent families. If that were the case, the solution to poverty would at the same time be one of its causes, and any attempts to increase the amount and the availability of AFDC would exacerbate the problem. The research on the relationship between AFDC grants and the formation of single-parent families is voluminous and somewhat contradictory. In sum, it does not suggest that welfare is a sufficient explanation for the increase in single-parent families.

The first thing to note in unraveling the connection between AFDC and the incidence of single-parent families is that the

25. Ibid., 8.
26. M. J. Bane and D. T. Ellwood, "Slipping into and out of Poverty: The Dynamics of Spells," National Bureau of Economic Research Working Paper, no. 1199, 1983; quoted in Wilson, "Poverty and Family Structure," 1985.
27. M. J. Bane and D. T. Ellwood, "Slipping," 36.

formation of single-parent families is not a single act.[28] All such cases, of course, involve sexual intercourse that results in conception. But after that the conscious acts are different for different groups of women. For some women there is a conscious decision not to terminate the pregnancy by abortion. Some women become single parents by not marrying the father of their child. Other women become single parents by separating from or divorcing the fathers of their children, and other women, who were either never married or are not currently married, prolong the state of being a single parent by not marrying or remarrying. The decision to form or to allow the formation of a single-parent household also involves two people, the mother and the father. Some of those decisions are probably joint decisions and some are unilateral.

There is no strong evidence that AFDC increases the number of extramarital births. Despite the wide variation in the administration of AFDC in different states, it is difficult to demonstrate a relationship between such births and either the level of AFDC payments or the acceptance rate of applications for AFDC.[29] Moreover, the public impression that the incidence of out-of-wedlock births is increasing is inaccurate. The number of such births did increase as the number of teenagers increased. But the rate of out-of-wedlock births per thousand teenagers actually declined between 1970 and 1980—a trend partly attributable to the legalization of abortions. (The out-of-wedlock birth rate had increased massively between 1950 and 1970 as a result of increased sexual activity among teenagers and an increasing tendency of pregnant teenagers not to marry.) What has changed recently is the ratio of out-of-wedlock births to all births. The percentage of out-of-wedlock births to all births has risen from 5.3 percent in 1960 to 17.1 in 1979.

The next decision that results in the formation of single-parent families is the decision of married couples to separate or divorce.

28. Much of this analysis of the effect of AFDC on the formation of single-parent families is taken from Robert Crawford, "The Causes of Female-Headed Households," Children's Policy Research Project, National Opinion Research Center, University of Chicago, 1981.
29. Barbara Janowitz, "The Impact of AFDC on Illegitimate Birth Rates," *Journal of Marriage and the Family* 38 (August 1976): 485–94; quoted in Crawford, "Causes of Female-Headed Households," 1981.

Once again the research shows a collection of studies with negative and positive findings about the relationship between AFDC rates and separation and dissolution rates. The difference between the null and the positive findings is probably caused by the particular group of variables that were controlled for in the regression equations.[30] Taken as a whole, they suggest that there is a modest relationship between AFDC rates and separation and dissolution rates. The studies that examine the relationship between AFDC rates and remarriage rates produce the same configuration—some null findings, some positive findings, with the balance of the evidence favoring the positive findings.[31]

Taken together, the studies on out-of-wedlock births and on marital disruption and dissolution do not warrant the conclusion that increasing AFDC rolls and rates of payment are the critical variables in the increase in single-parent families. (The last variable cannot explain any increases after the early 1970s, simply because there has been no real increase in AFDC payments nationwide since then.) No study is likely to pin down the causes with a strong degree of certainty. Some of the most important influences on sexual and marital behavior do not lend themselves to statistical analysis. Changing sexual mores affect the

30. Examples of studies that found that the level of AFDC has no effect on marital disruption rates are: Phillip Cutright and John Scanzoni, "Income Supplements and American Families," Paper No. 12, *Studies in Welfare*, for the Subcommittee on Fiscal Policy, Joint Economic Committee of the Congress (Washington, D.C.: Government Policy Office, 1973); and Isabel Sawhill, Gerald Peabody, Carol Jones, and Steven Caldwell, "Income Transfers and Family Structure," Working paper 979-03 (Washington, D.C.: Urban Institute, July 1975). Studies that found a positive relationship between the level of AFDC payments and marital disruption include: Marjorie Honig, "AFDC Income, Recipient Rates, and Family Dissolution," *Journal of Human Resources* 9 (Spring 1976): 250–60; and Saul Hoffman and John Holmes, "Husbands, Wives and Divorce," in *Five Thousand American Families: Patterns of Economic Progress*, vol. 4, ed. Greg J. Duncan and James N. Morgan (Ann Arbor, Mich.: Survey Research Center, Institute for Social Research, University of Michigan, 1976), 23–75.

31. One study that finds no relationship between AFDC payments and remarriage or reconciliations is Maurice McDonald, Thomas McDonald, and Irwin Garfinkel, "AFDC and Family Dissolution: A Skeptical Comment," Institute for Research on Poverty, University of Wisconsin, 1977. A study that found a negative relationship between levels of AFDC payments and remarriage rates is Robert M. Hutchens, "Welfare, Remarriage and Marital Search," *American Economic Review* 69 (June 1979): 369–79.

conception rate among the unmarried, and changing social customs have reduced the pressures on unmarried mothers to get married. The women's movement, with its stress on the capability of (and the need for) women to cope with their circumstances, adds a political rationale for women who are single parents to continue to manage on their own.

There is, however, another numerical indicator that is likely to increase our understanding of single parenthood. The concentration on AFDC as the prime cause of the huge increase in the formation of single-parent families ignores the condition that is prior to the nonformation or dissolution of a two-parent family— the dissatisfaction with that arrangement. Single parenthood is the result of two logically separate (though practically intertwined) cognitions: a distaste for marrying or staying married to the mother or father of one's child, and a decision to express that distaste in the act of staying or becoming single. While AFDC is an economic factor contributing to the second cognition, there is another economic factor that contributes to the first cognition. Several economic arguments explain the initial dissatisfaction with the possibility or fact of the married state in terms of the father's economic status.

The first of these arguments, labeled the income effect, predicts a positive relationship between income and marital stability and does so for several reasons. In families where one partner earns a reasonable salary and the other partner maintains the household, both partners have a lot to lose by breaking up the partnership.[32] The more assets that two partners have acquired through marriage, the more they have to lose through divorce. At the other end of the income scale, financial strain is likely to contribute to tensions in a marriage and reduce the economic disadvantages of marital dissolution. The second argument, another economic effect, is the independence effect, and this argument is particularly relevant to women whose mates are unemployed.[33] As a woman's economic capacity matches and exceeds her mate's, the value to her of continuing the relationship diminishes—particularly if, in addition to her economic

32. This theory is developed by Gary S. Becker, "A Theory of Marriage: Part I," *Journal of Political Economy* 81 (July–August 1973): 813–46.
33. Ibid.

role, she is also the major maintainer of the household. Finally, the third argument is a theory that is more sociological than economic—the role performance hypothesis. This theory argues that unemployed or low-paid males whose income is not the chief component of total household income have lost both in their own eyes and in their mate's eyes one of their major functions and are, therefore, failures. The spousal attribution and self-attribution of failure increase dissatisfaction with the relationship, which, in turn, increases the chance of a breakup.[34]

Each of these three pressures could have an influence on the lives of any couple, either separately or together, and it is probably not very sensible to expect to discover which has the greatest impact for which kinds of couples. There is, however, plenty of evidence that they have an effect. We know that there is a positive relationship between income, marital satisfaction, and marital stability.[35] Some studies also show that the greater the disparity between a man and a woman's contribution to family income in favor of the woman's contribution, the greater the probability of the disruption of that relationship.[36] As for the role hypothesis, there is both quantitative and qualitative data that demonstrate the destabilizing effects of a man's loss of his economic role.[37]

The disruptive effects of adverse economic conditions are particularly devastating in the black community—the community with the highest percentage of children living in single-parent families. The percentage of black males who are able to support a family from their own earnings is much lower than the percentage of white males who are economically independent.

34. The classic study of this phenomenon is Elliot Liebow, *Tally's Corner: A Study of Streetcorner Men* (Boston: Little, Brown, 1967).

35. Robert Hampton, "Marital Disruption: Some Economic Consequences," in *Five Thousand American Families: Patterns of Economic Progress*, vol. 3, ed. Greg J. Duncan and James N. Morgan (Ann Arbor, Mich.: Survey Research Center, Institute for Social Research, University of Michigan, 1975).

36. See Sawhill, Peabody, Jones, and Caldwell, "Income Transfers," 1975; Honig, "AFDC Income," 1976; and McDonald, McDonald, and Garfinkel, "AFDC and Family Dissolution," 1977.

37. See, for example, the discussion of this issue in William J. Wilson, *The Declining Significance of Race: Blacks and Changing American Institutions* (Chicago: University of Chicago Press, 1980).

This difference is due, first, to lower black labor force participation. The labor force participation rate of black men under the age of twenty-four declined severely in the 1970s. It is also due to higher incarceration rates for black males and higher mortality rates. William Wilson and Kathryn Neckerman have constructed a male marriageability index that estimates the ratio of economically independent young men to women of the same age and race.[38] In the mid-1960s, there were about 65 employed white men and black men aged twenty to twenty-four for every 100 women of the same age and race. By 1980, the white rate was 75 employed males per 100 females, and the black rate was 50 employed males per 100 females. For the twenty-five to thirty-four year-old age group in 1980, there were 85 white men to 100 white women and 60 black men to 100 black women. The chance for a black woman to find a mate of the same race and age who is in a position to support a family is significantly lower than for her white counterpart. This analysis, of course, does not reduce the irresponsibility of men who father and then desert their children. But an insistence on the dual imperatives of responsibility and opportunity makes a lot more sense than a call for either of them on their own.

The existence of a large group of single-parent families who are such because of a decision never to marry or a decision to separate or divorce is a striking discontinuity in the fabric of American society. Because for many people this phenomenon is a disturbing discontinuity, we may be tempted to find explanations for it in actions that can themselves be labeled aberrant. The existence of welfare and the extent and level of welfare payments cannot, however, be made to bear all the weight of explanation for this phenomenon. Adding the variable of economic opportunity brings us much closer to the reality of the families we are describing.

Toward Some Redefinitions of the Problem and the Solutions

The welfare and the economic opportunity explanations of single-parent families represent at their extremes two very

---

38. Wilson and Neckerman, "Poverty and Family Structure," 1985.

different views of the world. But they also point to the nature of explanation in matters of this complexity. Explanations are constructed in accordance with particular views and particular facts. As such they are always open to challenge from different perspectives and different constructions of the facts. This does not mean that one explanation is as good as any other; there are canons of explanation that result in some measure of agreement. It does mean, however, that explanations are rooted in particular premises and that we should know the premises before accepting the superstructures built on top of them. In the following discussion we will try to consider the broadest array of relevant facts about the lives of troubled families. As throughout the book, our goal is the development of strategies that sustain children in ways that will help them to a decent independence. And in the process we will continue to view children and their parents as citizens. This approach relieves us of the need to construct a "liberal" or a "conservative" perspective. We can instead recognize the devastating effects of lack of opportunity and demand that individuals exercise responsibility.

We will start with some improvements in the ways in which help can be given to poor families. These remedies have been constructed within the defining context of the notions of AFDC mothers and single-parent families. We conclude by questioning the defining context.

Several strategies will promote the sustenance of families within the structure of the AFDC program. But given what we have already described as the premier role of economic growth and employment in relieving destitution, it should be clear that AFDC can never be the major factor in reducing poverty or the stress that poverty produces. AFDC has improved the lot of many poor families, but the greatest influences on poverty since 1960 have been economic growth and Social Security transfers; the latter provide amounts of relief per family considerably in excess of that provided by AFDC.

In the first few years of the 1980s, unemployment increased as a direct result of government monetary policy aimed primarily at reducing the rate of inflation. If AFDC becomes part of that policy—providing some relief to the families of those thrown out of work by such federal policies—three deleterious consequences follow: (1) the number of families experiencing pretransfer poverty will increase; (2) the number of families experiencing post-transfer poverty will increase as AFDC and food stamps fail to take people over the poverty line; and (3) the effects of unemployment coupled with the effects of AFDC will probably increase the rate at which poor families dissolve into single-parent families. These effects will be strongest in minority communities.

It is not part of this study to describe the problems of reducing poverty by expanding the economy, but two points need to be made about previous efforts. First, the increase in economic growth during the 1960s (together with transfer programs) maintained the position of the poor vis-à-vis the not-poor. It did not increase the poor's share of the economic pie. Second, it is becoming apparent that a resurgence of economic growth in the context of the 1980s is not even likely to maintain that status quo. The increase in the number of people who are permanently unemployed or underemployed and the number of the working poor means that at present levels of the redistribution of the national wealth, even under conditions of economic growth, the position of the poor will actually get worse.

One link between employment and welfare is the issue of work incentives. If the combination of cash and in-kind transfers to poor families exceeds the available wage in poor communities, the combination of benefits will act as a work disincentive. While that disincentive may be a price worth paying for single mothers with small children, it may not be worth paying for single mothers with older children; by not working, these mothers pass up whatever chance exists to move on to jobs that pay more than the combined benefits.

The nature of the work disincentives inherent in AFDC depends on the context in which they are examined. On the one hand, the total benefit packet, including the average cost of Medicaid payments, looks attractive compared to the income of a household with a working adult earning the minimum wage. On the other hand, the problem is not the size of the benefit packet but the depressed condition of the poorest workers.

Welfare payments, as now constructed, act as a work disincentive because payment criteria contain very significant "notches"—points at which a very small increase in earned income causes a large reduction in benefits. The "notches," of course, are not just a function of the structure of AFDC payments. They are also a function of life on the other side of the line; of the costs faced by the working poor. An example constructed by President Carter's administration to describe some of the dilemmas of welfare reform captures the problem: "In Wisconsin . . . if a woman earning $2,500 in a half-time job switched to a full-time job, her total income would actually decline by $1,249 and being disqualified from receiving Medicaid could potentially add another $1,688 to the penalty."[39] This decrease in earnings is a function of the combined marginal tax rate on welfare programs—the amount by which benefits are reduced for every increase in earned income. In this example the notches are serious both because of the high marginal tax rate and because the earned income of working single mothers is low.

The other characteristic of the lives of the working poor relevant to the work disincentive in welfare packets is the high cost of medical care and the lack of reasonably priced insurance schemes in low-paying occupations. For any family receiving Medicaid as part of welfare benefits, the potential loss of those benefits is a major disincentive to pursuing earnings. In families with chronic health problems (a situation more likely among the poor than the nonpoor), the loss of Medicaid may be an insuperable barrier to moving back into the labor force. Indeed one conservative commentator on patterns of welfare use in New York City argues that the Medicaid notch is such a strong work disincentive that only the establishment of national health insurance will solve this problem.[40]

While work, work opportunities, and work disincentives are critical variables for the economic status of the poor, another important economic factor in the lives of single mothers is much more easily adjusted. Court-ordered child support payments provide income for a child whose mother or father has left the household. The absent parent is most often the father. The laws governing those payments are an assertion that fathers retain economic

39. Lawrence E. Lynn and David deF. Whitman, *The President as Policy Maker: Jimmy Carter and Welfare Reform* (Philadelphia: Temple University Press, 1981), 88.

40. Blanche Bernstein, *The Politics of Welfare: The New York City Experience* (Cambridge, Mass.: Abt Books, 1982), 148n–149n.

responsibility for children they have fathered, even when they have left the households their children inhabit. Since the vast majority of children living with only their mothers have a living father, those payments represent significant potential income. In most states that potential is not realized. The problem is three-fold. Many women who head single-parent families are not awarded child support payments; many women who are awarded child support payments receive comparatively low awards; and many of those same women receive either partial or no payments from fathers who have been ordered to pay child support. The 1980 census showed that only 48 percent of women who head families were awarded payments from the children's fathers, either by court order or by an informal agreement. Of these women, about half received the full amount, 23 percent less than the expected sum, and 28 percent received no payments at all.[41] The latest census survey shows that among those mothers who received some support, the average monthly payment came to $149.92.[42]

There is, of course, a relationship between awards, receipts, and the economic status of fathers: unemployed fathers cannot pay child support, and poorly paid fathers cannot pay as much as well-paid ones. Moreover, the federal program to encourage states to pursue fathers of children receiving AFDC payments does not directly affect the income of a mother already receiving AFDC.[43] The money collected from those fathers (over the first $50) is used to offset the federal and local costs of AFDC grants. A recent study calculated that full enforcement of custody awards would reduce poverty for mothers not on AFDC by a very small amount because the awards were so small.[44] But experiments in several states suggest that the rigorous collection, coupled with imaginative use of the proceeds, can

41. Hacker, *U/S*, 95.
42. Ibid.
43. Title IV D of the Social Security Act, 1974, requires as a condition of eligibility for AFDC that every applicant or recipient assign support rights to the state and cooperate with the state in establishing paternity and securing child support.
44. Philip K. Robins, "Child Support Enforcement as a Means of Reducing Welfare Dependency and Poverty," Discussion paper no. 758-84, Institute for Research on Poverty, University of Wisconsin, 1984.

make a difference to single-parent households. The state of Illinois used a massive increase in custody payment collections to leverage an increase in AFDC payment rates in the legislature in 1984. Wisconsin is capitalizing on higher custody payments to implement a demonstration project in which children living in single-parent households would be guaranteed a minimum benefit or a certain percentage of the absent parent's wage, whichever is higher. Initial calculations suggest that this system, which relies on the collection of a tax from the absent parent plus a much smaller surtax on the custodial parent's income, could produce significantly more generous rates of child benefits at a net savings to the state treasury.[45]

The routinized collection of higher custody payment awards would have several beneficial effects. For poor single mothers working at low-paying jobs, regular payments could make the difference between surviving without welfare and giving up a job in order to go on welfare. For mothers on welfare, the receipt of custody payments, some percent of which did count as earnings for AFDC eligibility, could relieve the burdens of acute poverty.

Whatever the merits of this last argument, there are several other characteristics of welfare payments that have been or could be altered to increase the likelihood that a mother and her children would retain the help and support of other adults. An important step was taken in 1968 when the U.S. Supreme Court ruled that Alabama's substitute father regulation, or more colloquially "man in the house" rule, was invalid.[46] The state of Alabama acting under a state regulation had cut off AFDC funds to a woman with four children because she entertained a man in her house on weekends; the state considered that man, by virtue of those visits, the children's substitute father. The intent of the regulation was to punish women who engaged in illicit sexual relations and to put such households on a par with those of regularly married couples who in Alabama were not eligible for AFDC. By this device Alabama cut its AFDC rolls

45. Irwin Garfinkel and Elizabeth Uhr, "A New Approach to Child Support," *The Public Interest* 74 (Spring 1984): 111–22.
46. King, Commissioner, Department of Pensions and Security, et al., V. Smith, et al., 392 U.S. 309, 88 S. Ct. 2128, 20 L.Ed. 2d, 118 (1968).

by about 20,000 persons, or over 20 percent, between 1964 and 1967. Judge Douglas, who wrote a concurring opinion, estimated that twenty other states had similar regulations in the AFDC plans they had submitted to the Department of Health, Education and Welfare. The Court was not itself interested in the family life of the mother. It ruled that the Alabama regulation conflicted with federal laws and policy. But by striking down the regulation, it had the effect of permitting mothers to establish nonmarital relationships that might help rather than hinder the task of raising children.

A current feature of the AFDC landscape discriminates against women who are married to and live with the fathers of their children. In the 1961 and 1962 amendments to the Social Security Act, AFDC coverage and federal financial participation were extended to two-parent families where both parents were unemployed. The purpose was to prevent discrimination against two-parent families and to reduce a clear economic incentive to marital dissolution. This action was taken in the context of a deepening concern about the rate of unemployment. The amendment, however, fails to live up to its possibilities. Individual states have been slow to use the provision of the amendments and, where they have adopted them, use them sparingly. Less than half the states use the provisions, and in most of the states where these provisions have been adopted, the AFDC-Unemployment caseload is less than 10 percent of the regular caseload.

The two-parent family is not the only family unit whose composition can be influenced by economic incentives that, in turn, affect a mother's capacity to cope. Teenage single mothers have a variety of living arrangements. The mothers' choice of living arrangement is affected by their economic capacity. Prior to 1976, in Illinois, a teenage mother's economic need was calculated for the purpose of assessing AFDC eligibility by including the income of her mother's family if her mother was receiving aid. Consequently, the grant to the teenage mother was less than it would have been if her mother's income had not been counted. The smaller grant meant that such mothers were likely to stay in their maternal homes. In 1976, this practice was changed as a result of a court ruling that made adolescent parents eligible to receive AFDC benefits in their own right. The ruling made it easier for such parents to establish their own households. But it turns out that there is a clear positive relationship between a teenage mother living with her parent(s) and her chances of staying in school. An increase in a mother's AFDC income that leads to the establishment of a separate household could, therefore, constitute a net loss in that mother's capacity.

This relationship is shown most dramatically in a comparison of black and other teenage mothers. An Illinois study surveyed 2,000 teenage mothers who were receiving AFDC payments.[47] The black teenagers were more likely to stay in school because they were more likely to be living with their mothers. In the sample 70 percent of the black mothers and about 44 percent of the white and Hispanic mothers were raising their offspring in the mother's parent's home. At the time they were interviewed, 57 percent of the black mothers were attending school, compared with 26 percent of the Hispanics and 21 percent of the whites. Living in their mothers' homes gave these young mothers the support they needed to keep up with their schooling.

There is more to a teenage mother's decision to stay in her maternal home than the economic possibility of making it on her own. The racial differences we have described are indicative of much greater patterns of familial support for teenage mothers in the black community than in the white and Hispanic communities. But the economic issue is important. Regulations that encourage single teenage parents to establish their own households may have the effect of robbing those parents of advice and sustenance they badly need. There will be situations where a young mother is forced to leave her parent's home, and those mothers should not be penalized. But in general, the demands of equal treatment should be weighed against the claims of a supportive environment. In later years the facts of having completed high school will be a much more important determinant of the mother's and the child's condition than grievances about the economic necessities that forced

47. These data are taken from Mark Testa, "The Social Support of Adolescent Parents: A Survey of Young Mothers on AFDC in Illinois," Interim Report, Children's Policy Research Project, National Opinion Research Center, University of Chicago, March 1983.

a mother to stay with her mother. And high school completion is just one of the benefits likely to accrue to young, single mothers who can count on substantial on-the-spot help in raising their children. The benefits extend beyond the teenage mother to her children. Girls who are raised in households that include their single mother and a grandparent are much less likely to become unwed mothers themselves than girls who live with their mothers alone.[48]

Conclusion

This description of revisions to the welfare system are a reminder that, even with the failure of the Nixon and Carter reforms, the system is not immutable. There is room for variation and change. It is possible to construct adjustments that sustain families and move them to independence. The reigning belief that welfare is simply a problem discourages these evolutionary improvements. But maximizing a family's chance for sustenance requires more than partial reforms of welfare. It requires an effort to consider the situation of poor families in a different context.

Lichtenberg, a contemporary of Linnaeus, wrote that nature does not create genera and species. Nature creates individuals, and it is our shortsightedness that compels us to look for similarities in order to handle a great many of these individuals at once. The larger the "families" we make for ourselves, the more inexact our concepts become.[49] By the same token nature does not create single parents. The federal government created the category AFDC, but it is precisely that—a federal category desig-

48. D. P. Hogan, "Demographic Trends in Human Fertility and Parenting Across the Life-Span" (Paper prepared for the Social Science Research Council Conference on Bio-Social Life-Span Approaches to Parental and Off-Spring Development, Elkridge, Md., May 1983); and "Structural and Normative Factors in Single Parenthood Among Black Adolescents" (Paper presented at the annual meeting of the American Sociological Association, San Antonio, Tex., August 1984), quoted in Wilson and Neckerman, "Poverty and Family Structure," 1985.

49. Georg Christoph Lichtenberg, *Schriften und Briefe*, vol. 1, *Sudelbucher*, ed. Wolfgang Promies (Munich: Carl Hanser, 1968), 13, quoted in Rodney Needham, *Against the Tranquility of Axioms* (Berkeley and Los Angeles: University of California Press, 1983), 5.

nating some people, by virtue of a few of their characteristics, eligible to receive aid.

When AFDC becomes the focus of attention, the problem for which it was a remedy, poverty, is moved off center stage. This transfer of attention becomes apparent when we consider the issue of the working poor. According to one scenario, the "problem" of AFDC would be relieved if poor AFDC mothers moved into the labor force. If they did, many of them would join the ranks of the working poor, whose condition has actually deteriorated in the past few years. But in this version of the problem, such a change would be an improvement. The situation would be even better, according to this view, if the number of single-parent families declined; yet some estimates indicate that the major increases in poverty during the past four years have been among persons—adults, but especially children—living in traditional husband-wife families. "In 1979 families headed by married couples made up 34.4 percent of the poor. Today they make up 40 percent, and 60 percent of the increase in poor families last year [1983] was made up of husband-wife families."[50] This trend was the result of changes in unemployment insurance rules, the tightening of eligibility criteria for in-kind assistance programs like food stamps and emergency energy assistance, and increased federal income and payroll taxes.

But as long as the receipt of AFDC is the issue, the structural conditions that keep working families in poverty and nonworking families out of the labor force can be ignored. The same focus pushes a number of other critical issues into the background. It conceals the general distribution of income and the issue of the range of incomes appropriate in a democratic society. This perspective obscures the changes in the job market that have resulted in the creation of a large number of low-wage jobs and the erosion of well-paying industrial employment. It hides the issue of private affluence and public squalor—the private creation of good surroundings (physical and institutional)

---

50. Timothy Sneeding, "Recent Increase in Poverty in the U.S.: What the Official Estimates Fail to Show," testimony before the U.S. House of Representatives Committee on Ways and Means, Subcommittees on Oversight and on Public Assistance and Unemployment Compensation, Washington D.C., 18 October 1983, 14–15, quoted in *Focus* 7, no. 1 (Winter 1984): 5.

for those who can afford them and the deterioration of those surroundings for the poor.

The second major consequence of the concentration on the issue of AFDC is that for AFDC recipients their participation in the program becomes their most salient characteristic. The result of that perspective is the concealment of important variation among those families. When the variety in the AFDC population is discussed, it is usually in terms of degrees of virtue—the distinction between families that use welfare for a short period of time to tide them over an acute problem, and those who use it for an extended period of time to address a chronic condition. That distinction is important, but there are other equally important distinctions that are seldom discussed.

For example, we could consider the conditions of three families receiving AFDC in three different types of housing. The first family lives in a high-rise project surrounded by other high-rise projects. In this situation the inhabitants are no longer in control of their environment. Gangs control the stairways and the elevators, which are frequently broken. Small children have to be kept in their apartments during the day because the playgrounds are out their mothers' sight. Occasionally someone crossing between the buildings is killed by random sniper fire. The group of buildings has no shopping center, no schools, and no churches. In a second example a poor family lives in the neighborhood the high rises were designed to replace. Here the decay of once adequate housing gives the appearance of a battle site. Empty lots are as common as houses, and the remaining houses are in the last stages of deterioration. The streets and sidewalks are broken, the stoplights are out, and the only sign of economic activity is the alley car wash and tire and hub cap shack. Lastly, there is the low-rise public housing site, built in the 1950s before the construction of multistorey dwellings, where the elements of a decent family life are much easier to maintain. The householders can exert some influence on their surroundings, and their children can play in enclosed spaces within sight and hearing of the kitchen window. In these examples the manipulation of just one characteristic of daily life creates situations significantly different for their inhabitants. Yet the spotlight on AFDC obscures this and other variations and reduces the problem of poverty to one dimension.

Just as AFDC is a partial description of poverty, so the description "single-parent family" is a partial description of family situation. It includes mothers without family or friends, who are, therefore, virtually isolated. It describes women who have husbands in all but law, and women whose male friends provide little or no support. In this same single category are mothers who live with and are supported by their mothers or their own grown-up siblings, and mothers who rely heavily on women in similar situations. The category encompasses teenage parents who have not graduated from high school, and mothers whose children are now teenagers and who have returned to the labor force. But the census does not recognize all these fine distinctions, despite their obvious importance for the condition of these women and their children.

The journalistic and sociological literature notices the differences, although individual writers do not always admit that they are describing a part, not the whole, of the population. These writers also make broader categorizations, which approach moral categories. A few examples will show the range. Susan Sheehan's *A Welfare Mother* describes a crowded, extended, Puerto Rican family in Brooklyn, whose lives can be summarized by saying that they remained unconnected to the imperatives of American society. Carol Stack's *All Our Kin* describes the triumph of solidarity of poor mothers who sustain each other through the worst times. Eliot Liebow's *Tally's Corner* looks at the male side of the equation and describes the economically marginal black man, his haphazard relationship with his women and children, and his noneconomic justifications for those patterns.

The real-world complexity is one of the reasons for the retreat into the homogeneity of the categories "AFDC recipient" and "single-parent families." But if we want to avoid that obscuring homogeneity, how are we to handle the complexity? It will not solve the problem to create one more interpretation of the patterns, because the patterns will be different in different circumstances and will be different for different purposes. Instead we need some guidelines for the act of creating categories. One caution suggested by the variety is that the categories public policy devises and acts upon represent situations that are interactions of personal circumstances, the effects of public policy, and poverty. To ignore the changing details of any of these three strands will produce an incomplete picture. The homogeneity of public policy is a shortcoming common in mass society. A unitary description of a significant minority in that society is not a virtue.

Another guideline we might adopt has to do with ambiguity. The homogenization of the poor relieves us of the problem of grappling with the distinction between the poor we support willingly and the poor we support grudgingly. But with that relief comes a one-dimensional portrait that serves neither us or the poor. The question of how far our tolerance extends—to which kind of poor in what kind of circumstances—should be a staple of the civic debate. And to be fair, it should not shrink from all the variety that actually exists. Under these conditions we could both celebrate the relief AFDC brings to some families and recognize at the same time that some actions of some of the poor worsen their situation and try our patience.

But the most important caution is the recognition that the categories are just that—categories. They are devised for our convenience, and the most subtle of them obscure and simplify. Writing about written images of the poor in the early industrial age, Gertrude Himmelfarb notes the lack of categories that could translate into policies and programs. The dominating images of Dickens's novels allowed no easy translation into legislation and regulations. But they accomplished a much more important task:

> This was the real triumph of the imagination, of the moral as well as the literary imagination: to accord to the poor all the complexity of character and situation that had always been the prerogative of the rich. The best of the novelists complicated their stories the most, interweaving the public and private, the social and domestic, the misery of poverty and the tragedy of discord, the virtues and vices of the rich and the virtues and vices of the poor.[51]

51. Gertrude Himmelfarb, *The Idea of Poverty: England in the Early Industrial Age* (New York: Vintage Books, 1985), 521.

This idea leads us back to the theme of civic participation and citizenship. As long as the poor are exiled by physical distance and caricature from the imagination of the rest of society, we cannot accord them, and they cannot seize, the rights and responsibilities of citizenship. The shrinking of that physical and cognitive distance should be the first step of any new construction of their plight and our response.

8

Professional Helpers and Sustenance

Strands in Social Work Theory

The link between social welfare legislation, social welfare bureaucracies, and clients is the social work profession. Social workers' interpretation of need and their assignment of limited resources creates the context of official helping. Just as welfare legislation creates categories of the poor, social work, which has a body of theories to classify the distressed and the needy, sorts clients for the purpose of assigning them to service programs and to different therapies. This context, constructed by the daily action of social workers, could logically be one that encourages and sustains troubled families or one that reduces their capacities. Our argument is that the profession's emphasis on personality rather than practical conditions reduces its ability to sustain families. The evidence we will examine is social work theory. This theory will not, of course, be an infallible guide to what social workers do in practice, but it is the cognitive context that guides some of their actions.

Social welfare involves the persistent choice between personal and situational explanations of distress. The psychoanalyst who examines the patient on the couch and the public aid clerk who mails out the biweekly welfare checks are at opposite ends of the spectrum. Social work claims to stand in the middle and to employ whatever mixture of those explanations is appropriate in the particular circumstance. Schools of social work teach social welfare policy and management in addition to more specialized social work theory. But that theory is the core of social work, and while it claims to look with equal ease at people's behavior and their situation, it concentrates much more on the former.

We will pursue our thesis through two questions: how did psychological explanations gain ascendancy in the profession of social work, and in what ways does that zeitgeist reduce the chances of family maintenance? We start with a caveat. There is a lot of social work theory, and there are intricate connections between different schools of thought. These complexities have been well described elsewhere.[1] In this chapter we examine some examples of the major strands.

The profession of social work had more than one progenitor. One crucial line of descent starts with the charity organization societies who at the turn of the century began to train their workers in "scientific" methods of philanthropy. The search for a method partly reflected the desire to do things well using science as the vehicle for increasing their effectiveness. The search also reflected a desire to distinguish the new social worker from the untrained charity worker of the recent past. The new science became largely dependent on psychology because the critical object of interest was human behavior. (The interest in psychiatry was well established in the United States by 1900.) One of the earliest organizations to adopt social work was the hospital (Massachusetts General was the first), and this association created an interest in developing a method that could hold up its head alongside medicine.

The organizations that first embraced a psychologically oriented casework shared a characteristic that encouraged the continued emphasis on behavior. The large city hospital, the juvenile court, and the public school each needed a mechanism for coping with the most difficult parts of their almost unlimited public responsibilities and with their most difficult clients. The hospital coped with the behavioral and environmental determinants of health with visiting social workers; the juvenile court

1. Carol Germaine, "Technological Advances," in *Handbook of Clinical Social Work,* ed. Aaron Rosenblatt and Diana Waldfogel (San Francisco: Jossey-Bass, 1983), 26–57.

coped with incorrigibility through the establishment of the probation service; and the public school coped with truancy through
the activities of visiting teachers and probation officers. Since the
early development of social work owed more to the demands of
these public institutions than to the immediate demands of the
slum, the lens through which the problems of the distressed poor
were viewed was that of the institutional task of coping with
aberrant and destructive behavior. By contrast the settlement
house lens was focused on the conditions in which the daily lives
of the poor took place—the facts of poor sanitation, housing,
employment conditions, and the basic struggles of the first generation of immigrant families to cope with the loss of their roots
and the demands of a strange society.

The first texts.   The consequences of this early orientation were profound. Many of the significant texts in social
work—from the first books to contemporary writing—reflect
the persuasion that client behavior and personality are central
to social work's concerns. The original text—*Social Diagnosis*,
written by Mary Richmond of the Charity Organization Department of the Russell Sage Foundation in 1917—claimed to be an
impartial study of the social situation and personality.[2] (While
Miss Richmond used the word *personality,* she was more concerned with what her contemporaries called *character.*) The
book's purpose was to discover the best route to "social reconstruction." Although its many references to the epistemologies
employed by law and medicine and its active hope for the development of a parallel methodology for social casework indicate
the seriousness of its "scientific" intent, the actual case examples reflect the other imperatives of the Charity Organization
Societies—that is, the prevention of pauperization and multiple
claims on different charities from the same resourceful or incor-
rigible individual. The key was the construction of a method for
distinguishing the worthy from the unworthy poor. The heart of
the practical advice in the book are methods for ferreting out
drunkenness, prostitution, and desertion, and for compiling a

2. Mary E. Richmond, *Social Diagnosis* (New York: Russell Sage Foundation, 1917).

list of relatives who could be persuaded to contribute to the destitute branch of the family.

Mary Richmond's second and equally influential book, *What Is Social Casework?*, retains the emphasis on the individual but changes the topic from direct manifestations of unworthiness to more theoretical concerns with personality.[3] The book's tone is set in the introduction, where she describes as a stellar example of preformal, unconscious casework Anne Mansfield Sullivan's work with the blind and deaf Helen Keller:

> Beneath all the handicaps of her charge and the unfortunate effects of those handicaps she [Sullivan] was able to divine the unusual character of the child. Building upon this discovery, she summoned up one environmental resource after another, first to release, then to develop, that highly socialized personality.[4]

While Richmond's understanding of Sullivan's use of the environment included the physical environment of the Keller's house, her main concern was the environment made up of interpersonal relationships. Helen Keller did not need a richer physical environment. She already possessed one. Her task was to figure out a way of becoming part of it.

For those whose environment was impoverished, mind was much important than economics. Richmond wrote in the conclusion of *What Is Social Casework?*: "Examples of social casework show that by direct and indirect insights, and direct and indirect action upon the minds of clients, their social relations can be improved and their personalities developed."[5] Economic help on its own was "so hopelessly undemocratic that its disgrace attaches to giver and receiver—it curses both."[6] It had no moral quality. She denied that any parts of the social condition could be aggregated for the purpose of social action. Treating people equally was a sham because no one person-environment interaction was the same.

This belief had a powerful effect on the central orientation of

3. Mary E. Richmond, *What Is Social Case Work? An Introductory Description* (New York: Russell Sage Foundation, 1922).
4. Richmond, *What Is Social Case Work?* 22.
5. Ibid., 255.
6. Ibid., 172.

her work. If human distress could not be described in aggregate terms, the profession could not prescribe aggregate remedies. The "social" in social work was for her not the "social" of social structures, units, or aggregations but the "social" that was truer to the roots *socialis* and *socius* with a psychological twist to the partnership or comradeship originally expressed by those terms. The strength of this orientation should not be underestimated. Writing about the unemployed, Richmond quotes approvingly from a report on unemployment written in 1908, which described the model charity organization society as one that would:

> Make a loan to one [of the unemployed], send another to the woodyard to work for all he gets, stave off the landlord's eviction notice for a third, find a chance to work outside for a fourth, place the fifth in a hospital, send the sixth and his whole family to the country, provide cash for the exceptionally provident buyer who is the seventh, relieve the improvident eighth sparingly with supplies plus a work test and instead of doing work twice over, turn the ninth over to the charity that is already caring for him.[7]

To be sure, this is the language of practical help. It is one of the few detailed descriptions of such in the book, and at some level the differentiations seem sensible. But they deny the possibility of similar underlying conditions, and in political terms they obey the injunction divide and conquer.

The influence of psychiatry and psychoanalysis.   Miss Richmond's interest in the psychology of personality was formed from pre-Freudian psychiatry. Freud is not mentioned in her two major books. The psychiatry available to her was the line dating from Benjamin Rush's *Medical Inquiries and Observations upon the Diseases of the Mind* published in 1812. In her generation it included the work of Adolf Meyer, William W. White, James J. Putnam, and most importantly, William Healy.[8] This contemporary psychiatry was reformist in the largeness of its view. It stood in contrast to the physiological psychology manifest in the work of asylum psychiatrists who performed autopsies on the brains of

---

7. Ibid., 209.
8. The major interpretative history of the development of social work is Roy Lubove, *The Professional Altruist: The Emergence of Social Work as a Career* (New York: Atheneum, 1977).

deceased inmates to discover the relationship between brain lesions and behavior. The reform psychiatry was prepared to discover multiple causes of mental illness and to try a variety of strategies to train the retarded. It regarded punishment as a futile response to mental impairment.

A central concern was forging links with the eugenics movement, which itself was fortified by a rediscovery of Mendel's work. This psychiatry retained a belief in the supremacy of individual characteristics and personality over context to explain bizarre behavior. Its subjects tended to be people labeled deviant by the mental health world or by the newly formed juvenile court. The thesis that many of the deviant were in fact retarded was tested and demonstrated by the rapidly spreading device of the mental test. Simon and Binet's mental age test was first published in Paris in 1905. The use of these tests spread dramatically, culminating in the rage for mental testing during World War I, when statistics demonstrated that 47.3 percent of white American draftees were feeble minded.[9] The mental test and the personality test gave psychologists and social workers a supposedly objective measure of their clients' status. The tests made it easier to ignore those clients' physical environments.

The Freudian legacy in contemporary casework is different from the impact it originally had on social work. The first of Freud's papers to be available in English was translated in 1909, and the same year Freud and Jung traveled to the United States, where Freud gave a series of lectures at Clark University. Mary Richmond's 1917 and 1922 texts may have escaped Freud's influence, but the third decade of the century saw an explosion of interest in psychoanalysis. The major historian of social work's early years records the words of one social worker, who said that her colleagues in the 1920s "peered anxiously into the faces of their comrades with the unspoken question: have you been psychoanalyzed?"[10] By the 1940s, however, under the influence of neo-Freudians such as Harry Stack Sullivan and Erich Fromm, clinical casework developed a particular interest in the ego and in the connections between personality and personal relationships.

9. Ibid., 69.
10. Ibid., 88.

The full flowering of this revised ego psychology approach, building on the writings of the social work theorists Gordon Hamilton and Charlotte Towle, came in Helen Harris Perlman's social work text *Social Casework* published in 1957.[11] While *Social Casework* bore all the marks of revisionist Freudianism, it was still determinedly psychoanalytic. Perlman explained in the introduction: "By practice, professional education and conviction I am psychoanalytically and diagnostically oriented."[12] Central to her analysis of the problems clients bring to their social workers was the interaction of mind, personality, and behavior. The critical task was to secure through changes in the client's behavior a better adaptation to his or her environment:

> But whatever the service the client asks for and whatever the agency is set up to do, the essence of social casework help is that it aims to facilitate the individual's social adaptation, to restore, reshape, or reinforce his functioning as a social being. To do these things is to affect a person's behavior.[13]

The pathway to the client's problems and treatment was through the understandings of ego psychology. The core of a client's problems was the fact that the ego's normal protection systems "have become so rigid, persistent, and chronic that, like walls, they constrict the ego's boundaries and bar its adaptive manoeuvers."[14] The process of helping was a matter of restoring a person's natural problem-solving capacity. In this regard *Social Casework* was more humane than Mary Richmond's work. It recognized the innate capacity of individuals to lead constructive lives and argued that the process of correcting what had gone wrong was not a matter of ensuring the triumph of moral rectitude over moral turpitude but of restoring the delicate mechanisms of the psyche. At this point, however, the argument reflects the paternalism inherent in much of clinical social work since its inception. The tool of restoration was to be the relationship between the caseworker and client, with the case-

---

11. Helen Harris Perlman, *Social Casework: A Problem-Solving Approach* (Chicago: University of Chicago Press, 1957).
12. Ibid., xc.
13. Ibid., 7.
14. Ibid., 13.

worker modifying the client's aims and aspirations where those were inappropriate. *Social Casework* thus recast the moral osmosis expected of friendly visiting in the psychoanalytically oriented language of the caseworker-client relationship.

What these formulations effectively accomplished was the denial of mutuality between helper and helped (there was no room for the client to insist that the caseworker was wrongheaded) and the consequent abandonment of the possibility of a political alliance between equals. They foreclosed the possibility of a common stake in the shape and structure of society, and—rhetorical bows to the idea of self-determination notwithstanding—these suppositions constituted a denial of the fundamental autonomy of the person in trouble. The essence of the supplicant's position was clienthood, and the supplicant had to be persuaded of that status before any rehabilitative work could begin: "In social casework practice perhaps more than in other helping professions, the caseworker's skills and energies may often have to be put into grappling first with just this problem: to help the person to want and then to will to be a client."[15] The unwillingness to recognize any valid reasons for refusing to submit to clienthood produced frustration when clients failed to show up for casework sessions—a frustration that could only be explained, within the canon, by the client's resistance.

A revisionist theory. We noted earlier how social work had both its triumph and a major setback in Washington in the 1960s: its triumph in the provisions of the 1962 amendments to the Social Security Act and a setback in the disillusionment of key federal officials at the end of the decade. The profession itself was not immune to such questioning, and in the early 1970s a major restatement of the object of casework appeared powered by a deep skepticism of previous claims. The restatement came in William Reid and Laura Epstein's *Task Centered Casework* published in 1972.[16] It sprang from the School of Social Service Administration at the University of Chicago, which, though it had spawned Perlman's book,

15. Ibid., 185.
16. William J. Reid and Laura Epstein, *Task Centered Casework* (New York: Columbia University Press, 1972).

had in the 1920s and 1930s tried to maintain the broadest conception of social welfare. This broad concept stood in contrast with the pattern in many other schools, which narrowed the guiding focus to the boundaries of the clinical.

The starting point of this restatement was a concise and explicit criticism of the claims of the current therapeutic models of casework. First, Reid and Epstein argued that the models were vague to the point of being useless in practical situations: "Most statements in most [therapeutic] models (and perhaps ours is no exception) have a relatively low information yield."[17] The vagueness not only inhibited practical applications, it also limited understanding and the possibility of testing propositions derived from the hypotheses the models asserted:

> We must bear in mind that psychoanalytical based models of casework have yet to prove their efficiency and psychoanalytical theory itself has serious shortcomings including a reliance upon propositions that are difficult to test, the imprecision of its language, and its general lack of empirical verification.[18]

Moreover, the models smacked of paternalism and denied autonomy to clients. Reid and Epstein pointed out that this paternalism encouraged the assumption that the values the caseworker assumed for the client were the same that the client would assume for himself or herself: "We are apt to assume that such states as 'mental health' and 'optimal social functioning' represent ideals that clients naturally wish to attain."[19] The authors' conclusion was that there was no necessary connection between the two sets of assumptions and that for philosophical and practical reasons the client's assumptions should take precedence. The philosophical premise was that the client's priorities had an a priori validity: they were valid simply because they were the client's. But a practical consideration reinforced that philosophical respect. The main rationale for accepting the client's definition of a problem "is simply that the client will not let us do much else anyway—his conception of what he wants altered placed stringent limits upon our helping efforts no matter

17. Ibid., 10.
18. Ibid., 30.
19. Ibid., 18.

how well justified these may be in our value and theoretical systems."[20]

The keys to the book were a humbleness in the face of the size of the task and a respect for the person of the client. This premise led to the central argument that social casework interventions should be brief, concrete, and aimed at practical improvements in clients' lives. Such interventions were more likely to ease some of the stress of those lives than the nostrums of ego psychology. But to the degree that the task-centered prescription concentrated on the client's maladaptive behaviors, it ignored the environment in which those behaviors were shaped and that sometimes threatened the effectiveness of the most adaptive behavior.[21]

Casework and behaviorism.   *Task Centered Casework* was a deliberately atheoretical attempt to describe a set of interventions to relieve distress. The 1970s also saw the first major theoretical attempt in social work to elucidate both problem and solution in behavioral terms. While Freudian psychology infiltrated social work practice fairly rapidly after its introduction in 1908, the fate of behaviorism was different. John Broadus Watson's first book, *Psychology from the Standpoint of a Behaviorist,* was published in 1919. It was not, however, until the 1950s that behaviorism took a strong hold in some departments of psychology (B.F. Skinner's *Science and Human Behavior* was published in 1953), and only in the 1960s did it come to be regarded as a competitor in the therapeutic marketplace.[22] The

20. Ibid., 79.
21. It should be pointed out in fairness to Laura Epstein that one of her more recent statements of the ends of social work practice espouses a very different goal: "The predicament of social work practice today is to link its top heavy investment in reduction of personal deficiencies to its weak and unsystematic investment in the improvement of personal environments. . . . Located in a university with leadership power, we have no right to fiddle while Rome burns. What people need are resources, social skills, and consolation—in that order." Comment prepared for the 75th Anniversary Faculty Conference, the School of Social Service Administration, University of Chicago, November 1983.
22. For a brief history of the advent of behaviorism in social work, see Edwin J. Thomas, "Behavioral Modification and Casework," in *Theories of Social Casework,* ed. Robert W. Roberts and Robert H. Nee (Chicago: University of Chicago Press, 1970), 181–218.

first behavioral texts for social workers were written in the 1960s, and in 1975 the behavioral psychologist Israel Goldiamond and the social worker Arthur Schwartz published *Social Casework: A Behavioral Approach*.[23]

The Schwartz and Goldiamond text took issue with the intrapsychic orientation of previous social work texts in an attempt to set the problems of social work clients in an environmental context. But the environment that these two authors analyzed was identical to, and therefore as circumscribed as, the environment that Perlman considered—the environment of interpersonal relations. The emphasis, of course, was very different. Schwartz and Goldiamond were interested in describing the therapeutic powers of respondent and operant conditioning (and somewhat less enthusiastically of social learning theory). But in terms of our definition of the environment, their work stayed in the narrow mainstream that most social work had moved in since the 1930s. Their rejection of a broader analysis was clear and somewhat simple-minded:

> We believe that the issue currently dividing the field of social work—whether the main thrust of its efforts should be helping the individual or changing the system itself—posits an artificial dichotomy. True, much goes on that can be described as system failure, however, this translates into the human suffering of individuals. Systems do not become depressed, suicidal, hungry. Systems are concepts, but human beings, whose sufferings are very real and very painful, are the recipients of a system's functioning.[24]

With the environment thus dismissed, the core of human distress could emerge.

> Client problems are viewed as problems in social functioning; that is problems of clients involved in relationships that maintain behaviors that have undesirable effects, or are preventing the individual from obtaining desirable effects.[25]

The reasoning that led to this view was not blindness to the consequences of social arrangements. It was attributable to the

23. Arthur Schwartz and Israel Goldiamond, *Social Casework: A Behavioral Approach* (New York: Columbia University Press, 1975).
24. Ibid., 2–3.
25. Ibid., 2.

belief that individual behavior was the proper unit for the scientific investigation of the human condition, and that the redress of social ills required scientific techniques that partialized solutions to the level of individual behavior.

The problems of a unified theory.   The profession, however, remained dissatisfied with this dismissal of the environment, and in the 1980s several attempts have been made to redress the balance. One of them, Carol Meyer's *Clinical Social Work in the Eco-Systems Perspective,* appeared to promise an integrated study of individual behavior, social behavior, and social and institutional structures.[26] An occasional sentence can be found in the book to demonstrate that commitment. But the book is not about understanding people in trouble in all their relevant contexts. It is instead a thinly veiled attempt to cover up the differences in social work theory. Moreover, the differences with which it is concerned are not the inevitable difficulties with assigning responsibility between personal action and social context but the disagreements among the claims of individual therapies.

The anguish that prompted the book was caused by the embarrassment that psychoanalytic, behavioral, and task-centered caseworkers went their own ways, not according to the dictates of the particular problems as justified by demonstrated success, but according to the accidents of their own training and personal predilections. Consequently, social work could not present a united front to the world and, worse still, could not answer the basic question of which approach was preferable in what kind of situations.

The solution to this dilemma was a not very elaborate charade. Social workers would be united by their practice of looking at problems *in the first instance*—in a broad perspective. But once that common act has been performed, each worker was at liberty to employ whatever method he or she thought appropriate. Moreover, the choice of treatment would not be overly influenced by the initial broad analysis of the problem:

26. Carol H. Meyer, ed., *Clinical Social Work in the Eco-Systems Perspective* (New York: Columbia University Press, 1983).

The underlying assumption that drives us is that an all-encompassing perspective is needed to account for the real-life person and environment complexity in social work situations. Such a perspective cannot prescribe interventions, it can only focus our vision and lead us to notice the presence and interrelatedness of the features of a case. Once having accomplished this comprehension of the phenomena at hand—and only then—differential models, modalities, methods, and skills can be called upon for individualized use where appropriate. . . . Both perspective and methods are needed to achieve coherence, accountability and effectiveness. There is no competition between perspective and method; they are complementary to each other in clinical practice.[27]

But what then would determine action if not the broad view of the problem? At this point the thinness of the strategy to unify social work theory becomes apparent. It is not an intellectual, empirical, or a theoretical effort at all. Rather it is a peace-at-any-price strategy:

The analytical framework used in this book was intended to be helpful in the social work clinician's choice of practice models to be used at particular times, with particular cases. Are the clinician's ideological and value commitments syntonic with those explicated in one or another model? Does the staff situation require a clinical model that would allow for differential use of various levels of staff? Does the client seem to be sufficiently verbal to engage in a clinical encounter requiring thoughtful reflection, or is the client more apt to be responsive to work based upon defining behavioral tasks? Is the clinician interested in evaluation of his or her practice? Does that particular model make it possible to define outcomes and evaluate effectiveness? Does the issue of time impose on the clinician the use of a short-term versus a long-term model? Does the model allow for environmental interventions of a particular type? The analytic framework used to explicate the practice models should help the eclectic clinical practitioner to decide which models to use, when, and under what conditions. The eco-systems perspective is proposed as the unifying conceptualization to make coherent and cohesive the application of any or all of the models chosen.[28]

27. Ibid., 26.
28. Ibid., 239–40.

In between the apparently sensible differentiations the real message to social workers is clear: do whatever you feel like doing. The ecosystems perspective turns out to be a fig leaf for covering the embarrassment of not only the radically different prescriptions existing within the same profession but also the lack of evidence to evaluate their competing claims rationally. In this guise the environment, far from being the crucial and inescapable stage for individual behavior, is such an unimportant part of the real enterprise that it can serve as a common, though meaningless, litany for all the subgroups within the profession who cannot agree on anything else.

The Consequences of Social Work Theory

This brief summary of the main strands in social work education illustrates some straightforward ways in which the prevailing temper prevents a catholic enough view of human distress—a view that would allow the broadest possible set of responses. It does not describe the full range of social work's theories, but the vast majority of social work students define themselves as clinicians and are trained in the theoretical schools just described.

These mainstream theoretical commitments reduce the emphasis on family maintenance in specific ways. One consequence is a narrowing of vision—the decontextualization of the client. This contraction results in a redefinition of the environment relevant to social work action. The earliest social workers and their predecessors, the friendly visitors, whatever their political or emerging professional views, placed the personality in its context simply because they were constant witnesses to the details of their clients' lives. As a result, advice on how to cope with a husband's anger came hand in hand with information about the possibilities of a temporary job and a source of warm winter clothing. The strengthening of psychological theories of distress and the private sector's retreat from quasi-public responsibilities put a wider physical and intellectual distance between social workers and their clients. It takes a great deal of imagination to see the constraints that govern other people's behavior. Similarly it is very hard, absent close observation of a person in his or her setting, to notice adaptive behaviors among the maladaptive. The more the theory and practice of social work distances itself from the lives of its clients, the less likely the professional definition of the problem will do justice to the range of causes, and the less likely the remedy will take into account all the possibilities. In particular the psychologically stylized version of the critical events will tend to miss the relationship between client capacity and social opportunity.

The present catechism of social work theory relies on the phrase "the person in the environment" to cope with the tensions among the accounts of distress and remediation. The problem with that formulation is twofold: the dichotomy encourages the notion that it is useful to pursue one-half the equation separately, and it encourages the belief that the relevant unit of analysis is the unique individual. This opinion precludes the equally important possibility that the construction of social welfare responses requires an analysis of relevant classes of people inhabiting common environments.

The emphasis on psychological explanation encourages another kind of distortion: an underestimation of capacity or the exaggeration of incapacity. As we have suggested, such distortion results partly from the distance between worker and client, but it is also a consequence of the establishment of extreme psychological disorders as the touchstone for understanding distress. In the words of a medical critic of the organization of medical services, the tendency is for the extreme to become the mean; the diagnoses and interventions justified in extreme cases become the norm for much less severe cases.[29] The expectation is that even apparently capable clients have underlying incapacities that, if ignored, will manifest themselves in "worse" forms in the future.

Evidence of both sorts of distortion are found in social workers' case records.[30] These records exhibit a distinct tendency to elide the practical nature of distress and seize on the smallest

29. See Dr. Robert S. Mendelsohn, *Confessions of a Medical Heretic* (Chicago: Contemporary Books, 1979).

30. For a description of this phenomenon, see Malcolm Bush, "The Public and Private Purposes of Case Records," *Children and Youth Services Review* 6, no. 1 (1984), 1–18.

clues of psychological determinants as explanations. At their worst they leave open the possibility of the client's decline into severe states of psychological incapacity but offer virtually no supporting evidence. Erving Goffman in his essay "The Moral Career of the Mental Patient" suggests some reasons for this tendency when the clients are the institutionalized mentally ill:

> However, since he [the patient] will be held against his will in the hospital, his next-of-kin and the hospital staff will be in great need of a rationale for the hardships they are sponsoring. The medical elements of the staff will also need evidence that they are still in the trade they were trained for. These problems are eased, no doubt unintentionally, by the case history construction that is placed on the patient's past life, this having the effect of demonstrating all along he had been becoming sick, that he finally became very sick, and that if he had not been hospitalized much worse things would have happened to him.[31]

Another way in which social work's particular use of psychological explanation distracts from the analysis of a situation is what might be called the "myth of intimacy." Most of the social work texts we have described emphasize the importance of the relationship between the client and the social worker. For most texts that relationship is the central strategy. So Perlman writes:

> The casework process, like every other process intended to promote growth, must use relationship as its basic means. The labors of body and mind involved in problem solving may feel less arduous when they take place within the warmth and security of a strong relationship.[32]

Moreover, the relationship, which is such a central part of the helping strategy, is charged with emotion and intimacy. Those feelings are essential because they begin to change the client:

> As the client tells of himself and his feelings, he gives over or deposits something of himself in the caseworker; as he feels at one with the caseworker's responses, he begins to take back into himself some of the caseworker's attitudes, qualities and val-

---

31. Erving Goffman, *Asylums: Essays on the Social Situation of Mental Patients and Other Essays* (Garden City, N.Y.: Anchor Books, 1961), 145.
32. Perlman, *Social Casework*, 65.

ues. . . . Thus a client may be nourished and fortified by his feeling of union with his caseworker that not only has augmented his sense of wholeness but also may considerably alter his inner reactions and overt behavior.[33]

The epistemological status of statements like this is unclear. But our main concern is the influence they have on the definition of a client's problem and the construction of solutions that sustain clients in their own environments. The evidence indicates that these relationships are one-sided; the client opens up while the social worker prods, explores, or in pseudo-technical language "facilitates." The roles are never reversed. The act of casework, therefore, creates an artificial intimacy in which one participant's private life is revealed in order to be interpreted by the other higher status person acting under bureaucratic, professional, and legislative constraints.

One effect of this relationship is that definitions of problems and suggestions for treatments will be oriented to social work rather than to the client. They will reflect the constraints and opportunities under which the social worker is operating more than those affecting the client. They will, therefore, tend to be blind to the possibilities and limitations of help centered on the client's context as opposed to help that can be delivered from the official institutions of helping. Institutional restraints are not the only phenomenon responsible for this bias. It is a commonplace of social psychology that when the subjects and observers of behavior make attributions about the cause of the behavior, the subjects tend to attribute the behavior to situational influences and the observers to personality variables. The practical dominance of the caseworker in a situation where the client's behavior is the reason for the interaction ensures the dominance of the observer's (the personality) explanation over the client's (the situational) explanation.

The concentration on the relationship as a cure, together with the concentration on the interpersonal as a cause, reduces the possibility of either situational or combined situational and personal explanations. The complexities of interpersonal etiologies of distress require an attention that takes time and energy

33. Ibid., 73.

away from strategies for helping. Anecdotal and systematic evidence describes the considerable degree to which poor clients are turned off by the concentration on relationships and feeling, and this distaste reduces the possibility of their cooperation even when that cooperation is a necessary condition for effective help.

One aspect of the myth of intimacy guards it from critical analysis. The emphasis on relationships, which carries with it the assumption that the social worker cares for the client, makes hard-headed criticism of the caseworker process difficult. The declaration of care and sympathy for clients in trouble is justification for the intrusion into the private parts of a client's life. The good intentions subdue the necessity to demonstrate the efficacy of the strategy.[34]

The last way in which some elements of social work theory and practice reduce the possibility of family maintenance can be described as the denial of politics and the clientage of the citizen. Social workers have often been involved in political action on behalf of their clients. Often the target of the action has been reform that would increase the capacity of families to cope on their own. Settlement house workers supported mothers' pension acts, and a few leading social workers were crucial figures in the establishment of the Children's Bureau, which fought hard for the inclusion of the Aid to Dependent Children provisions in the 1935 Social Security Act. Social work groups throughout the country organized against the social service cuts of the Reagan Administration. In Illinois a coalition representing agencies with different internal agendas agreed to concentrate their efforts on preventing cuts to day care programs—a decision that testified to their commitment to the priority of family maintenance.[35]

But there has always been a line of thought in the profession that goes in the opposite direction—that argues the problem of social welfare in a way that depoliticizes political issues and ig-

34. For an elaboration of this argument, see John McKnight's essay, "Professionalized Service and Disabling Professions," in *Disabling Professions*, ed. John McKnight et al. (London: Marion Boyers, 1978), 69–91.

35. The coalition was named ICARE, the Illinois Coalition against Reagan Economics.

nores opportunities for changing the social context to allow families to cope on their own. This denial of the appropriate place of politics is most obvious in the omission of reference to the political realm in the social work texts we have described. It is also seen in attempts to reduce politics—in particular the legitimate debate over the distribution of resources—to a matter of technique. This reductionism is most apparent in some forms of behavioral writing where social and economic contexts are redescribed as contingencies that shape behavior and that can themselves be modified by behavioral techniques. In the Schwartz and Goldiamond text the political context is effectively denied in the very passage in which it is apparently asserted.

> We are not advocating blind adherence to the status quo, nor is it always advisable to help people "adapt" to the social system. Moreover, if a social system is lacking or deficient in any way, and nearly all social systems evidence some deficits, then the operant approach lends itself well to work toward changing that system, as well as toward helping the client with his individual problem.[36]

When political processes are reduced to putting systems right, the legitimate clash of interest among competing groups is ignored, as is the particular distribution of political power that maintains the ascendency of some of those groups.

This criticism is about a blindness to the politics of groups. Another political issue is the place of an individual in his or her society, or the politics of citizenship. The premise of our argument is that some aspects of the role of client and citizen are contradictory—that in some ways the more a person is a client, the less he or she is a citizen. The most obvious way in which this premise is true has to do with control over the possibilities of one's behavior. An inmate of a mental hospital has fewer options than a person living outside the walls of such an institution. There is a similar disparity in the distribution of resources. Persons regarded as normal are likely to have greater access to the resources that will maintain that status than people who have been defined as being outside that range. This relationship is true, for example, of people's access to jobs.

36. Schwartz and Goldiamond, *Social Casework*, 2.

Some social work writing emphasizes the clienthood of people in trouble to a degree that may well reduce the priority given to maintaining their citizenship. Indeed in some accounts the recognition of clienthood is a condition of receiving help. The difference between an extreme condition of clienthood and citizenship is not merely external to the person. It also affects people's view of themselves and, consequently, their capacity for extracting from their context what they need to sustain themselves.

The social work profession, which is aware of this problem, has argued the possibility of the coexistence of self-determination with professional help. The philosophical thinness of that argument has been systematically exposed. The case for the incompatibility of the imposition of others' ideas on a person and that person's freedom has been stated most forcibly in relation to a different set of problems. Writing about the idea of ideology and the end of ideology, Alisdair MacIntyre put the case this way:

> But what are rational goals for those within the consensus [in our case, expert social work knowledge] to lay down, explicitly or implicitly, for those outside the consensus are not rational goals for those outside the consensus to lay down for themselves, if only because of the force of that always to be remembered truism that not only in the end, but even in the relatively short run, nobody can know what an agent wants better than the man himself. Every restriction upon the right of men to speak for themselves in this respect involves either some unjustified claim that others can know better than they what they want, or some claim that their wants are irrelevant, perhaps because what they want is not good for them.[37]

The problem here is not the fact that social benefits and restrictions have to be decided upon by people other than, or in addition to, the clients but the claim that such actions are perfectly compatible with self-determination. The goal of maximizing the possibilities for citizenship would be better served by a recognition of the legitimacy of some coercive acts and of the possibility of unintended coercion in professional acts of helping.

37. Alasdair MacIntyre, "The End of Ideology and the End of the End of Ideology," in *Against the Self-Images of the Age: Essays on Ideology and Politics* (Notre Dame, Ind.: University of Notre Dame Press, 1978), 9–10.

Conclusion

According to this chapter's analysis, the mainstream of social work theory is debilitating, not sustaining, from the client's perspective. The question that remains is whether in the future the profession's theorists will be able to recognize the fullness of the world its clients inhabit. Without that broadness of vision the child in trouble will be the delinquency petition or the episode of running away, and the child's parents will be the instances of neglect and the occasions when they could not cope. Moreover, the prime solution offered to those infirmities will be "casework," an ill-defined concept embedded in confused fragments of psychoanalytic thought that prompts the obvious but unanswered question: "case of what?"[38]

Several characteristics of the profession suggest the pessimistic response that this characteristic of social work will be hard to change. One reason for pessimism is the eagerness with which other groups in contemporary society have embraced psychological goals. Psychological social work is part of a critical cultural change that has taken our attention away from the condition of groups of people to the condition of the individual psyche. This change has consequences for the relationship between helpers and the helped. This notion is developed in Philip Rieff's *The Triumph of the Therapeutic*. Rieff argues that the conscious and unconscious predicates that tie the nondistressed to the distressed and that fashion the nature of the responsibility of the latter to the former have been eroded. The dissolution of Christianity as a unitary system of belief in the Western world opened the door to the spread of the therapeutic ideal—an ideal that had as its highest good the manipulation of the *individual's* sense of well-being.[39] For our purposes, the critical difference between the two systems is that the former contains a moral demand system that protected communal purposes from the impulses of individuality and autonomy. The latter system frees the individual from those controls and

---

38. For the original use of this remark, see Barbara Wootten, *Social Science and Social Pathology* (London: Allen and Unwin, 1959), 290.

39. Philip Rieff, *The Triumph of the Therapeutic: Uses of Faith After Freud* (New York: Harper Torchbooks, 1968).

speaks instead in the language of releases from constraint so that the individual has nothing more at stake than the achievement of "well-being." Such an ethic can have disastrous consequences for the internal life of a distressed community and for the relationship between that community and more fortunate communities.

Another reason for pessimism is the particular way in which the profession has embraced science. From its earliest days the profession has been uneasy about its status and has sought to bolster its image through the trappings of "scientific" methodology.[40] The rise of the profession coincided with the burst of energy in first pre-Freudian and later Freudian psychiatry, and the profession clung to those rising stars in order to share their insights and prestige. Changing the psyche was a grand task, and while the elaboration of theories past their practical benefit would not help families in trouble, it would allow social workers to hold up their heads in the professional meeting and the academic seminar.

But the recognition that the troubled family inhabits a context that is relevant to its problems suggest the possibility that the solution involves some humble tasks and some political tasks. This possibility is at odds with professional status. Professional training is not necessary for humble tasks, and it is inappropriate for professionals to engage in political tasks. When highly trained social workers are confronted with humble tasks, they sometimes avoid them and sometimes dress them up to become professional tasks. The social service agency for the elderly that insists on psychosocial assessments for people requesting a home meal service has taken the latter course. One theory we described, task-centered social work, faced the dilemma and embraced the importance of humble work. But precisely because it did that it could not become the vehicle for transforming the profession's view of its role.

The social work profession has recently found an additional way to embrace "science" by attempting to measure the outcomes of social work action and by teaching social workers some of the tools of social science methodologies. This change

40. See Roy Lubove, *The Professional Altruist*.

has had the salutary consequence of forcing social workers to enumerate specific actions and their effect on specific outcomes. But the effort to evaluate the profession's techniques has produced comparatively few positive results. The hope remains that refinements in research methods will produce refinements in social work technique.

This hope is in some ways delusionary for reasons we have already rehearsed in relation to the psychological aspects of social work. It is certainly possible to compare techniques for teaching an autistic child to learn such tasks as dressing himself or taking care of his body. But the task of helping a sixteen-year-old to an honorable independence when her family cannot help her and when her neighborhood is dangerous is a task of a very different kind. It can be broken down into more discrete tasks, but it cannot be separated from the profound effects of an inhospitable and *changing* environment. Here the task is not the identification of independent and dependent variables and their relationship, while all else is conveniently held constant, but the acceptance of the dialectical forces that constantly shape and reshape the situation. "Holding all other things equal" is another expression for ignoring the environment. The person in the environment is the situation, and the separation of one from the other for the purpose of research is a denial of the situation.

While contemporary social work claims to study the individual in the environment, its clinical practitioners are taught a method of research that makes that broader aim impossible. The method, called "single subject design," consists of the therapist choosing a client behavior to modify and then monitoring the incidence of that behavior before, during, and after therapy. The method has serious flaws as a theory-testing research technique, but more importantly, it refutes the claim that social work is interested in the situated person. Not only does the method exclude all but one aspect of the client, it is unable to comprehend any relationship between that single client behavior and the context in which that behavior is performed.

Another problem with the more recent attempt at science is connected with the scientist's discomfort with politics. Any group of people, including people in trouble, can choose to reshape their situation while recognizing that they will still be limited by what their situation denies them. But changes that improve their condition will not come from the disembodied examination of single elements of the situation. They will come from grappling with all the relevant and interacting parts of their environment. This process is not research but praxis— meaningful or purposeful action. If social work researchers wish to help, they must first become situated and then involved in the actual complexities of overcoming the limiting characteristics of their fellow citizens' environment.

The usual response to suggestions of this kind is that by becoming involved researchers will lose their objectivity. But by not becoming at least situated they will never get to see the object they are studying. Moreover, since social welfare decisions are finally political, the refusal to become situated has the unintended consequence of situating the researcher in the group that is not being studied, a group that has economic and political interests different from "clients."

In this chapter we have discussed the context that social work theory provides to people who help troubled families. The theory will not determine each action of every social worker, but it is bound to influence the way in which social workers see problems and solutions. Many social workers are, of course, engaged in both humble tasks and tasks that involve such skills as negotiating with organizations and complex regulations on behalf of their clients. They are, however, less likely to concentrate on their clients' situation or regard their clients as fellow and equal citizens as long as social work theory denigrates both possibilities.

9

Organizations, Clients, and Citizenship

Organizations

This book has described how organizations respond to need. We have also examined the relationship between citizenship, civic action, and need. In this chapter we will pull together some of these other themes. But first we should conclude our examination of organizations.

Public and private organizations. The terms *public* and *private* are crucial ideas. They rank in importance with the term *social* for describing the arenas that are important to each of us. The opportunities and restrictions they present are part of the web of everyone's life. The terms *public* and *private* are also important parts of the way social welfare organizations perceive themselves. These organizational designations have practical consequences and create choices for legislatures and policy makers. The existence of two kinds of organization in the social welfare enterprise is the basis of a complicated set of relationships that is interesting in its own right.

Much more can be said about public and private organizations. For example, we could consider the effects of political patronage, civil service procedures, and union agreements on the work of the public sector. Sometimes these phenomena may make the public sector less "public"—that is, they diminish the attention paid to the *res publica*. We have not examined the third sector in social welfare—private for-profit organizations. They are not immune from some of the constraints public and not-for-profit organizations face, and they have the added constraint of providing a return on their owners' investments. The turbulent history of for-profit nursing homes and the less visible condition of for-profit day care centers suggest that the profit motive in social welfare makes it harder, not easier, to create organizations that sustain poor clients.[1]

But this book argues that the designation of an organization as public or private, its relation to government, and its sources of funding are not the critical variables in determining how effectively it responds to people in trouble. There is an important caveat: the survival of a variety of organizations that are different from each other on a range of characteristics is important, both as a source of variation for the definition of problems and for variation in strategies for attacking problems. Variation aside, the organizational characteristics "public" and "private" do not seem to relate to the issues of maintaining the citizenship of people in trouble.

One reason for this lack of connection is the variation that exists under the two labels. A public organization can be a large service agency, operating under its own complex regulations. There may be little effective appeal against agency decisions, and the agency's street-level bureaucrats may be dismissive of their clients. By contrast, the latest variation in public organization is the tenant-managed public housing development, where duly elected tenants collect the rent, pay the bills, screen prospective residents, and maintain the property. All this is done under the umbrella of local and federal legislation and regulations, and is funded out of tax dollars. By the criteria we have

---

1. The tribulations of for-profit nursing homes are well known. The differences between for-profit and not-for-profit day care centers are not so well publicized. A nationwide study by ABT Associates indicates that proprietary day care centers spend about 30 percent less per child than do nonprofit operations. They maintain lower caregiver–child ratios; they utilize fewer noncaregivers; they pay lower wage rates; and they provide supplemental services with far less frequency. Richard Ruopp, Jeffrey Travers, Frederic Glantz, and Craig Coelen, *Children at the Center* (Cambridge, Mass.: Abt Books, 1979), 133.

developed, a world of difference exists between these two organizations, both of which operate under the rubric "public."

Similar variations exist in the private sector. On the one hand, a few large private agencies possess endowments and enjoy large-scale support from local United Ways. Some of these agencies reacted to the growth of federal and state involvement in social welfare by moving away from street-level work and by developing a reputation for setting the tone in the field of therapy and family counseling. They may have as many middle-class as poor clients; their boards of trustees may live in the wealthier suburbs and rely on their staff's descriptions for their image of the world of the poor. Here, at its worst, the privateness of the agency provides the comforts of a "private life" for its staff—a life free from the pressures of public need.

On the other hand, there is the newer private social welfare agency, which is partly funded by a township that helped to develop a publicly determined agenda for the organization. On the agency's staff are former clients and parents of current clients, who interpret that publicly determined agenda according to their first-hand knowledge of the lives of the people in trouble.

This analysis of the terms *public* and *private* is not meant to suggest that the terms lack real descriptive meaning. There are important differences between the large state child welfare department and the small private agency. But the demands of sustaining troubled families do not fit neatly into that dichotomy. The energy spent on the public–private debate may be better spent elsewhere.

But if the critical traits of social service organizations are not whether they are public or private (and this subsumes the issues of financing, jurisdiction, and auspices), what is critical? In broad terms the critical issue is the relationship between the helping organizations and families in trouble, not the relationship between the organizations and the government. The heart of the matter is the status of the person in trouble and the ways the helping organizations affect that status. There are some legitimate conflicts between the demands of troubled families and relief delivered by helping organizations. What is not legitimate is the resolution of those differences through the objectification of the person in trouble. When this happens, the organization is the acting subject and the person in trouble the object of its attention. The person then becomes decontextualized—abstracted from his or her own context—and becomes an object in the context of the organization's world.

We have described some examples of this process. One instance is the tension between delivering help to the family (the family maintenance services) and offering help away from the family (placement services). The process is exemplified in the distance between the world of the helpers and the world of the helped, and in the difficulty helpers have entering the world of troubled families. Decontextualization is also present in the management reforms that attempt to make sense out of diversity and incomprehensibility by information systems that oversimplify clients' lives. In this process the relevant heterogeneity of particular situations is homogenized by the construction of a few simple categories of need, interventions, and outcomes.

Several reform strategies are a staple of the debate about "responsiveness." In this context *responsiveness* means the process of the subjects seeing the objects more clearly. But the objects are still objects. Since the reforms are rooted in the world of organizations rather than in the nature of the connection between the world of organizations and the world of families, they miss the point.

The first strategy is that of decentralization. Large social welfare bureaucracies gain their understanding of the local and familial contexts of their clients from the lowliest of their workers and from the most decentralized of their units. The reform argument is that in a decentralized bureaucracy decision makers will be closer to the actual world of their clients and will, therefore, make better decisions. But decentralized organizations can be just as bound up in organizational and professional analyses of problems as centralized organizations, and in spirit they can be just as far away from their clients. Moreover, the arguments for maintaining centralized structures are as pressing as the organizational arguments in the other direction. In the words of one sociologist, "a dialectical tension exists in social service delivery systems between advocates of a strongly centralized structure and advocates of a strongly decentralized structure."[2] Too much local discretion produces inequity, waste, lack of coordination, and concealment from public accountability. Too much central authority produces unresponsiveness. So the capacity of a large organization to decentralize authority will be circumscribed by pressures in the opposite direction.

The second reform strategy argues that the problem of representing people in trouble to unresponsive centralized bureaucracies can be accomplished by another set of organizations called "mediating institutions."[3] According to this argument, mediating institutions include such diverse organizations as churches, voluntary associations, and the media and trade unions. The notion is that these collectivities can mediate between the private lives of citizens and the public realm, thus "reducing both economic precariousness of individual existence in isolation from society and the threat of alienation to the public order."[4]

We will make the argument later that some variety of these institutions can enlarge the possibilities of relevant and nonintrusive helping. But the claims made for mediating institutions raise serious questions. The first problem is whether mediating institutions really are Janus-like—whether they have acuity of vision in both directions. Perhaps the more attuned they are to the world of the large bureaucracies and aggregated public and private power, the more blind they are to the private worlds of families. By the same token, if they are habituated to those private worlds, they may be lost in the public realm.

Another problem is whether the most distressed are represented by mediating institutions at all. In fact the destitution of the most distressed is often accompanied by, or caused by, isolation from such groups. Deviants from any social class are likely to be suspect in the voluntary associations of the nondeviant.

The argument also has a more fundamental flaw. If there is

2. Howard Aldrich, "Centralization versus Decentralization in the Design of Human Service Delivery Systems: A Response to Gouldner's Lament," in *The Management of Human Services*, ed. Rosemary Sarri and Yeshekel Hasenfeld (New York: Columbia University Press, 1978), 51.

3. For an explication of the role of mediating institutions, see Peter L. Berger and Richard John Neuhaus, *To Empower People: The Role of Mediating Structures in Public Policy* (Washington, D.C.: American Enterprise Institute for Public Policy Research, 1977).

4. Ibid., 3.

need for mediation between the citizen and unresponsive units of government (or government-funded social welfare organizations), the fault may lie not in the absence of connecting links but in the need for those links. The problem may be the distribution of authority that makes those links necessary in the first place. The key to bringing the vital facts of the condition of the distressed to those in authority is to move some of that authority to a place where those conditions are visible. (The tenant-managed housing development is an example of such a solution.) Thus the issue is not about communication, representation, or decentralization but access to resources and power. Paying attention to the local without transferring power is an incomplete solution. As one critic of the theory of mediating institutions commented:

> But to become the vehicle for social identification, local initiative must be given a substantial political content. This remains the blind spot of conservatives who celebrate the vitality of churches, kinship networks and voluntary associations. The capacity of such groups to resist encroaching power on the modern scale [in our terms objectification] is severely limited. They can flourish only under a benign sovereign.[5]

This analysis does not preclude the construction of organizations that guard against the objectification of the people they try to help. But the key to these organizations is not their capacity to represent clients to aggregated power. They are different by virtue of their relationship to the people in trouble. Scattered throughout the book are references to the characteristics of such organizations. We can now bring these references together in a description of existing organizations that sustain their clients and avoid some of the unintended negative consequences of organized helping.

Responsive organizations.   What follows is a description of an ideal type of organization—ideal in the sociological sense of having a heuristic purpose. Not all the organizations we will describe have all the characteristics in the construction.

5. Andrew J. Polsky, "Welfare Policy: Why the Past Has No Future," *Urban Prospects*, 1982.

Indeed some of them have characteristics that might be maladaptive outside their particular context. This fact should not be surprising. If an agency fits into this category, it is because the agency is sensitive to local contexts. An organization that is suited to one particular context might not be so effective in a different context. As a result such organizations cannot be imposed on a community by a centralized public helping system. They either have to spring from a community (a context) or be developed by people who are sensitive to the characteristics of that community.

This sensitivity or awareness is the first characteristic of such organizations, and it comes from geographical and temporal proximity. The settlement house is one model, but there are plenty of other organizations that develop such an awareness. The awareness springs from a view of all the relevant problems in a community, the pressures under which people organize their lives, and the possibilities the people and the community possess. This awareness of the totality of the lives of the distressed discourages caricature and premature classification. There is one important variation on geographical proximity. Some organizations deliberately reject responsibility for a particular problem. They assert instead responsibility based on all the relevant problems and opportunities in a particular area. As a report on youth serving agencies in San Diego put it:

> The youth serving agencies maintain strong ties to geographic communities. Because of this community focus, the agencies see their responsibility for youth as extending beyond any one categorical group. They tend to consider the needs of youth in the social and economic context of their families, their neighborhoods, and other institutions with which the youth interact.[6]

This assertion of broad responsibility leads to the second characteristic of these organizations—the development of broad, flexible, nondogmatic definitions of the problems they address.

6. Frank Farrow and Sally Diamond, "Draft Report on Social Welfare Organizations in San Diego County, California, for the Study on the Changing Role of Voluntary Organizations in the Provision of Social Services," Center for the Study of Social Policy, University of Chicago and Washington, D.C., January 1982, 2.

The lens they use is wider than the lens of a particular profession or therapeutic approach. Relevant skills are still represented on their staffs, but no single theory of human behavior or remediation is dominant. One way agencies accomplish this broadening is by expanding the group of people who shape the agencies' work. The rule at Aunt Martha's was: "In everything we do we involve young people in every stage of the planning. That is what makes us suspect with the young professionals."[7]

Two corollaries of this resistance to a particular view of distress are that such agencies are concerned less with the etiology of a problem than with the current condition of their clients, and they are not bewildered by clients who in professional terms come from "multiproblem families." Multiproblem families create havoc with simple models of cause and single-stranded interventions. They cause fewer problems in agencies where staff are willing to meet any condition that requires attention without first constructing a formal theory of either the condition or the attention. This catholicity allows a mixture of the granting of sustenance, opportunity, and attempts to reduce maladaptive behavior without insisting a priori on the supremacy of any one of those strategies.

An example of such an approach from contemporary Brazil resembles some of the tactics Charles Loring Brace used in New York City in the 1870s. Between 3 and 20 million Brazilian children have been abandoned—"orphans of living parents." A good portion of these children survive by petty and not so petty crime.[8] In the town of Ipameri, 140 miles south of Brasilia, a community organization brought together guilds of shoeshine boys, office boys, gardeners, and popsicle vendors out of children who would otherwise have joined street gangs. The organization provided their parents with discount food to help keep the families together, and on Sundays and early weekday mornings organizers gave lectures to the participants on topics like

7. Interview with Cathy Miner, Aunt Martha's, Forest Park, Ill., 13 August 1980.
8. For estimates of the number of homeless children in Brazil, see Warren Hoge, "Brazil's Waifs Find Town That Cares," *New York Times,* 23 September 1983, 6. A dramatization of the plight of Brazil's homeless chidren can be seen in Hector Babenco's film, *Pixote,* which was reviewed by Pauline Kael in the *New Yorker* Magazine, 9 November 1981, 170–77.

tolerance, forgivenesss, rights and duties, work, and solidarity. Participation in the program, which paid a minimum wage of $45 a month, depended on decent behavior and school attendance.[9] Here is an unself-conscious mix of practical helping, training, and family sustenance with the mix dictated, not by an overarching theory, but by the very particular facts of the local situation.

A third characteristic of organizations that seem capable of sustaining is the sometimes tacit, and sometimes explicit, insistence on capacity. One aspect of this characteristic is an insistence on moving a client toward independence wherever that is appropriate. Another aspect is the insistence that the children of troubled families have talents and should have opportunities beyond those that lead to a bare competence.

The Better Boys Foundation, located in one of Chicago's worst slums, was originally called Archie Moore's Gym, reflecting what an earlier generation thought was needed to move a young person to independence.[10] Now the emphasis is on after-school tutorials and a social development program that teaches basic skills. But the Better Boys Foundation also developed a program in the cultural arts—theater, painting, and dancing. A private school for poor black boys, many of whom had dropped out of the public schools in Chicago, takes a similar approach. After first teaching the boys that bringing guns and knives to school is not acceptable behavior, the vicar of the Anglican Choir School of Saint Gregory coaxes them through the Episcopal Liturgy.[11] Equal attention is paid to schoolwork, but the notion is that the distressed have the same capacities as those who grow up accustomed to a variety of opportunities. There is also the historic example of the Bolshoi Ballet, which started in 1773 as the dancing school of the Moscow Orphanage.

Belief in the capacity of the apparently downtrodden may seem quixotic in paradigms that emphasize the incapacity of the

9. Warren Hoge, "Brazil's Waifs."

10. See Harold Goldman, "Reforming Youth Services in Illinois in the 1980's: Governor James Thompson's Special Task Force on Troubled Adolescents" (Ph.D. diss., School of Social Service Administration, University of Chicago, 1982), 135.

11. Adrian Ayres, "A Hopeful Noise," *Reader* (Chicago's Free Weekly), 18 November 1983, sec. 1, pp. 8–39.

distressed. But insistence on the capacity of those who are in some respects disabled stops the drift toward defining them totally in terms of clienthood and puts them back in the world of citizens.

Insistence on capacity need not be restricted to those who are able to achieve full independence. For those who primarily need sustenance, the relevant capacity is the ability to benefit from living in a community—the opposite of community is being sent into exile. A person in an institution (or on the streets) is exiled from the world of familiars and from the world of people, where there are some bonds of reciprocity, mutual responsibility, and sympathy. Some communities for the severely disabled avoid those characteristics of exile by emphasizing the connections between staff and clients. In the small village of Trosly in the Compiègne forest in France, mentally disabled young men live in several village houses. They are cared for by a mixture of short-term and long-term staff, who have the common characteristic that they share at least part of their normal lives (eating, working, playing, attending religious services) with the young men.[12] The emphasis is on not just the personhood of the disabled but the relevance of the normal lives of the nondisabled to the disabled and vice versa. The nondisabled bring to the disabled a contact with a larger world and capacities that the disabled lack. The disabled bring to the nondisabled a sense of humility that comes from the recognition that people who are outcasts by the standards of mainstream society have a strong capacity for delight in simple things: compassion, affection, and the sympathetic perception of the condition of other people's lives. The humility is accompanied by a reaffirmation of those values.

The emphasis on capacity is itself an element of citizenship. The citizenship of both the able and the less able in this kind of community relies on a respect for maximizing autonomy. It also relies on a sense of the underlying equality of the helpers and the helped based on a recognition of both the capacities of the

12. The organization responsible for the mentally disabled at Trosly is called the Ark or L'Arche, and was founded by the Canadian Jean Vanier. It is described in Bill Clarke, *Enough Room for Joy: Jean Vanier's L'Arche. A Message for Our Time* (Toronto: McClelland and Stewart, 1974).

helped and the limitations of the helpers. This equality also depends on the recognition that the helpers can derive some sustenance from the company of the helped. Thus there is a sense of mutuality—the common fact that both sets of people face the realities of the human condition and count on interdependence to live with those realities.[13]

Community is also vital for those clients who are being helped to move to independent adulthood. The program at Ipameri refused to feed the boys lunch, thereby motivating them to return home to have lunch with their families. Aunt Martha's had parents on its staff and encouraged youth to sort out their problems with their parents. The organizers of the program in Trosly encouraged the young people's forays out and the neighbors' forays into the residences. This emphasis on community reflects the belief that the organized programs of helping cannot be sufficient sustenance for young people: poor families, inadequate families, and external associations remain vital to sustenance.

What makes these characteristics possible is in formal terms bureaucratic flexibility and, less formally, a tolerance for untidiness. This flexibility allows organizations to perceive and respond to the untidiness in the clients' lives. At St. Gregory's such tolerance sprang from the perception that the boys had been subject to a good deal of the wrong kind of control—control aimed merely at preventing them being a nuisance to other people—and that they needed space and time in between the formal lessons to express themselves in any nonharmful way they chose. In this case the opportunity for self-expression reaffirms their citizenship: one of the deprivations of extreme clienthood is the insistence that clients behave at all times of the day in the precise manner the helping organizations consider appropriate.

At L'Arche, the French program for mentally disabled young men, the flexibility emerged in several ways. Most important was the understanding that the men possessed a variety of possibilities and limitations. Some men would live and work outside

---

13. I am indebted to Stanley Hallett for his assessment of the four elements of citizenship: sharing knowledge, respecting autonomy, restoring equality, and accepting mutuality.

the sheltered homes, while others might spend their lives inside them. The increasing capacities of one person and the declining capacities of another were each greeted with encouragement and sympathy. In comparison with systems for the mentally handicapped that diagnose, prescribe, and predict according to formal systems, this tolerance for untidiness, and indeed for ambiguity, allowed the facts that did not fit a particular diagnosis to emerge, collide with the diagnosis, and assert themselves.

There was a parallel tolerance at L'Arche for allowing the men the opportunity to take part in the daily work of the place, no matter that the work might consequently be slowed down or diverted. Work allowed some of them to move closer to independence, but just as important it established the position of all of them as part of the active fabric of the community. By contrast, inmates of the old back wards of mental hospitals were only acted upon.

These various forms of flexibility were themselves made possible by the organizations' reliance on a broad array of volunteers. The task of helping clients as individual actors and of encouraging their capacities is enormously time consuming. In most organizations it is beyond the scope of a paid, professional staff. In the organizations described here the connection between helper and helped varied according to the clients' situation, the organization, and the community (physical or otherwise) in which both were set. At Aunt Martha's the community of helpers consisted of relatives of clients and former clients themselves. In a scheme sponsored by the Catholic Archdiocese of Chicago, where staff organized volunteers in twenty-two parishes to provide clothing, food, babysitting, and counseling to those who needed it, the community was both geographical and religious.[14] At L'Arche the community was originally a community of strangers. At a Ford Foundation project in Harlem, where experienced mothers taught and encouraged new mothers, community was a group of neighbors with the competence to help those with fewer skills and less experience.[15] These dif-

---

14. Interview with Rev. Roger Coughlin, Catholic Charities of Chicago, 2 August 1979.

15. This story was reported in the *New York Times*, 29 November 1983, sec. 1, pp. 1 and 36.

ferences reflect different motivations. For the organizations, the differences in motivations are probably not very important. Their task is to tap whatever connections and motivations exist to accomplish their work.

This brief conclusion about organizations has touched on some of the other themes of the book. But these themes are important enough to be looked at in their own right, not just through the lens of organizations. This tactic is also a conclusion. Many social service organizations owe their origins to concerns about needy people who had no place or person to turn to. But social service organizations are still only part of the dialectic between need and response. We turn now to the other parts of the puzzle.

Citizenship

In the introduction we pointed to the maintenance of citizenship as an element of the dialectic between need and response. We can now reexamine the dichotomy between citizenship and clienthood. Citizens and clients are under different obligations. Citizens have the responsibility to maintain their independence by using the opportunities provided by the market and government action. Clients are obliged to accept the conditions of a particular service or service system so that *later* they can become citizens. Sometimes the service enhances their chances of citizenship, sometimes it has no effect, and sometimes it diminishes their capacities.

Help can disable for a variety of reasons. When the condition of service is separation from family and friends, the service can exacerbate the problem it was designed to relieve. Some families do fail to sustain their children. But the task of sustenance becomes more difficult when children are removed from contact with parents, who whatever their inadequacies, still have something to offer their families.

The acceptance of service often results in a loss of power and a sense of impotence. Parents who lose custody of their children find themselves unable to influence the decisions made about their children and are discouraged from taking even minor responsibility for their lives. Children who are moved in and out of surrogate placements soon realize that they can always be moved again and that no single adult will maintain responsibility for their care.

No organization, either public or private, possesses the qualities required of adequate parents. The *parens patriae* power works only if the state can quickly restore the authority and responsibility of parenthood back to the natural parents, or when that fails, transfers them to long-term surrogate parents. Absent these outcomes, the state can be a custodian but not a parent. Children are sustained by the "illogical" affection of their parents—affection and regard that outsiders would not give to children, particularly when they misbehave or if, by various criteria, they are unattractive. The state can never provide that affection, and many surrogate parents cannot maintain it in the face of deviant behavior.

The assignment of the status "client" exposes people in trouble to a series of categorizations that, while necessary for organizational purposes, diminishes the richness of their lives. The analysis of categories of clients gives us useful insights into their "careers." But from the perspective of the client, any act of categorization is a procrustean bed. Vital characteristics are lopped off to make the category stick, and very often what is lopped off are capacities and strengths.

Even reforms instituted to improve the condition of client children can disable when they are viewed as total solutions, or when they obscure important variations among clients. The permanency movement, which focused attention on the disabling delays and indecisions in the child welfare system, does not help those older adolescents who are halfway to independence and no longer willing to accept another surrogate family. The child abuse legislation that laid down emergency action for cases of the worst physical abuse disables families where poverty and difficult conditions demand support and material help, not police action.

Service sometimes concentrates on means at the cost of ends. Then the measures of service replace the goal of citizenship. So attendance at counseling sessions becomes a substitute for achieving a normal childhood, and adjusting to the requirements of an institution becomes a substitute for attaining maturity.

One cause of these problems is that one generation's solutions are inappropriate for the next generation's conditions. The independence that the westward migration brought to the street urchins of New York depended on the expanding frontier and the demand for agricultural labor. When the frontier closed, the builders of child welfare institutions, concerned with the dangers of the city, placed many of them in the country. But while the farm offered the reality of independence, the rural institution was merely a symbol of independence. Country air and distance from the distractions of the city were puny measures in the absence of an expanding rural market for labor.

The history of the juvenile court is another example of a situation changing faster than reforms. The juvenile court, established to protect children from the harshness of the adult criminal court, so eroded children's rights that Gerald Gault received a maximum punishment of six years in an industrial school for admitting to dialing the telephone number for a call in which a friend made an obscene remark. The changes that followed the Supreme Court's opinion in *Gault*—that juveniles facing incarceration were entitled to due process—restored the appearance of protection to juvenile proceedings. But in large urban areas the change had the effect of denying justice by contributing to intolerable delays.

There are, however, counterstrategies that recognize the inevitability of such twists of fortune and help to limit the damage. The most important strategy is the reiteration of independence (and interdependence among citizens) as the goal of intervention.

Insisting on Independence

The goal of independence requires, first, the strategy of keeping people out of trouble wherever possible. For the families with whom we are concerned, this goal means pushing back the boundaries of poverty. A number of tactics would currently address this goal. Some are appropriate for families whose only problem is financial hardship. In 1985, the Legal Aid Society of New York filed a suit against New York City charging that the city had routinely placed hundreds of children in foster care because their parents were homeless or living in substandard housing.[16] By this act the city was subsidizing surrogate parents in an amount that, had it been paid to the natural parents, would probably have ended the emergency. Moreover, the moment the children left their parents' homes, the parents became ineligible for renovated apartments and other help that would have enabled them to get their children back. It is, of course, cheaper for a public department to subsidize the surrogate care of a few children than to subsidize the parents of all children who are homeless or who are living in substandard housing. It may also be easier to arrange for placement than to find housing for a family in a very tight housing market. But the failure to find creative and affordable solutions that help desperate families results in a policy that meets trouble with the strategy of dependence.

Problems of this kind can probably be resolved by imaginative redistribution of current service dollars. There are other ways in which the redistribution of current expenditures could push back the edges of poverty, but they will be much more difficult to achieve. They require changing the terms of the debate about help to poor families. They also mean admitting to the calculations items that are not always included in the discussions about poverty and assistance. One important issue is the gradual increase in expenditures for services at the expense of cash assistance or in-kind help. Another is the cutback in assistance to the working poor at the same time that tax expenditures (taxes not collected on account of tax deductions and credits) for the middle class have been protected. The costs of food stamps and health insurance for the unemployed are rarely discussed in the context of the $40 billion tax expenditures for home mortgage and property tax relief. Another issue, which is even harder to bring into the public debate, is the connection between poor physical environments and troubled families. This issue is partly a matter of expenditures—expenditures on the infrastructure of decaying neighborhoods and tax breaks for the rehabilitation of decaying housing. It is also a matter of the physical concentration or segregation of the poor in large cities and their consequent loss of the amenities (including jobs) that nonpoor neighborhoods enjoy.

16. See the account in the *New York Times*, 8 November 1985, p. 13.

Such large-scale issues admit no simple solutions. It is much easier to discuss the workings of foster care and adoption for children whose parents have reached the limits of their capacity to cope with trouble and hardship. But they are part of the conditions of troubled families and play a role in the events that lead from citizenship to clientage.

Once people enter a service system, the strategy for restoring independence is the provision of the most enabling alternative. This strategy has some success stories. Subsidized adoption for the handicapped enlarged the circle of dependent children who could regain the security of a permanent family. Changing attitudes about juveniles whose behavior was a nuisance rather than seriously delinquent restored some of them from detention centers to their natural families. Specialized foster care provided a home for children whose only alternative was an institution.

The disposition of delinquent children raises another issue—the dialectic between opportunity and responsibility. So far we have emphasized lack of opportunity, but responsibility is an equal part of our definition of citizenship. The key to a fruitful debate, however, is the simultaneous consideration of both sides of the equation. For example, attitudes toward single, teenage mothers have become the litmus test of attitudes to welfare, but the couching of that debate in terms of either assistance *or* self-reliance ignores the dialectic. There is no reason why support for programs for poor teenage males that discuss contraception, child support payments, and responsibility for children they father should not go hand in hand with an analysis of job opportunities in poor neighborhoods and job placement programs. Nor is there any reason why stressing to poor teenage girls the economic consequences of single parenthood should not be accompanied by programs for teenage mothers that give them the practical support they need to keep their children and stay in school.

The critical task is to avoid the simplification that comes from stereotypes of race, virtue, and deviance. Our discussion of the black teenage mothers who stayed in school at twice the rate of their white peers is an interesting lesson in the complexities of trouble and help. In the case of those black women, their own efforts, the sustenance offered to them by their mothers in

whose houses they lived, and the help of infant and child nurser-
ies in supportive public schools gave them a chance to get back
on the track to independence.

The problem of simplification is a problem of definition and
that leads to the next strategy for citizenship.

Redistributing the Power to Define

The key ingredient for definitions of trouble and the
help that maintains citizenship is that the troubled themselves
have a role in their construction. There are a number of reasons
for this conclusion. Trouble is very often not a single incident
but a collection of problems. Consequently, the label a needy
person is given is a result of a choice. The choice could often
have been different since it depends on a particular description
of the situation. No description of the context of need and response will be adequate if the experience and perspective of the
needy are absent. For example, the fact that an organization has
trouble coping with a child does not constitute a priori evidence
that the child is troubled and requires coercive interventions.
Proxies of need, help, and success are essential but are often
flawed. If official codes do not make sense to the people they
describe, they may be inauthentic. The use of one part of a
condition—single parenthood—or a blanket description—the
underclass—sheds darkness as well as light and encourages the
caricature that prevents informed action. In a stable society
power comes not out of the barrel of a gun but, among other
things, from participation in the construction of crucial definitions and categories.

There have been many scattered attempts to restore the clients' voice to the debate about the needy, although they are
described in different language by different people. Our suggestion is that they fit under the rubric of sustaining citizenship and
that they be seen as a necessary and constant part of the response to need, not just as exceptional reform efforts. The practice of opening case records to the people whose lives are described in them will curtail the worst distortions of inadequate
or one-sided descriptions. By giving clients a protected part in
the processes of monitoring and making judgments, citizen re-

view boards allow for a more critical examination of the official definitions of need and response. Advocacy, the representation of a client's case by other people, gives it enough stature to be heard. The latest attempt to secure fair representation in the juvenile court, Court Appointed Special Advocates, connects each child before the court with a trained volunteer whose job it is to concentrate on the child's interests.[17] It remains to be seen whether such volunteers can resist being coopted by the daily organizational demands of the court, but it is an honest attempt by citizens and the association of juvenile court judges to make up for the deficiencies in the court process.

At a different level, neighborhood dispute centers, where adolescents, their parents, and aggrieved citizens hammer out the details and the consequences of uncivil or even minor delinquent behavior, put the power and responsibility on the people with the most knowledge and the largest stake.

None of these examples suggests the overruling of official decisions when there is no other recourse. They suggest instead a readjustment of the balance between official definitions and citizens' definitions. Social workers who give wards of the state a choice between several substitute homes recognize the child's official status but allow the child some power of definition within that status. The aim here is not a large range of choices; that would be impracticable and might not improve the child's chances. But it gives children, at a minimum, a veto over prospective caretakers and, at best, the chance of finding a surrogate home where they sense they will be comfortable. A different kind of readjustment was attempted in Illinois when a group of legislators introduced a bill that would have added another category to the roster of juvenile court adjudications—no-fault dependency. The legislation was introduced by suburban Republicans on behalf of middle-class families who wanted official help with adolescent children, but who did not wish themselves to be categorized as inadequate, or to have their children labeled delinquent. This bill was a clear attempt to reshape the boundaries and the consequences of official definitions. It failed

17. See National Council of Juvenile and Family Court Judges, *Court Appointed Special Advocate: A Guide for Your Court* (n.p., National Council of Juvenile and Family Court Judges, n.d.).

because the state feared a rush of new demands for its already scarce services, but it is an example of formal ways of redistributing the power to define.

These issues of redefinition are part of a larger issue—adjusting the balance between organized helping and clients. The premise emerging from some of the issues analyzed in previous chapters is that the ordinary pressures faced by helping organizations every day are sometimes resolved by honorable people in ways that reduce the capacity and hence the citizenship of families in trouble. A number of strategies will serve as counterpressures.

One strategy is to open up more of the helping organizations' work to inspection. Public action should not be opaque, and private agencies should not employ their particular status to protect their privacy. We discussed some ways to achieve this goal in chapter 6. Openness to the concerns of clients is, however, not just a matter of inspection. It is also a matter of the balance of power. One of the thorniest examples is the place of union activity in human services. While it protects the legitimate interests of employees, at some point the creation of decent working conditions inhibits the energy and creativity needed to attend to the problems of people who live in indecent conditions. Some of what is good for the social worker will be good for the client and some will not.

Another strategy is the notion that even effective organizations should recognize the limits of their capacity to sustain. Specifically they should limit their protection when their actions are likely to reduce the confidence and capacity of their clients. Charles Loring Brace had a clear sense of this, perhaps because of his fear of pauperism. The protection of what Erving Goffman calls a "total institution" has this effect, and the protection of troubled teenagers against the demands of the job market or the rules of law will do the same. Marillac House, the settlement house described in chapter 3, had a program for mothers whose children had been adjudicated neglected or abused. The program was the women's last chance of keeping their children. The workers and other community mothers taught the women how to budget their welfare checks, how to shop effectively, and how to cook. It also negotiated with their landlords to get the heat turned on and the buildings cleaned up. At the same time, the program workers made it absolutely clear that if the mothers' behavior became a threat to their children's well-being, they would return the mothers to juvenile court and recommend that the children be placed in surrogate care.

Recognizing the limits of action is not the same as "being tough." It is instead a recognition of the reality of the world in which the distressed live—a world where eventually, no matter how bad their conditions, they are responsible for their actions. Marillac House was not preaching that its clients should adjust to their conditions. They were teaching their clients to survive in their conditions while at the same time making every effort to improve the worst features of their devastated neighborhood.

One of the disabling pressures we noted in our discussion of difficult children was the tendency to exaggerate the incidence of difficult behavior and to use difficult behavior as the touchstone for children who were not difficult. There is the parallel problem of determining the appropriate allocation of resources between the average and the most troubled children. There are many examples of difficult cases becoming the tail that wags the dog. The overclassification of nondifficult children and the diversion of resources from the care of the average client deny those children enabling help. One reason for this tendency is the relationship between "difficulty" and professional status. The segmentation of trouble into fine categories justifies specialist intervention. Professional stature increases as the incapacities professionals treat worsen. So the normal complexities of allocating scarce resources are exacerbated by the pressures of the guild.

The day care action council that fought the governor of Illinois on the extraordinary cuts made in day care grants demonstrated one counterpressure—political action on behalf of ordinary children. One director of the Department of Children and Family Services had a novel solution for the overlabeling of children. He suggested a limit to the number of children who could be classified as "dangerous." Once the state's allotment had been reached, no new name could be added to the list until a listed name was removed. The suggestion recognized the artificiality of such labels, the need to create counterpressures to the normal tendencies to expand the list, and the importance of dramatizing the problem.[18]

The last counterpressure is not a matter of bureaucratic practice but a matter of theory. It is the issue of putting psychology in its place. The rhetoric of contemporary social work theory suggests a continuum between psychological and situational accounts of distress. But in practice that continuum has turned into a dichotomy with psychology as the dominant partner. When psychological insights are the defining characteristic of a profession, the professsion will attract students amenable to those insights and produce graduates eager to use them. But the dominance of psychological theories has consequences that diminish citizenship. It reduces the emphasis on both responsibility and opportunity as treatment and cure become the critical terms.

This criticism does not deny the proven role of particular therapies in particular circumstances. But the use of a single theory to explain and treat diverse categories of distress, or the employment of an "eclectic" approach that does not specify the treatment of choice for a particular condition, is justified only by the predilections of the practitioners.

This point is not just an issue of the diagnosis of individuals. More importantly, this characteristic of social work drowns out the place of the social and the situation. The apparently value-neutral, scientific act of psychological diagnosis in social casework has heavy political consequences. It denies citizenship because it denies the situation. And this denial is built into the cognitive structures of the enterprise. Writing about the difficulties of psychologists analyzing social problems (in this case the government of Salvador Allende in Chile between 1970 and 1973), a social psychologist expressed it this way:

> The redefinition of a social problem in terms of the attribution of centrality to psychological variables usually implies a radical shift in the object of inquiry. Since the definition of the problem determines the research strategy, the selection of a social action

18. Personal communication, Jerome Miller, Director of the Illinois Department of Children and Family Services, 1973.

delivery system and the criteria for evaluation, a tendency to assign causal significance to person-centered variables produces a significant shift in understanding. If industrial productivity is studied as worker productivity; if political education is analyzed as attitude change; if ideology is understood in terms of motives; if alienation is defined in psychological terms, in all these cases the analysis of the social situation has been effectively displaced to a marginally explanatory role. Such an organization of research will not necessarily show the arbitrariness of the problem transformation. Verification methods don't have the power to alter the definition of the problem under study.[19]

This analysis suggests that the problem of psychological interpretation is much broader than the topic of social work or social welfare. It will not be answered by professional slogans.

Civic Action

In the introduction we suggested that civic action on behalf of the distressed had gradually been crowded out by the development of the helping bureaucracies and professions. Today civic action—at one time the mainstay of helping—is often reduced to money raising. This reduction of civic involvement is not justified by the success of professional helping, and as we have seen in isolated incidents, citizen action has a vital role.

The first issue is the definition of civic participation. In the introduction we defined it formally as the process of hammering out compromises between different interests by people directly affected. Via civic participation, judgments are made about public matters and responsibilities are assigned. We can now expand this definition in the light of the events we have described. Our definition will, however, be limited and provisional. There are several reasons for this caution. Changing circumstances and changing need will alter the shape and appearance of civic action. Civic participation is broader than this particular application to the world of the needy. And lastly, we must avoid the risk of

19. Ricardo B. Zuniga, "The Experimenting Society and Radical Social Reform: The Role of the Social Scientist in Chile's Unidad Popular Experience" (Paper delivered as the invited address at the 82nd Annual Convention of the American Psychological Association in New Orleans, 1 September 1974).

defining a utopia—a phenomenon aptly described as "a form of nostalgia for an imagined past projected on to the future as a wish."[20]

Civic action as source of legitimacy. We have described occasions when small groups of citizens challenged the dogmas of the helping bureaucracies. Civic groups raised the issue of racial discrimination at times when black children were excluded from the range of help available to white children. Civil rights activists also challenged the treatment of "difficult" children when they became lost to view. On a national scale, organizations like the Children's Defense Fund analyze national policy on a variety of topics for its effects on children.

These activities could be described as the interjection of one more voice—part of a balance of authority for the well-being of the nation's children. The delegitimization of that voice by the claims of professional and bureaucratic expertise increases the need to restore that source of understanding to a greater prominence. Another kind of civic participation is the role of commentator of last resort when the regular mechanisms for responding to need break down. When child abuse scandals hit the press, or when a child welfare institution is found to be seriously wanting, popular opinion and blue-ribbon panels force the problem into the light of day and allow a reassessment of past practice. Citizen review boards are attempts to correct the oversights of state action on a child-by-child basis.

We can, however, make a case for assigning to civic participation a much more fundamental role. In this perspective, groups of citizens acting in these various ways are expressing the community's moral sense. They are not merely one more voice but the legitimator of all organized, extrafamilial action taken on behalf of children. Public and private agencies then become the surrogates for civic action; both are public servants. One premise of this perspective is that legislation—surrogate rule-making—expresses only the broad outlines of the community's sense of what is proper. It cannot recognize the variety of situations in

20. Michael Ignatieff, *The Needs of Strangers: An Essay on Privacy, Solidarity, and the Politics of Being Human* (New York: Viking, 1984), 107.

which it will be applied or the variety of outcomes it will produce. The other premise is that the best bureaucracy or professional helper is in the same boat; they cannot be aware of all the possibilities and, moreover, cannot always submerge their own interests when they clash with the clients' interests. As a corollary, organizational and professional criteria for judging action are valid only if they are consonant with civic criteria. Professional understandings will occasionally influence civic criteria, but their ultimate validity comes from the fact that they are accepted by the relevant group of citizens.

This definition of the role of civic participation suggests a particular definition of the volunteer. The voluntary action that occurred in the most responsive organizations involved nonprofessionals as a central part of the enterprise. They volunteered their time, not simply for the convenience of the agency, but to directly reduce or mitigate the problems of troubled families. They were variously involved in the definition of the problem and the definition of the response; they were often legitimate members of the community in which the needy lived; their experience legitimated their presence as much as the training of the professional actors legitimated their involvement.

This perspective reshapes the current relationship between citizens, clients, and paid helpers. It recognizes the reality of the division of labor and the broad role of organized helping. It suggests, however, that the exercise of civic action puts the basic authority and responsibility for the needy back where they belong. The resurgence of civic authority offers the possibility of reducing disjunctions between need and help by resituating the crucial power of definition with people whose interest and legitimacy are communal rather than professional.

Civic action as a source of sustenance.   Another lesson of our analysis is that, while social service agencies arrange help for people in trouble and give help of a limited kind, the largest source of helping is extrabureaucratic—the actions of individual citizens. For example, foster parents are at once the Cinderellas and the work horses of the child welfare system. They are suspect because foster care is a second best—a temporary home that sometimes degenerates into a series of temporary homes.

They are the work horses because they take children who have
no other place to go and generally offer those children sustenance and affection.[21] In some social work texts they have been
described as semiprofessionals, and in others they have been
described as semiclients—the argument here is that someone
who would undertake such a thankless task must be inadequate
themselves. They are neither. Whatever their motives and whatever their rewards, they perform the civic function of taking
care of children who desperately need care. From the accounts
of those children themselves, we know that they are more likely
to receive the care they think they need from foster parents than
from many other sources of help.[22]

In like manner, families who adopt handicapped children
give those children a measure of help and sustenance they might
otherwise not have received. The personal costs are often very
high, and the evidence suggests that only certain families—
families who can accept children who will never achieve success
by customary standards—can cope with the task.

What these two examples show is that civic helping is an
ingredient in clients' transition to citizenship. The child in the
foster home is in a setting different from that of a child living in
his or her natural home but is much more part of the ordinary
community than the child in the institution. The more foster
parents are able to treat their foster children as normal children
with turbulent histories, rather than as clients, the less the distance between those children's experience and the lives of other
children.

These are acts of individual citizens who in the aggregate
perform a civic function. Civic action also includes collective
acts of sustenance, which range from the commitment of time,

21. Foster placements are considered "bad" because some foster children
move from placement to placement and because natural homes or adoptive
homes are considered "good." A survey of almost 400 children in a variety of
surrogate homes showed, however, that foster homes are rated better than
institutions, group homes, and even some natural homes on qualities such as the
amount of care, affection, attention, and help that foster parents give their
foster children. Malcolm Bush, "Institutions for Dependent and Neglected Children: A Therapeutic Option of Choice or a Last Resort?" *American Journal of
Orthopsychiatry* 50, no. 2 (1980): 239–55.
22. Ibid.

energy, and resources to the distressed to the display of tolerance for those of the distressed who are also considered deviant.

The civic act of tolerance—tolerance for the needy living close by and tolerance for admitting the deviant to our leisure time associations and our children's schools—has always been a hard issue, if only because of the dialectic it represents. Growing intolerance threatens more people with exile, and growing tolerance threatens the sense of common bonds that are the bedrock of communities of citizens. It is a crucial issue in our field. The acceptance of wards of the state into local schools on equal terms with other children, the tolerance of annoying adolescent behavior, the acceptance into our neighborhoods of group homes for mentally and physically handicapped children, and a broad rather than a narrow response to the complex issue of single, teenage parenthood have immediate consequences for children in trouble. In these cases a tolerant response (coupled with an insistence on the exercise of responsibility) is more likely to sustain children than the attempt to solve the problem by pushing the children out of sight. But there are also limits to the tolerance each of us is prepared to display. Moreover, there are limits to our capacity for civic behavior. And so the issue of tolerance raises the question of whether our description of civic participation has strayed too close to the utopian.

The reality of civic action.   We can easily construct a list of the shortcomings of civic and communal action that is as long as the virtues of such action. Civic action can be exclusive (and especially exclusive of the interests of troubled families); it can be disconnected, as when blue-ribbon panels comment on public action toward people who are different by class and race; it can be uninformed; and it can be "private" in the sense of being wielded to protect the comforts of the comfortable. Civic action can also be spasmodic and unreliable. The history of child welfare shows that organized helping filled a void left by the incapacity of civic and communal helping. When the particular ties of small communities were dissolved, the destitute quickly learned that general expressions of concerns not backed up by either real connection or organization left them still destitute. As a commentator on *King Lear* put it: "Woe betide any man who depends on

the abstract humanity of another for his food and protection. . . .
Lear learns too late that it is power and violence that rule the
heath [the streets?], not obligation."[23]

Thus civic helping has its share of shortcomings. There is a
disjunction between the possibilities of the civic and the fragility
it sometimes exhibits in the real world. But while the dialectic of
need and response demonstrates limitations, it also demonstrates possibilities. One possibility is that the condition of the
troubled can be improved by a shift in the balance toward civic
participation. Among other things, this possibility means the
nurturing of ties and connections between needy and nonneedy
citizens; the recognition that civic and communal action has
been vital in the recent past and has its own place in the present;
the recognition, as a corollary, that civic action should not be
subsumed under the authority or definitions of bureaucratic and
professional action; and the insistence that, however infre-
quently we exercise our authority as citizens over surrogate paid
helpers, they remain our surrogates.

The consequence of this conclusion is that troubled families
need much more (from at least some of us on some occasions)
than our tax payments and our tacit support for the organizations
of helping. If we want to improve the lot of dependent and neglected children, or of young people who are not making the
passage to independence, or of children who are permanently
handicapped, we will have to do something about it. The organizations of helping have not solved the problem the Good Samaritan tackled on his own, nor can they. The citizenship of the
troubled still depends on the rest of us exercising our citizenship.

23. Michael Ignatieff, *Needs of Strangers*, 53.

Bibliography

Addams, Jane. *Twenty Years at Hull House.* 1910. Reprint. New York: Signet, 1960.

Aldrich, Howard. "Centralization versus Decentralization in the Design of Human Service Delivery Systems: A Response to Gouldner's Lament." In *The Management of Human Services,* edited by Rosemary Sarri and Yeshekel Hasenfeld, 51–79. New York: Columbia University Press, 1978.

———. *Organizations and Their Environments.* Englewood Cliffs, N.J.: Prentice-Hall, 1979.

Alexander, Carole J. "An Analysis of the Cook County Children in Foster Care Two Years or More, under the Age of Thirteen." Chicago: Illinois Department of Children and Family Services, October 1978. Photocopy.

American Humane Association, Children's Division. *Evaluation and Consultation, Cook County CPS Program, Illinois Department of Children and Family Services.* Chicago: American Humane Association, 1977.

American Public Welfare Association. "Poverty Reaches Highest Level Since 1965: Hits Young Hardest." *Washington Reports.* 18 no. 7 (September 1983): 1–7.

Arthur Young and Company. *Report to the Department of Children and Family Services: Review of Current Operations in Cook County Region.* Chicago: Arthur Young and Company, 1980.

Ashby, LeRoy. *Saving the Waifs: Reformers and Dependent Children, 1890–1917.* Philadelphia: Temple University Press, 1984.

Becker, Gary S. "A Theory of Marriage: Part II." *Journal of Political Economy* 81 (July–August 1973): 813–46.

Berger, Peter L., and Richard J. Neuhaus. *To Empower People: The*

Role of Mediating Structures in Public Policy. Washington, D.C.: American Enterprise Institute for Public Policy Research, 1977.

Bernstein, Blanche. *The Politics of Welfare: The New York City Experience.* Cambridge, Mass.: Abt Books, 1982.

Berzy, Barry. "The Governor's Cook County Court Project: Presentation and Analysis of Selected Issues." M.A. thesis, School of Social Service Administration, University of Chicago, 1981. Photocopy.

Better Government Association, Child Advocacy Project. *The State and the Child in Need: A White Paper.* Chicago: Better Government Association, 1979.

Blades, Leslie Burton. "Why Institutions Fail." *Survey Midmonthly* 77 (1941): 291–92.

Boehm, Bernice. "The Child in Foster Care." In *Foster Care in Question: A National Reassessment by Twenty-One Experts,* edited by Helen Stone, 270–77. New York: Child Welfare League of America, 1970.

Brace, Charles Loring. *The Dangerous Classes of New York and Twenty Years Work Among Them.* New York: Wynkoop and Hallenbeck, 1872. Reprint. Washington, D.C.: National Organization of Social Workers Classic Series, 1973.

Bremner, Robert H., ed. *Children and Youth in America: A Documentary History.* 3 vols. Cambridge, Mass.: Harvard University Press, 1971–1974.

Brown, H. Frederick. "Policies and Practices of the Child Protective Services System in Cook County." Chicago: Jane Addams College of Social Work, University of Illinois at Chicago Circle, 1979. Photocopy.

Bush, Haydn. "Care." *Science 84,* September 1984, 34–35.

Bush, Malcolm. "A Client Evaluation of Foster Care." Ph.D. diss., Northwestern University, 1976.

———. "Institutions for Dependent and Neglected Children: Therapeutic Option of Choice or Last Resort?" *American Journal of Orthopsychiatry* 50 (April 1980): 239–55.

———. "The Public and Private Purposes of Case Records." *Children and Youth Services Review* 6, no. 1 (1984): 1–18.

Bush, Malcolm, and Mark Testa. "Racial Bias in Child Welfare Services." Paper presented at the National Association of Social Workers Minority Issues Conference, "Color in a White Society," Los Angeles, California, 9–12 June 1982.

Caffey, J. "Multiple Fractures in the Large Bones of Children Suffering from Chronic Subdural Hematoma." *American Journal of Roentgenology* 56 (1946):163–73.

Caputo, Richard. "Welfare and Freedom American Style: A Study of the Influence of Segmented Authority on the Development of Social and Child Welfare Reforms through an Examination of the Role and Activities of the Federal Government, 1900–1940." Ph.D. diss., University of Chicago, 1982.

Children's Defense Fund. *American Children in Poverty*. Washington, D.C.: Children's Defense Fund, 1984.

Clarke, Bill. *Enough Room for Joy: Jean Vanier's L'Arche: A Message for Our Time*. Toronto: McClelland and Stewart, 1974.

Coughlin, Roger, and Cathryn A. Rippler. *The Story of Charitable Care in the Archdiocese of Chicago, 1844–1959*. Chicago: Catholic Charities of Chicago, 1981.

Council of Social Agencies. *Survey of Resources for Negro Children*. Chicago: Council of Social Agencies of Chicago, 1945, Chicago Historical Society.

Council of Social Agencies of Chicago, and the Graduate School of Social Service Administration of the University of Chicago. *The South Side Survey: A Survey of Social and Philanthropic Agencies Available for Negroes in Chicago, Summary Report*. Chicago: Council of Social Agencies of Chicago, and the Graduate School of Social Service Administration of the University of Chicago, n.d., Chicago Historical Society.

Crawford, Robert. "The Causes of Female-Headed Households." National Opinion Research Center, University of Chicago, 1981.

Cutright, Phillip, and John Scanzoni. "Income Supplements and American Families." *Studies in Welfare* for the Subcommittee on Fiscal Policy, Joint Economic Committee of the Congress. Washington, D.C., Government Policy Office, 1973.

Derthick, Martha. *Uncontrollable Spending for Social Service Grants*. Washington, D.C.: Brookings Institute, 1975.

Designs for Change. *Caught in the Web: Misplaced Children in Chicago's Classes for the Mentally Retarded*. Chicago: Designs for Change, 1982.

Douglas, Paul H. *Real Wages in the United States, 1890–1926*. Boston: Houghton Mifflin, 1930.

Easterlin, Richard. "Interregional Differences in Per Capita Income, Population and Total Income, 1840–1950." In *Trends in the American Economy in the Nineteenth Century: Studies in Income and Wealth*. National Bureau of Economic Research ed. vol. 24. Princeton, N.J.: Princeton University Press, 1960.

Fanshel, David. "The Exit of Children from Foster Care: An Interim Research Report." *Child Welfare* 50, no. 1 (January 1971): 65–82.

————. "Status Changes in Foster Care: Final Results of the Columbia University Longitudinal Study." *Child Welfare* 55, no. 3 (March 1976): 143–73.

Farrow, Frank, and Sally Diamond. "Draft Report on Social Welfare Organizations in San Diego County, California, for the Study on the Changing Role of Voluntary Organizations in the Provision of Social Services." Center for the Study of Social Policy, University of Chicago and Washington, D.C., 1982. Photocopy.

Folks, Homer. *The Care of Destitute, Neglected, and Delinquent Children.* New York: Macmillan, 1902.

Garfinkel, Irwin, and Elizabeth Uhr. "A New Approach to Child Support." *Public Interest* 74 (Spring 1984): 111–22.

Germaine, Carol. "Technological Advances." In *Handbook of Clinical Social Work,* edited by Aaron Rosenblatt and Diana Waldfogel, 26–57. San Francisco: Jossey-Bass, 1983.

Giovannoni, Jeanne. *Defining Child Abuse.* New York: Free Press, 1979.

Gittens, Joan. "The Children of the State: Dependent Children in Illinois, 1818–1980s." Chapin Hall Center for Children at the University of Chicago, 1986.

Goffman, Erving. *Asylums: Essays on the Social Situation of Mental Patients and Other Essays.* Garden City, N.Y.: Anchor Books, 1961.

Goldman, Harold. "Reforming Youth Services in Illinois in the 1980s: Governor James R. Thompson's Special Task Force on Troubled Adolescents." Ph.D. diss., University of Chicago, 1982.

Goldstein, Joseph, Anna Freud, and Albert J. Solnit. *Beyond the Best Interests of the Child.* New York: Free Press, 1973.

Gordon, Andrew, Margo Gordon, John McKnight, and Malcolm Bush. "Experiences of Wardship: Interim Report II to the Office of Child Development, U.S. Department of Health, Education and Welfare." Center for Urban Affairs, Northwestern University, 1975.

Greenstone, J. David. "Dorothea Dix and Jane Addams: From Transcendentalism to Pragmatism in American Social Reform." *Social Service Review* 53 (December 1979): 527–60.

Group for Action Planning. Files. Children's Home and Aid Society of Illinois, Chicago, Illinois.

Hacker, Andrew, ed. *U/S: A Statistical Portrait of the American People.* New York: Viking Books, 1983.

Hadas, Susan, and Mary Ann Jones. *Sources of Voluntary Agency Income 1979–1980.* New York: Child Welfare League of America, 1981.

Hampton, Robert. "Marital Disruption: Some Economic Conse-
    quences." In *Five Thousand American Families: Patterns of Eco-
    nomic Progress,* vol. 3, edited by Greg J. Duncan and James N.
    Morgan, 163–87. Ann Arbor, Mich.: Survey Research Center, Insti-
    tute for Social Research, University of Michigan, 1975.
Haremski, Roman L. "Logical Features of Public Agencies in Behalf
    of Children." Paper presented at the National Conference of Social
    Work, Cleveland, June 1949.
Himmelfarb, Gertrude. *The Idea of Poverty: England in the Early
    Industrial Age.* New York: Vintage Books, 1985.
Hirshorn, Seth I., and Jean Covington. "Evaluation of the Governor's
    Cook County Project, Final Report (First Draft) vols. 1 and 2." SIH
    Inc., Ann Arbor, Mich., 1980. Photocopy.
Hoffman, Saul, and John Holmes. "Husbands, Wives and Divorce." In
    Five Thousand American Families: Patterns of Economic Progress,
    vol. 4, edited by Greg J. Duncan and James N. Morgan, 23–75.
    Ann Arbor, Mich.: Survey Research Center, Institute for Social
    Research, University of Michigan, 1976.
Honig, Marjorie. "AFDC Income, Recipient Rates and Family Disso-
    lution." *Journal of Human Resources* 9 (Spring 1976): 250–60.
Hurley, Timothy. "Origins of the Illinois Juvenile Court Law." In *The
    Child, the Clinic, and the Court,* edited by Julia Lathrop, 322–30.
    New York: New Republic, 1927.
Hutchens, Robert M. "Welfare, Remarriage and Marital Search."
    American Economic Review 69 (June 1979): 369–79.
Ignatieff, Michael. *The Needs of Strangers: An Essay on Privacy, Soli-
    darity, and the Politics of Being Human.* New York: Elizabeth
    Sifton Books, Viking, 1984.
Illinois Children's Home and Aid Society. Archives. Children's Home
    and Aid Society of Illinois, Chicago, Illinois.
Illinois Commission on Children. *Report of a Committee for a Compre-
    hensive Family and Child Welfare Program in Illinois.* Springfield,
    Ill.: Illinois Commission on Children, 1962.
Illinois Department of Children and Family Services. *Biennial Report.*
    Springfield, Ill.: State of Illinois, 1964.
————. *Statistical Handbook: Available Data 1949 through 1969.* Spring-
    field, Ill.: State of Illinois, 1970.
————. *A Family: Every Child's Right* (Annual Report). Springfield,
    Ill.: State of Illinois, 1975.
Illinois Department of Corrections. "Population and Capacity Re-
    port." In *Illinois Human Services Data Report.* Springfield, Ill.:
    State of Illinois, 1982.

Illinois Legislative Commission on Services for Children and Their Families. *Report.* Springfield, Ill.: State of Illinois, 1963.

Institute for Research on Poverty, University of Wisconsin. "Measuring the Effects of the Reagan Welfare Changes on the Work Effort and Well-Being of Single Parents." *Focus* 8 (Spring 1985), 1–8.

Kahlert, John. *Child Dependency in Illinois.* Springfield, Ill.: Illinois Department of Public Aid, Division of Child Welfare, 1940.

Kotter, Philip, and Michael Murray. "Third Sector Management—The Role of Marketing." *Public Administration Review* 35 (September–October 1975): 467–72.

Kramer, Ralph. "The Future of the Voluntary Service Organization." *Social Work* 18 (November 1973): 59–69.

———. *Voluntary Agencies in the Welfare State.* Berkeley and Los Angeles: University of California Press, 1981.

Lane, F. T. *A Study of the Need of Facilities for Negro Children under the Supervision of the Juvenile Court of Cook County.* Chicago: Chicago Urban League, 1944.

Lash, Trudy, and Heidi Sigal. *State of the Child: New York.* New York: Foundation for Child Development, 1976.

Lebergoh, Stanley. *The American Economy: Income, Wealth and Want.* Princeton, N.J.: Princeton University Press, 1976.

Lerman, Paul. *Deinstitutionalization and the Welfare State.* New Brunswick, N.J.: Rutgers University Press, 1982.

Liebow, Elliot. *Tally's Corner: A Study of Streetcorner Men.* Boston: Little, Brown, 1967.

Linn, Janice, Kim Zalent, William Geller, and Harris Meyer. *Minors in Need: A Study of Status Offenders at the Juvenile Court of Cook County.* Chicago: Chicago Law Enforcement Study Group, 1979.

Lipsky, Michael. *Street Level Bureaucracy: Dilemmas of the Individual in Public Services.* New York: Russell Sage Foundation, 1980.

Long, Clarence D. *Wages and Earnings in the United States, 1860–1890.* Princeton, N.J.: Princeton University Press, 1960.

Lubove, Roy. *The Professional Altruist: The Emergence of Social Work as a Career.* New York: Atheneum, 1965.

Lynn, Laurence E., and David deF. Whitman. *The President as Policy Maker: Jimmy Carter and Welfare Reform.* Philadelphia: Temple University Press, 1981.

MacIntyre, Alasdair. "The End of Ideology and the End of the End of Ideology." Chap. 1 in *Against the Self-Images of the Age: Essays in Ideology and Philosophy.* Notre Dame, Ind.: University of Notre Dame Press, 1978.

———. "Psychoanalysis: The Future of an Illusion?" Chap. 3 ibid.

McDonald, Maurice, Thomas McDonald, and Irwin Garfinkel. "AFDC and Family Dissolution: A Skeptical Comment." Institute for Research on Poverty, University of Wisconsin, 1977.

McKnight, John L. "Professionalized Service and Disabling Help." In *Disabling Professions,* edited by Ivan Illich, 69–91. London: Marion Boyers, 1978.

Mendelsohn, Robert S., M.D. *Confessions of a Medical Heretic.* Chicago: Contemporary Books, 1979.

Meyer, Carol H., ed. *Clinical Social Work in the Eco-Systems Perspective.* New York: Columbia University Press, 1983.

Miller, C. Arden. "Infant Mortality in the U.S." *Scientific American* 253 (July 1985): 31–37.

Moscovice, Ira, and William Craig. "The Omnibus Budget Reconciliation Act and the Working Poor." *Social Service Review* 58 (March 1984): 49–62.

Moynihan, Daniel Patrick. *The Politics of a Guaranteed Income: The Nixon Administration and the Family Assistance Plan.* New York: Vintage Books, 1973.

Murray, Charles. *Losing Ground: American Social Policy 1950–1980.* New York: Basic Books, 1984.

Needham, Rodney. *Against the Tranquility of Axioms.* Berkeley and Los Angeles: University of California Press, 1983.

Netting, Ellen. "The Sectarian Social Service Agency and the Meaning of its Religious Connection: Three Case Studies." Ph.D. diss., University of Chicago, 1982.

O'Connell, Mary. "Mother Johnson's House of Good Repute." *Salt* (July–August 1981): 12–16.

Perlman, Helen Harris. *Social Casework: A Problem-Solving Approach.* Chicago: University of Chicago Press, 1957.

Pifer, Alan. *The Nongovernmental Organization at Bay.* New York: Carnegie Corporation Annual Report, 1966.

Polsky, Andrew J. "Welfare Policy: Why the Past Has No Future." *Urban Prospects* 1982.

Reid, William, and Laura Epstein. *Task Centered Casework.* New York: Columbia University Press, 1972.

Richmond, Mary. *Friendly Visiting Among the Poor: A Handbook for Charity Workers.* New York: Macmillan, 1899.

———. *Social Diagnosis.* New York: Russell Sage Foundation, 1917.

———. *What Is Social Casework? An Introductory Description.* New York: Russell Sage Foundation, 1922.

Rieff, Philip. *The Triumph of the Therapeutic: Uses of Faith After Freud.* New York: Harper Torchbooks, 1968.

Rizzini, Irene. "Report on the Child Abuse Case Load at Children's Memorial Hospital, Chicago, Illinois." School of Social Service Administration, University of Chicago, 1982. Photocopy.

Robins, Philip K. "Child Support Enforcement as a Means of Reducing Welfare Dependency and Poverty." Institute for Research on Poverty, University of Wisconsin, Discussion paper 758–84, 1984.

Ruopp, Richard, Jeffrey Travers, Frederic Glantz, and Craig Coelen. *Children at the Center.* Cambridge, Mass.: Abt Books, 1979.

Sartre, Jean-Paul. *Search for a Method.* Translated by Hazel Barnes. New York: Vintage Books, 1968.

Sawhill, Isabel, Gerald Peabody, Carol Jones, and Steven Caldwell. "Income Transfers and Family Structure." Washington, D.C.: Urban Institute, Working Paper 979-03, 1975.

Schlossman, Steven, and Michael Sedlak. *The Chicago Area Project Revisited.* Santa Monica, Calif.: Rand Corporation, 1983.

Schwartz, Arthur, and Israel Goldiamond. *Social Casework: A Behavioral Approach.* New York: Columbia University Press, 1975.

Scott, Robert A. *The Making of Blind Men: A Study of Adult Socialization.* New York: Russell Sage Foundation, 1969.

Silverman, F. M. "The Roentgen Manifestations of Unrecognized Skeletal Trauma in Infants." *American Journal of Roentgenology and Radium Therapy* 69 (1953): 413–27.

Stack, Carol. *All Our Kin: Strategies for Survival in a Black Community.* New York: Harper and Row, 1975.

Stehno, Sandy. "Foster Care for Dependent Black Children in Chicago." Ph.D. diss., University of Chicago, 1985.

Testa, Mark. "The Social Support of Adolescent Parents: A Survey of Young Mothers on AFDC in Illinois." Children's Policy Research Project, National Opinion Research Center, University of Chicago, 1983.

———. "Child Placement, Deinstitutionalization and Social Change." Ph.D. diss., University of Chicago, 1984.

Testa, Mark, and Edward Lawlor. *The State of the Child: 1985.* Chicago: Chapin Hall Center for Children at the University of Chicago, 1985.

Testa, Mark, and Fred Wulczyn. *The Child in Illinois: A Series of Research Reports,* vol. 1, *The State of the Child.* Chicago: Children's Policy Research Project, School of Social Service Administration, University of Chicago, 1980.

Thomas, Edwin J. "Behavioral Modification and Casework." In *Theories of Social Casework,* edited by Robert W. Roberts and Robert H. Nee, 181–218. Chicago: University of Chicago Press, 1972.

Thurston, Henry. *The Dependent Child: A Story of Changing Aims and Methods in the Care of Dependent Children*. New York: Columbia University Press, 1930.

Titmuss, Richard. "Choice and 'The Welfare State.'" Chap. 12 of *Commitment to Welfare*. 2nd ed. London: Allen and Unwin, 1976.

Trast, Merton Julius. "A Study of the Joint Service Bureau of the Protestant and Non-Sectarian Child Caring Agencies of Chicago." M.A. thesis, University of Chicago, 1934.

U.S. Bureau of the Census. *Historical Statistics of the United States. Bicentennial Edition: Colonial Times to 1970*. Washington, D.C.: Bureau of the Census, 1975.

————. *Statistical Abstracts of the United States*. Washington, D.C.: Bureau of the Census, 1978 and 1979.

U.S. Congress. House. Committee on Ways and Means. *Hearings on the Public Welfare Amendments of 1962*. 87th Cong., 2d sess., 1962.

U.S. Congress. Senate. Committee on Finance. *Hearings on S. 1130. A Bill to Alleviate the Hazards of Old Age, Unemployment, Illness, and Dependency, to Establish a Social Insurance Board in the Department of Labor, to Raise Revenue and Other Purposes*. 74th Cong., 1st sess., 1935.

Valentine, Charles A. *Culture and Poverty: Critique and Counter Proposals*. Chicago: University of Chicago Press, 1968.

Weisbrod, Burton A. *The Voluntary Nonprofit Sector: An Economic Analysis*. Lexington, Mass.: Lexington Books, 1977.

Welfare Council of Metropolitan Chicago. *Facts Establishing the Need for a Child Placement Service in Metropolitan Chicago*. Chicago: Welfare Council of Metropolitan Chicago, 1954.

————. *Report of the Committee on Institutional Care*. Chicago: Welfare Council of Metropolitan Chicago, 1956.

————. *Selected Information on Children's Institutions with Membership in the Welfare Council of Metropolitan Chicago and Serving School Aged Children*. Chicago: Welfare Council of Metropolitan Chicago, 1967.

Wilson, William Julius. *The Declining Significance of Race: Blacks and Changing American Institutions*. Chicago: University of Chicago Press, 1980.

Wilson, William Julius, and Kathryn M. Neckerman. "Poverty and Family Structure: The Widening Gap Between Evidence and Public Policy Issues." Department of Sociology, University of Chicago, 1985. Photocopy.

Wisconsin Division of Community Services. "Alternate Case Inventory." N.p. State of Wisconsin, 1983.

Wootten, Barbara. *Social Science and Social Pathology.* London: Allen and Unwin, 1959.

Zuniga, Ricardo. "The Experimenting Society and Radical Social Reform. The Role of the Social Scientist in Chile's Unidad Popular Experiment." Paper read at annual convention of the American Psychological Association, New Orleans, September 1974.

Index

Compositor: Huron Valley Graphics
Text: 10/12 Times Roman
Display: Goudy Bold Roman
Printer: Braun-Brumfield, Inc.
Binder: Braun-Brumfield, Inc.